PRENTICE HALL

The
American
Nation

★ ★ ★ ★ ★ ★ ★ ★

Reading
and
Vocabulary
Study Guide

PEARSON

Prentice
Hall

Upper Saddle River, New Jersey
Needham, Massachusetts

Pearson Prentice Hall™ is a trademark of Pearson Education, Inc.

Pearson® is a registered trademark of Pearson plc.

Prentice Hall® is a registered trademark of Pearson Education, Inc.

ISBN 0-13-128362-6

5 6 7 8 9 10   08 07 06 05

Table of Contents

Success in social studies comes from doing three things well—reading, testing, and writing. The following pages present strategies to help you read for meaning, understand test questions, and write well for social studies.

Reading for Meaning

Do you have trouble remembering what you read? Here are some tips from experts that will improve your ability to recall and understand what you read:

▶ Before You Read

Preview the text to identify important information.

Like watching the coming attractions at a movie theater, previewing the text helps you know what to expect. Study the questions and strategies below to learn how to preview what you read.

Ask yourself these questions:	Use these strategies to find the answers:
• What is the text about?	Read the headings, subheadings, and captions. Study the photos, maps, tables, or graphs.
• What do I already know about the topic?	Read the questions at the end of the text to see if you can answer any of them.
• What is the purpose of the text?	Turn the headings into *who, what, when, where, why,* or *how* questions. This will help you decide if the text compares things, tells a chain of events, or explains causes and effects.

► As You Read

Organize information in a way that helps you see meaningful connections or relationships.

Taking notes as you read will improve your understanding. Use graphic organizers like the ones below to record the information you read. Study these descriptions and examples to learn how to create each type of organizer.

Sequencing

A **flowchart** helps you see how one event led to another. It can also display the steps in a process.

Use a flowchart if the text—
• tells about a chain of events.
• explains a method of doing something.

TIP ► List the events or steps in order.

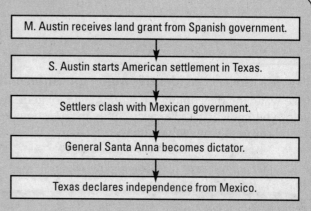

M. Austin receives land grant from Spanish government.

↓

S. Austin starts American settlement in Texas.

↓

Settlers clash with Mexican government.

↓

General Santa Anna becomes dictator.

↓

Texas declares independence from Mexico.

Comparing and Contrasting

A **Venn diagram** displays similarities and differences.

Use a Venn diagram if the text—
• compares and contrasts two individuals, groups, places, things, or events.

TIP ► Label the outside section of each circle and list differences.
Label the shared section and list similarities.

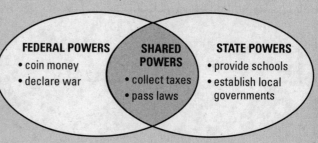

FEDERAL POWERS
• coin money
• declare war

SHARED POWERS
• collect taxes
• pass laws

STATE POWERS
• provide schools
• establish local governments

► As You Read *(continued)*

Categorizing Information

A **table** organizes information in categories.

Use a table if the text—
- lists similar facts about several places or things.
- presents characteristics of different groups.

TIP► Write an appropriate heading for each column in the table to identify its category.

COLONY	FOUNDED	LEADERS
Massachusetts	1620	William Bradford John Winthrop
New Hampshire	1623	John Wentworth
Connecticut	1636	Thomas Hooker
Rhode Island	1636	Roger Williams

Identifying Main Ideas and Details

A **concept web** helps you understand relationships among ideas.

Use a concept web if the text—
- provides examples to support a main idea.
- links several ideas to a main topic.

TIP► Write the main idea in the largest circle. Write details in smaller circles and draw lines to show relationships.

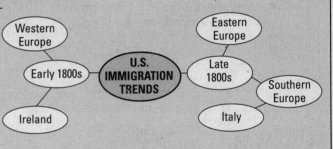

Organizing Information

An **outline** provides an overview, or a kind of blueprint for reading.

Use an outline to organize ideas—
- according to their importance.
- according to the order in which they are presented.

TIP▶ Use roman numerals for main ideas, capital letters for secondary ideas, arabic numerals for supporting details.

> **I. Differences Between the North and the South**
>   **A.** Views on slavery
>   **1.** Northern abolitionists
>   **2.** Southern slave owners
>   **B.** Economies
>   **1.** Northern manufacturing
>   **2.** Southern agriculture

Identifying Cause and Effect

A **cause-and-effect** chart shows the relationship between what happened (effect) and the reason why it happened (cause).

Use a cause-and-effect chart if the text—
- lists one or more causes for an event.
- lists one or more results of an event.

TIP▶ Label causes and effects. Draw arrows to indicate how ideas are related.

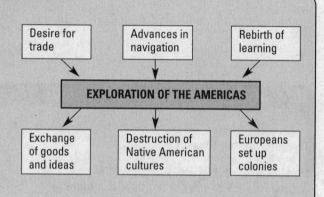

▶ After You Read

Test yourself to find out what you learned from reading the text.
Go back to the questions you asked yourself before you read the text. You should be able to give more complete answers to these questions:
- What is the text about?
- What is the purpose of the text?

You should also be able to make connections between the new information you learned from the text and what you already knew about the topic.

Study your graphic organizer. Use this information as the *answers*. Make up a meaningful *question* about each piece of information.

Writing for Social Studies

When you face a writing assignment, do you think, "How will I ever get through this?" Here are some tips to guide you through any writing project from start to finish.

▶ The Writing Process

Follow each step of the writing process to communicate effectively.

Step 1. Prewrite

- Establish the purpose.
- Define the topic.
- Determine the audience.
- Gather details.

Step 2. Draft

- Organize information logically in an outline or graphic organizer.
- Write an introduction, body, and conclusion.
- State main ideas clearly.
- Include relevant details to support your ideas.

Step 3. Revise

- Edit for clarity of ideas and elaboration.

Step 4. Proofread

- Correct any errors in spelling, grammar, and punctuation.

Step 5. Publish and Present

- Copy text neatly by hand, typewriter, or word processor.
- Illustrate as needed.
- Create a cover if appropriate.

► Types of Writing for Social Studies

Identify the purpose for your writing.

Each type of writing assignment has a specific purpose, and each purpose needs a different plan for development. The following descriptions and examples will help you identify the three purposes for social studies writing. The lists of steps will help you plan your writing.

Writing to Inform

Purpose: to present facts or ideas

Example

During the 1960s, research indicated the dangers of the insecticide DDT. It killed insects but also had long-term effects. When birds and fish ate poisoned insects, DDT built up in their fatty tissue. The poison also showed up in human beings who ate birds and fish contaminated by DDT.

TIP► Look for these **key terms** in the assignment: explain, describe, report, narrate

How to get started:
• Determine the topic you will write about.
• Write a topic sentence that tells the main idea.
• List all the ideas you can think of that are related to the topic.
• Arrange the ideas in logical order.

Writing to Persuade

Purpose: to influence someone

Example

Teaching computer skills in the classroom uses time that could be spent teaching students how to think for themselves or how to interact with others. Students who can reason well, express themselves clearly, and get along with other people will be better prepared for life than those who can use a computer.

TIP► Look for these **key terms** in the assignment: convince, argue, request

How to get started:
• Make sure you understand the problem or issue clearly.
• Determine your position.
• List evidence to support your arguments.
• Predict opposing views.
• List evidence you can use to overcome the opposing arguments.

Writing to Provide Historical Interpretation

Purpose: to present the perspective of someone in a different era

Example

The crossing took a week, but the steamship voyage was hard. We were cramped in steerage with hundreds of others. At last we saw the huge statue of the lady with the torch. In the reception center, my mother held my hand while the doctor examined me. Then, my father showed our papers to the official, and we collected our bags. I was scared as we headed off to find a home in our new country.

TIP► Look for these **key terms** in the assignment: go back in time, create, suppose that, if you were

How to get started:
• Study the events or issues of the time period you will write about.
• Consider how these events or issues might have affected different people at the time.
• Choose a person whose views you would like to present.
• Identify the thoughts and feelings this person might have experienced.

▶ Research for Writing

Follow each step of the writing process to communicate effectively.

After you have identified the purpose for your writing, you may need to do research. The following steps will help you plan, gather, organize, and present information.

Step 1. Ask Questions

Ask yourself questions to help guide your research.	What do I already know about the topic? What do I want to find out about the topic?

Step 2. Acquire Information

Locate and use appropriate sources of information about the topic.	Library Internet search Interviews
Take notes.	Follow accepted format for listing sources.

Step 3. Analyze Information

Evaluate the information you find.	Is it relevant to the topic? Is it up to date? Is it accurate? Is the writer an authority on the topic? Is there any bias?

Step 4. Use Information

Answer your research questions with the information you have found. (You may find that you need to do more research.)	Do I have all the information I need?
Organize your information into the main points you want to make. Identify supporting details.	Arrange ideas in outline form or in a graphic organizer.

Step 5. Communicate What You've Learned

Review the purpose for your writing and choose an appropriate way to present the information.

Purpose	Presentation
inform	formal paper, documentary, multimedia
persuade	essay, letter to the editor, speech
interpret	journal, newspaper account, drama

Draft and revise your writing, then evaluate it. Use a rubric for self-evaluation.

▶ Evaluating Your Writing

Use the following rubric to help you evaluate your writing.

	Excellent	Good	Acceptable	Unacceptable
Purpose	Achieves purpose—to inform, persuade, or provide historical interpretation—very well	Informs, persuades, or provides historical interpretation reasonably well	Reader cannot easily tell if the purpose is to inform, persuade, or provide historical interpretation	Lacks purpose
Organization	Develops ideas in a very clear and logical way	Presents ideas in a reasonably well-organized way	Reader has difficulty following the organization	Lacks organization
Elaboration	Explains all ideas with facts and details	Explains most ideas with facts and details	Includes some supporting facts and details	Lacks supporting details
Use of Language	Uses excellent vocabulary and sentence structure with no errors in spelling, grammar, or punctuation	Uses good vocabulary and sentence structure with very few errors in spelling, grammar, or punctuation	Includes some errors in grammar, punctuation, and spelling	Includes many errors in grammar, punctuation, and spelling

How To Use This Book

The purpose of *Reading and Vocabulary Study Guide* is to help you strengthen reading and language skills that you can use both inside and outside the classroom. These skills will help you as you read your history textbook, *The American Nation*.

There are four types of worksheets in *Reading and Vocabulary Study Guide*.

Vocabulary Development

Each group of chapter worksheets begins with Vocabulary Development. With this worksheet you can

Guide to the Essentials

There is one Guide to the Essentials worksheet for each section in your textbook. With these worksheets, you can

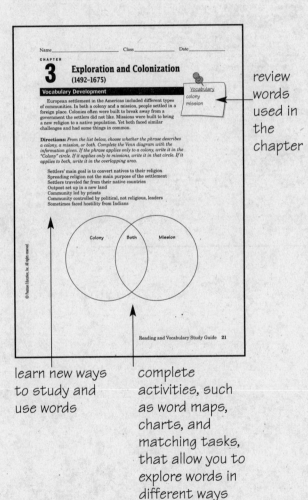

review words used in the chapter

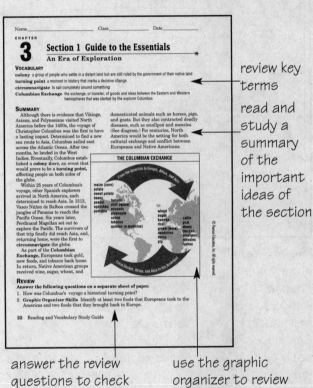

review key terms

read and study a summary of the important ideas of the section

learn new ways to study and use words

complete activities, such as word maps, charts, and matching tasks, that allow you to explore words in different ways

answer the review questions to check your understanding of what you have read

use the graphic organizer to review content

At times, some of the Vocabulary Worksheets will have writing activities. These activities will help you use the words you have learned and help you develop your composition skills.

Guided Reading and Review

The Guided Reading and Review worksheets will help you understand what you have read after you complete the assigned reading.

Chapter Test

Once you finish a chapter, the Chapter Test is a good way to see if you have mastered the chapter content. Use the Guide to the Essentials worksheet to review those ideas you did not understand on the chapter test.

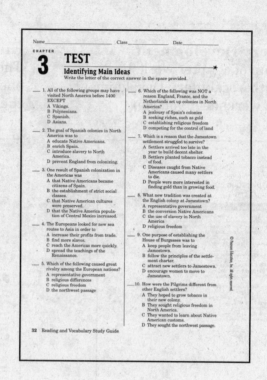

"As You Read" gives you a chance to review what you read in the section. Complete the activity to make sure that you know the content.

"Reviewing Key Terms" and "Key People" helps you review the key terms and key people discussed in the section.

CHAPTER

1 Geography, History, and the Social Sciences

Vocabulary Development

Vocabulary
latitude
longitude

Latitude and longitude are used to describe locations on a map or globe. Lines of latitude (from a Latin word meaning "broad") are horizontal on a map and measure distance north or south of the equator. Lines of longitude (from a Latin word meaning "long") are vertical on a map and measure distance east or west of a line through the Greenwich Observatory, near London, England.

Look at the maps of the world and the United States in the reference atlas of your textbook. In each of the following situations, one of the measurements for the two locations is about the same, and one is different. For each pair, which coordinate differs the most?

1. Your friend in Austin, Texas, is about to fly to visit her grand-
   mother, who lives in Bismarck, North Dakota.

   latitude   longitude

2. You live in San Francisco, California, and want to travel to
   Tokyo, Japan.

   latitude   longitude

3. A ship plans to sail from the Bahamas, near Florida, to the
   Canary Islands, off the coast of Africa.

   latitude   longitude

4. You are leaving on a trip from Miami, Florida, and want to know
   what the weather is like in Pittsburgh, Pennsylvania.

   latitude   longitude

Name_____ Class_____ Date_____

Section 1 Guide to the Essentials
Thinking Geographically

VOCABULARY

geography the study of people, their environment, and their resources

natural resource material that humans can take from the environment to survive and satisfy their needs

irrigation a method of bringing water to dry lands

cartographer a mapmaker

SUMMARY

To understand the history of the United States, one must also understand the nation's **geography.** United States history is directly affected by people and their relationship to their environment and their **natural resources.**

For example, when desert dwellers **irrigate** their crops, they not only change the landscape, they also change history. Because of the new water supply, a village, or even a great civilization, can take root.

In the 1700s, people lived near the Atlantic Ocean, which provided transportation and food. As the United States expanded westward, people followed. Today, many of the largest city populations in the nation are located in the Southwest.

Maps and globes are one way of visualizing geography. Early maps were made by explorers and travelers. Today, sophisticated technology helps **cartographers** draw accurate maps.

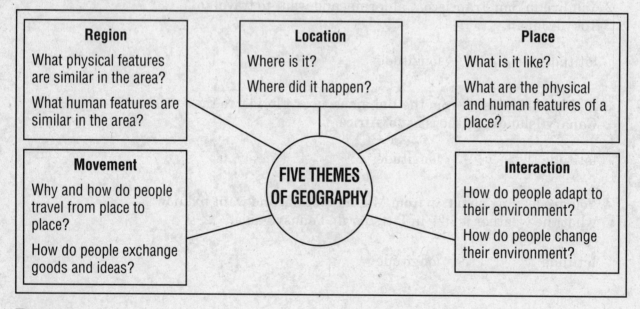

Region	Location	Place
What physical features are similar in the area? What human features are similar in the area?	Where is it? Where did it happen?	What is it like? What are the physical and human features of a place?

FIVE THEMES OF GEOGRAPHY

Movement	Interaction
Why and how do people travel from place to place? How do people exchange goods and ideas?	How do people adapt to their environment? How do people change their environment?

REVIEW
Answer the following questions on a separate sheet of paper.

1. How could irrigation change history?

2. **Graphic Organizer Skills** What are the five themes of geography?

CHAPTER

1 Section 1 Guided Reading and Review
Thinking Geographically

A. As You Read

Directions: Complete the chart below as you read Section 1 in your textbook. Fill in details about the five themes of geography.

The Five Themes of Geography	
1. location	
2. place	
3. interaction	
4. movement	
5. regions	

B. Reviewing Key Terms

Directions: Explain how the following terms relate either to the five themes of geography or to maps and globes.

6. latitude _____

_____

7. longitude _____

_____

8. natural resources _____

_____

9. cartographer _____

10. map projection _____

11. thematic map _____

CHAPTER

1

Section 2 Guide to the Essentials

Lands and Climates of the United States

VOCABULARY

tributary a stream or smaller river that flows into a larger one

precipitation water that falls in the form of rain, sleet, hail, or snow

altitude height of land above sea level

SUMMARY

Geographers divide the United States into several different physical regions with contrasting landforms. The Hawaiian Islands, located in the North Pacific Ocean, consist of a chain of islands more than 1,500 miles long. The Pacific Coast is the mainland's westernmost region, with high mountain ranges stretching from Alaska to Mexico. To the east is the Intermountain Region, made up of mountains, plateaus, canyons, and deserts. The Rocky Mountains stretch from Alaska into the western United States and include some of the highest peaks in North America.

The Interior Plains are rich in natural resources and fertile soil. The Appalachian Mountains run from Canada down to Georgia and Mississippi. The Canadian Shield, a lowland region extending from Canada into Michigan, Wisconsin, and Minnesota, is rich in minerals. The Coastal Plains, the easternmost region of the United States, is divided into two subregions: the Atlantic Plain, which lies between the Atlantic Ocean and the Appalachian Mountains; and the Gulf Plain, which lies along the Gulf of Mexico.

The rivers of the United States crisscross the country linking many different physical regions. The Mississippi and Missouri Rivers (and their **tributaries**) are the longest and most important river systems in the United States. The Great Lakes—Superior, Michigan, Huron, Erie, and Ontario—form the largest freshwater supply in the world.

The United States has 10 types of climates. (See chart.) Two features that define climate are temperature and **precipitation.** The location and **altitude** of a region also influences its climate.

CLIMATES IN THE UNITED STATES		
Climate	**Region**	**Characteristics**
Marine	Southern Alaska to Northern California	warm summers, cool winters
Mediterranean	California	mild, wet winters; hot, dry summers
Highland	Western Mountains	cool temperatures
Desert	Southwest	hot days, cold nights; very dry
Steppe	Great Plains	hot summers, cold winters; dry
Humid Continental	Central Plains, Northeast	mild summers, cold winters
Tropical	Southern Florida, Hawaii	hot and humid
Humid Subtropical	Southeast	warm, regular rainfall
Tundra	Coastal Regions of Alaska	cold all year
Subarctic	Alaska	long, cold winters; short summers

REVIEW

Answer the following questions on a separate sheet of paper.

1. What are the two most important river systems in the United States?

2. **Chart Skills** Which locations would be considered dry regions?

CHAPTER

1 Section 2 Guided Reading and Review

Lands and Climates of the United States

A. Main Ideas

Directions: As you read Section 2 in your textbook, complete the chart with a brief description of each physical region or climate of the United States.

Physical Region	Climate
1. Pacific Coast	9. marine
2. Intermountain Region	10. Mediterranean
3. Rocky Mountains	11. highland
4. Interior Plains	12. desert/steppe
5. Appalachian Mountains	13. humid continental
6. Canadian Shield	14. tropical/humid subtropical
7. Coastal Plains	15. tundra/subarctic
8. Hawaiian Islands	

B. Reviewing Key Terms

Directions: Match the terms in Column I with the descriptions in Column II. Write the letter of the correct answer in the space provided.

Column I

_____ 16. isthmus

_____ 17. erosion

_____ 18. tributary

_____ 19. precipitation

_____ 20. altitude

Column II

a. rain, snow, sleet, or hail

b. height of the land above sea level

c. narrow strip of land

d. gradual wearing away of land

e. stream or river that flows into a larger river

CHAPTER

1

Section 3 Guide to the Essentials
The Tools of History

VOCABULARY

authenticity the quality and reliability of a source

bias a leaning toward or against a certain person, group, or idea

artifact an object made by a human

culture a way of life that a people has developed

SUMMARY

History is the study of people in different times and places. Historians use different tools to study the past. Primary sources are just one of these tools. They give firsthand information about people or events. Primary sources include diaries, letters, speeches, photographs, and videos.

A secondary source is written after the event by people who were not there. Secondary sources are always based on primary sources. Historians must decide on the **authenticity** and reliability of a source. Some sources may show **bias.**

Sometimes no primary or secondary sources exist. **Artifacts,** or objects, help

historians learn about an ancient **culture.** Pottery, tools, and bones are examples of artifacts. Archaeology is the study of evidence left by early people. Archaeologists study these artifacts, and technology helps them form ideas about the early cultures.

History is divided into eras, or major periods of time. (See time line.) Chronology puts events in the order in which they happened. Chronology helps people understand the connections between events. Studying history gives people information for solving today's problems.

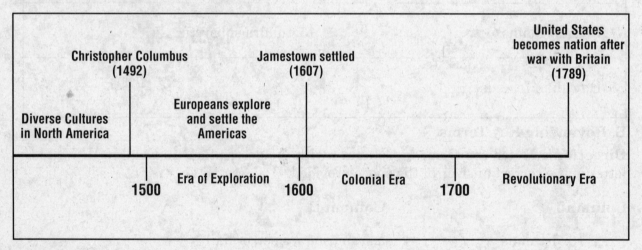

REVIEW
Answer the following questions on a separate sheet of paper.

1. What two types of evidence do historians study?
2. **Graphic Organizer Skills** When did Europeans begin to explore North America?

CHAPTER

1

Section 3 Guided Reading and Review

The Tools of History

A. As You Read

Directions: As you read Section 3 in your textbook, correct each of the following false statements.

1. A secondary source is firsthand information about people or events.

_____

2. A historian must first determine if a primary source is historic.

_____

3. When evaluating authenticity, a historian must look for bias.

_____

4. History is the study of evidence left by early people and civilizations.

_____

5. Historians never study ordinary people who do the everyday things that shape the community.

_____

6. Absolute chronology shows the time of an event in relation to other events.

_____

B. Reviewing Key Terms

Directions: Define the following terms.

7. bias _____

_____

8. artifact _____

_____

_____

9. archaeology _____

_____

10. culture _____

_____

11. chronology _____

_____

CHAPTER

1

Section 4 Guide to the Essentials
Economics and Other Social Sciences

VOCABULARY

cash economy an economy in which people exchange money for goods and services

consumer a user of goods and services

SUMMARY

Economics is the study of how people use resources to survive and to satisfy their wants and needs. A society must answer three basic economic questions. What goods and services should we produce? How should we produce these goods and services? For whom should we produce them? People need food, shelter, and clothing. Some resources may remain after these basic needs are met. These resources can be used to make other goods. Years ago, each family produced the food and goods it needed. Today, factories produce most products. In a **cash economy,** income determines the goods and services a **consumer** can buy.

The United States has a free enterprise system. A free enterprise system offers several benefits, but the government plays a limited role. (See chart.)

Economics is one of the social sciences. The social sciences help us understand people and their societies. Political science is the study of government. Civics looks at the rights and responsibilities of citizens. Anthropology examines how people and cultures develop. Sociology is the study of how people behave in groups. Psychology looks at how people think and feel.

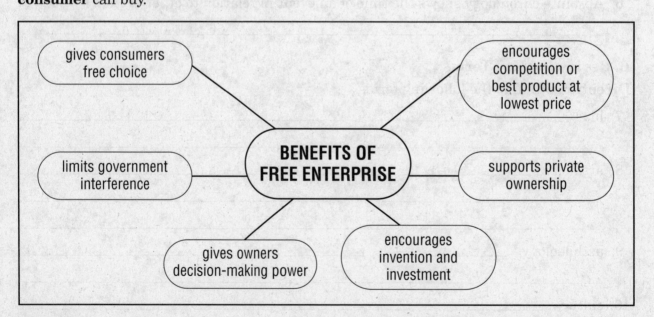

REVIEW
Answer the following questions on a separate sheet of paper.

1. What are the three basic economic questions every society must answer?

2. **Graphic Organizer Skills** What are two benefits that a free enterprise system offers to consumers?

CHAPTER

1

Section 4 Guided Reading and Review
Economics and Other Social Sciences

A. As You Read

Directions: As you read Section 4 in your textbook, complete the chart below by writing supporting details under each main idea.

> **Main Idea A:** There are three basic economic questions each society must answer.
>
> 1. _____
> 2. _____
> 3. _____
>
> **Main Idea B:** The American economic system is based on free enterprise.
>
> 4. _____
> 5. _____
>
> **Main Idea C:** Other social sciences besides economics are important to the study of history.
>
> 6. _____
> 7. _____
> 8. _____

B. Reviewing Key Terms

Directions: Complete each sentence below by writing the correct term in the blank.

9. The study of how people manage their limited resources to satisfy their wants and needs is called _____.

10. A _____ is based on the exchange of money for goods and services.

11. _____ is the study of the rights and responsibilities of citizens.

12. The study of how peoples and cultures develop is called _____.

CHAPTER
1 TEST
Identifying Main Ideas
Write the letter of the correct answer in the space provided.

____ 1. The five themes of geography show the connection between geography and
   A region.
   B movement.
   C history.
   D location.

____ 2. When the United States expanded, settlers moved to the
   A North.
   B West.
   C South.
   D East.

____ 3. Physical regions in the United States are marked by
   A contrasting landforms.
   B similar climates.
   C high elevations.
   D heavy precipitation.

____ 4. Which of the following are the two most important river systems in the United States?
   A Ohio and Tennessee
   B Superior and Huron
   C Mississippi and Missouri
   D Arkansas and Platte

____ 5. Two features that define climate are
   A temperature and precipitation.
   B warm summers and cool winters.
   C rain and snow.
   D tropical and marine.

____ 6. Which of the following is NOT a primary source?
   A a textbook
   B a diary entry
   C a photograph
   D a personal letter

____ 7. Chronology is a key tool for historians because it
   A identifies how people use their resources.
   B shows the order of past events.
   C illustrates where and when people move.
   D describes Earth's climates.

____ 8. Which of the following is NOT a question economists ask about society?
   A What goods and services should we produce?
   B How should we produce goods and services?
   C For whom should we produce goods and services?
   D Where should we sell our goods and services?

____ 9. Which of the following is an example of a person's basic need?
   A transportation
   B clothing
   C education
   D entertainment

____10. Which social science deals with the rights and responsibilities of citizens?
   A psychology
   B economics
   C civics
   D anthropology

CHAPTER

2 Before the First Global Age
(Prehistory–1600)

Vocabulary Development

Some of these words are used in Chapter 2 to describe types of land that people live on. Others are used when talking about how people live together in groups.

Vocabulary
clan
culture
glacier
sachem
savanna
terrace
tribe

Directions: *Draw a line to match each word to its definition.*

1. tribe   a. the way of life of a group of people

2. terrace   b. a thick sheet of ice

3. culture   c. the leader of a tribe

4. savanna   d. a region of grasslands

5. sachem   e. a group of related families

6. clan   f. a wide step of land on a mountainside

7. glacier   g. a community of people who share customs, language, and rituals

Directions: *Using at least four of the listed vocabulary words, write a paragraph about the chapter on the lines below. Be sure to use complete sentences and correct spelling in your writing.*

_____

_____

_____

_____

_____

_____

_____

_____

_____

_____

CHAPTER 2

Section 1 Guide to the Essentials

The First Civilizations of the Americas

VOCABULARY

terrace wide step cut into the land

culture the way of life of a people

SUMMARY

Many scientists believe that people reached North and South America during the last ice age. Hunters may have followed herds of animals across a land bridge that joined Siberia to Alaska.

Some scientists believe that people traveled in boats from Asia to North America; others think that people reached the continents from Europe, Africa, or islands in the South Pacific.

The Olmecs in Central America were successful farmers. They also studied the stars and created a calendar to track the seasons. The Mayas, located in present-day Guatemala, Mexico, and Belize, built cities and trade networks. Mayas also made advances in astronomy and mathematics.

The Aztecs lived in present-day central Mexico and grew rich from trade and conquest. The Incas ruled a large empire of more than 10 million people in South America. They kept government records, constructed a system of roads, and built **terraces** for farming.

Trade and migration carried ideas and goods from Central America and Mexico to North America. These ideas influenced **cultures** in the present-day American Southwest. The Hohokams lived in present-day Arizona and dug irrigation ditches so they could farm desert land. The Anasazis, in addition to irrigating the desert to farm, built a network of roads to link dozens of towns.

AZTEC SOCIETY

Emperor
chosen by nobles and priests to lead in war

Priests
performed rituals, gave advice, and ran schools

Nobles
served as officials, judges, and governors

Warriors
could become nobles by killing or capturing enemies

Merchants
often acted as spies for the empire

Artisans
passed skills on to their children

Farmers
made up most of the population

Slaves
were mostly captives or criminals

REVIEW

Answer the following questions on a separate sheet of paper.

1. How do scientists believe the first people came to America?

2. **Graphic Organizer Skills** Who could advance to a higher social class by killing or capturing enemies?

CHAPTER

2 Section 1 Guided Reading and Review
The First Civilizations of the Americas

A. As You Read

Directions: Complete the chart below as you read Section 1 in your textbook. Fill in details about each civilization.

1. Olmec	
2. Maya	
3. Aztec	
4. Inca	
5. Southwestern	
6. Mound Builders	

B. Reviewing Key Terms

Directions: Define the following terms.

7. surplus _____

_____

8. quipu _____

_____

9. terrace _____

10. pueblo _____

_____

CHAPTER

2 Section 2 Guide to the Essentials

Native American Cultures

★

VOCABULARY

tribe a community of people that share common customs, language, and rituals

pit house a house dug into the ground and covered with wood and skins

kachina a spirit represented by masked dancers in Pueblo cultures

potlatch ceremonial dinner held by cultures of the Pacific Northwest

SUMMARY

As early peoples settled in North America, they formed groups and developed unique cultures. By the time Europeans arrived in the 1490s, there were hundreds of Native American **tribes,** languages, and religions in North America.

Native Americans were all influenced by geography, climate, and resources. Depending on where they lived, Native American people might farm, fish, hunt, or trade for food and other resources. In the arctic climate of the Far North, the Inuits lived in **pit houses** and lived off the sea. In the milder Northwest, tribes settled in villages and traded goods. In the fertile Southeast, the Natchez farmed and hunted. (See chart.)

Despite geographical differences, Native American peoples shared some key beliefs. They respected nature and believed that the world was filled with unseen and powerful forces. They held special ceremonies and performed regular rituals to honor these forces. In the Southwest, the Pueblos held ceremonies celebrating the **kachinas.** In the Northwest, families celebrated by holding **potlatch** ceremonies.

The Iroquois people of the Eastern Woodlands had a unique society. Women had the power to own property and to elect tribal leaders.

ARCTIC/SUBARCTIC	**Beavers, Crees, Inuits, Hutchins, Montagnais** Lived as nomadic hunters and food gatherers.
CALIFORNIA/GREAT BASIN/PLATEAU	**Nez Percés, Pomos, Shoshones** Lived as hunters and gatherers in small family groups.
SOUTHWEST	**Apaches, Hohokams, Hopis, Navajos, Pueblos** Lived in villages in homes made of adobe; built irrigation systems to grow corn and other crops.
SOUTHEAST	**Cherokees, Natchez** Grew corn, squash, beans, and other crops.
GREAT PLAINS	**Arapahos, Blackfeet, Cheyennes, Comanches, Crows, Lakotas, Mandans, Osages** Lived in tepees; animals hunted by men; crops grown by women; relied on buffalo to meet basic needs of food, shelter, and clothing.
EASTERN WOODLANDS	**Algonquins, Ojibwas, Hurons, Iroquois, Leni-Lenapes, Miamis, Pequots, Shawnees** Lived in farming vilages, but also hunted for food.
NORTHWEST COAST	**Bella Coolas, Coos, Kwakiutis, Tlingits** Benefited from rich natural resources in forests, rivers, and ocean.

REVIEW

Answer the following questions on a separate sheet of paper.

1. What were two beliefs that all Native American peoples shared?

2. **Chart Skills** In which culture areas did Native Americans farm?

CHAPTER

2 Section 2 Guided Reading and Review

Native American Cultures

A. As You Read

Directions: As you read Section 2 in your textbook, cross out the term or name that does not belong in each group below. Then explain how the remaining terms are related.

1. driftwood   pit houses   seal oil   corn

_____

_____

2. potlatch   buffalo   canoes   villages

_____

_____

3. calendar   Natchez   igloo   Stinkard

_____

_____

4. adobe   tepees   buffalo   Great Plains

_____

_____

5. long house   confederacy   maple sugar   kachina

_____

_____

B. Reviewing Key Terms

Directions: Match the terms in Column I with the descriptions in Column II. Write the letter of the correct answer in the space provided.

Column I

_____ 6. tribe

_____ 7. pit house

_____ 8. kachina

_____ 9. clan

_____ 10. sachem

Column II

a. group of related families

b. community of people that share common customs, language, and rituals

c. house dug into the ground and covered with wood and skins

d. spirit represented by a masked dancer

e. Iroquois tribal leader

CHAPTER

2

Section 3 Guide to the Essentials

Trade Networks of Africa and Asia

VOCABULARY

first global age in the 1400s, the first time that faraway places became linked through trade

Islam religion founded in the A.D. 600s in the Arab world by the prophet Muhammad

city-state large town that has its own government and controls the surrounding countryside

kinship the sharing of a common ancestor

extended family several generations living in a single household

SUMMARY

Long before Europeans reached North America, the **first global age** was underway. For the first time, places separated by great distances were linked through trade. The Silk Road was a key overland route that connected China, India, and Africa. Thanks to this and other routes, cities in Asia, Africa, the Mediterranean region, and the Middle East were now connected.

The Middle East was an important center of trade. Arab merchants played a large role in this growing trade. The growth of trade was also linked to the spread of the new religion **Islam**. The followers of Islam are Muslims.

Trade routes connected cities within the vast continent of Africa as well. The **city-states** in Zimbabwe in East Africa were in contact with the trading kingdoms of Mali and Songhai in West Africa. Trade brought goods, as well as Islam, to Africa. In Africa, most people lived in villages and hunted, fished, and farmed for survival. Africans valued relationships based on **kinship** and **extended family**. People who shared common ancestors were loyal to one another.

In the early 1400s, people in African coastal cities might have seen a fleet of Chinese trading ships led by Zheng He. The fleet expanded Chinese trade routes and influence, and opened China to the world. Although Chinese expeditions never reached North America, some historians speculate that if those expeditions had crossed the Pacific Ocean, American history might be very different.

CAUSE	Arab merchants expand their trade routes into Africa, Spain, and southwestern Asia.
EFFECTS	• The religion of Islam spreads throughout the known world. • People around the world, including African leaders, speak Arabic and make pilgrimages to Mecca. • New goods and treasures make their way to the rest of the world.

REVIEW

Answer the following questions on a separate sheet of paper.

1. What areas of the world were connected by trade routes in the 1400s?

2. **Chart Skills** What effect did Arab merchants have on the world in the 1400s?

CHAPTER

2 Section 3 Guided Reading and Review

Trade Networks of Africa and Asia

A. As You Read

Directions: As you read Section 3 in your textbook, answer the following questions.

1. Why do the 1400s mark the beginning of the first global age? _____

_____

2. Who founded Islam, and what do Muslims believe? _____

_____

3. How was the growth of trade in the Middle East linked to the growth of Islam?

_____

4. What were the major trade routes Muslim traders traveled? _____

_____

5. What are some aspects of African village life? _____

_____

6. Why did China not trade with outsiders until 1402? _____

_____

B. Reviewing Key Terms

Directions: Complete each sentence below by writing the correct term in the blank.

7. Muslims practice a religion called _____, which was founded by the prophet Muhammad.

8. The _____ is the sacred book of Islam.

9. The _____ was an overland trade route that linked China and the Middle East.

10. _____ were groups of people who traveled together for safety.

11. A _____ is a large town whose government controls the surrounding countryside.

12. Several generations of an _____ live in one household.

CHAPTER

2 Section 4 Guide to the Essentials

Tradition and Change in Europe

VOCABULARY

salvation in Christian teachings, everlasting life

republic a system of government in which citizens choose representatives to govern them

Crusades a series of wars fought by Christians against Muslims to control the Holy Land of Jerusalem and surrounding areas

Renaissance a French word meaning "rebirth" given to a time of great learning and discovery in Europe

SUMMARY

Life in Europe in the 1400s was influenced by two religions, Judaism and Christianity. Judaism's emphasis on law and tradition provided followers with an identity based on moral teachings and customs. Christianity, with its emphasis on love and **salvation,** offered followers a hope for everlasting life after death. The Christian church in particular became a central institution in European life.

The Christian church's roots in the ancient world was one reason that the lessons of ancient Greece and Rome were preserved. Around 500 B.C., the city-state of Athens, Greece, experienced a golden age of art, literature, and politics. During the same period, the **republic** of Rome was established. Many of our modern ideas about equality and government came from the writings of this period, which were preserved by the church.

Another source of learning came from the documents preserved by Muslim scholars in the Middle East. These were made available to Europeans as a result of the **Crusades** in the 1300s, when Europeans waged a series of wars against Muslims. The crusaders did not win the wars, but they did establish trade routes and gained access to new ideas.

By the 1400s, a **Renaissance** was under way in Europe. Europeans, through trading, travel, and scholarship, made great gains in their knowledge of science, art, and history. During the Renaissance, Europeans came out of a long period of isolation and began to explore the globe. The rulers of Portugal, Spain, France, England, and Holland began to fund expeditions to Africa, Asia, and North and South America.

WORLD TRADITIONS		
Greek Tradition	**Roman Tradition**	**European Tradition**
• direct democracy • all citizens make laws • all citizens may attend assembly • only free men are citizens	• republic • citizens elect representative • everyone is equal before the law	• feudalism • king gives land to lords • lords fight when king asks • people who work land are not free to leave

REVIEW

Answer the following questions on a separate sheet of paper.

1. What effects did the Crusades have on learning in Europe?

2. **Chart Skills** Which tradition in the chart organizer is most like the tradition we have in the United States today?

CHAPTER

2

Section 4 Guided Reading and Review

Tradition and Change in Europe

A. As You Read

Directions: As you read Section 4 in your textbook, complete the chart below by writing supporting details under each main idea.

Main Idea A: Judaism and Christianity, two religions of the ancient Middle East, shaped European beliefs.

1. _____

2. _____

3. _____

Main Idea B: The customs of two ancient civilizations, Greece and Rome, shaped European traditions.

4. _____

5. _____

Main Idea C: The Middle Ages was a transition from the decline of the Roman empire to the modern era.

6. _____

7. _____

Main Idea D: The Renaissance expanded European geographical and intellectual horizons.

8. _____

9. _____

10. _____

B. Reviewing Key Terms

Directions: Define each term below, and identify the civilization or era with which it is associated: Jewish, Christian, Greek, Roman, Middle Ages, or Renaissance.

11. salvation _____

12. missionary _____

13. direct democracy _____

14. republic _____

15. feudalism _____

16. manor _____

17. Crusades _____

18. astrolabe _____

CHAPTER 2 TEST

Identifying Main Ideas

Write the letter of the correct answer in the space provided.

____ 1. Which theory of early migration to North America do many scientists believe?
A People walked along the coast of California.
B People traveled by boat from England.
C People crossed a land bridge.
D People came from Europe and Africa.

____ 2. What did the early peoples of North America learn from the peoples who settled in Central and South America?
A how to write
B how to keep records
C how to build boats
D how to irrigate crops

____ 3. What influenced the development of Native American culture in North America?
A climate and tradition
B climate, geography, and resources
C resources and religion
D Europeans and tradition

____ 4. Native Americans developed different cultures because they
A came to the Americas from different parts of the world.
B were from different social classes.
C adapted their ways of life to different environments.
D could not agree on one common way of life.

____ 5. Despite geographic differences, all Native American cultures in North America believed
A that the world was full of unseen and powerful forces.
B in celebrating the harvest.
C that all Europeans were dangerous.
D in sharing wealth with others.

____ 6. By the 1400s, people in Africa and the Middle East shared all of the following EXCEPT
A religion.
B trade routes.
C respect for nature.
D language.

____ 7. Which of the following first happened during the same century that Columbus reached the Americas?
A Africa and Asia were linked by trading routes.
B Chinese trading fleets visited India and Africa.
C The Iroquois nations formed an alliance.
D The Renaissance began.

____ 8. Which of the following traditions did NOT influence the development of European civilization?
A Christianity
B the Roman republic
C Chinese trading fleets
D Judaism

____ 9. What was one important result of the Crusades?
A Modern weapons were developed.
B New trade routes were opened.
C Europe became an isolated region.
D Religious wars came to an end.

____ 10. Which of the following was NOT a result of the Renaissance in Europe?
A More people traded and traveled.
B European rulers discouraged exploration.
C Gains were made in science, art, and history.
D Europe came out of a long period of isolation.

CHAPTER

3 Exploration and Colonization
(1492–1675)

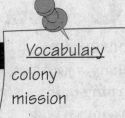

Vocabulary
colony
mission

Vocabulary Development

European settlement in the Americas included different types of communities. In both a colony and a mission, people settled in a foreign place. Colonies often were built to break away from a government the settlers did not like. Missions were built to bring a new religion to a native population. Yet both faced similar challenges and had some things in common.

Directions: *From the list below, choose whether the phrase describes a colony, a mission, or both. Complete the Venn diagram with the information given. If the phrase applies only to a colony, write it in the "Colony" circle. If it applies only to missions, write it in that circle. If it applies to both, write it in the overlapping area.*

Settlers' main goal is to convert natives to their religion
Spreading religion not the main purpose of the settlement
Settlers traveled far from their native countries
Outpost set up in a new land
Community led by priests
Community controlled by political, not religious, leaders
Sometimes faced hostility from Indians

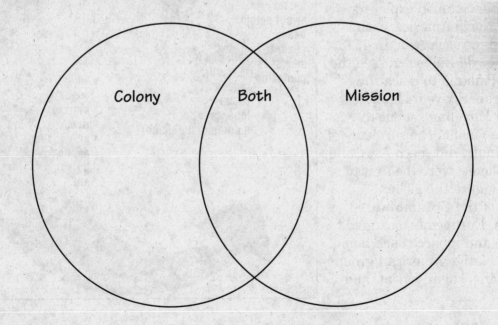

Colony   Both   Mission

Section 1 Guide to the Essentials
An Era of Exploration

VOCABULARY

colony a group of people who settle in a distant land but are still ruled by the government of their native land

turning point a moment in history that marks a decisive change

circumnavigate to sail completely around something

Columbian Exchange the exchange, or transfer, of goods and ideas between the Eastern and Western hemispheres that was started by the explorer Columbus

SUMMARY

Although there is evidence that Vikings, Asians, and Polynesians visited North America before the 1400s, the voyage of Christopher Columbus was the first to have a lasting impact. Determined to find a new sea route to Asia, Columbus sailed east across the Atlantic Ocean. After two months, he landed in the West Indies. Eventually, Columbus established a **colony** there, an event that would prove to be a **turning point,** affecting people on both sides of the globe.

Within 25 years of Columbus's voyage, other Spanish explorers arrived in North America, each determined to reach Asia. In 1513, Vasco Núñez de Balboa crossed the jungles of Panama to reach the Pacific Ocean. Six years later, Ferdinand Magellan set out to explore the Pacific. The survivors of that trip finally did reach Asia, and, returning home, were the first to **circumnavigate** the globe.

As part of the **Columbian Exchange,** Europeans took gold, new foods, and tobacco back home. In return, Native American groups received wine, sugar, wheat, and

domesticated animals such as horses, pigs, and goats. But they also contracted deadly diseases, such as smallpox and measles. (See diagram.) For centuries, North America would be the setting for both cultural exchange and conflict between Europeans and Native Americans.

THE COLUMBIAN EXCHANGE

From the Americas to Europe, Africa, and Asia

maize (corn)
potato
sweet potato
beans
peanut
squashes
pumpkin

tomato
chili pepper
avocado
pineapple
cocoa
tobacco
quinine (a medicine)

wheat
sugar
banana
rice
grape (wine)
dandelion
horse
pig

cattle
goat
sheep
chicken
smallpox
measles
typhus

From Europe, Africa, and Asia to the Americas

REVIEW

Answer the following questions on a separate sheet of paper.

1. How was Columbus's voyage a historical turning point?

2. **Graphic Organizer Skills** Identify at least two foods that Europeans took to the Americas and two foods that they brought back to Europe.

Name_____ Class_____ Date_____

Section 1 Guided Reading and Review

An Era of Exploration

A. As You Read

Directions: Complete the chart below as you read Section 1 in your textbook. Fill in the missing causes and effects.

Causes	Effects
1.	Vikings left behind detailed records of their voyages.
Spain wanted a share of the Asian spice trade.	2.
Columbus returned to Spain with exotic gifts such as parrots and pearls.	3.
4.	Contact with the Europeans wiped out much of the Taino population of the West Indies.
5.	Europeans learned the true size of the Earth.
Europeans brought the first horses to North America.	6.

B. Reviewing Key People

Directions: Identify each of the following people. Include the country or region for which each sailed and the areas each explored, claimed, and/or settled.

7. Leif Ericson _____

_____

8. Christopher Columbus _____

_____

9. Vasco Núñez de Balboa _____

_____

10. Ferdinand Magellan _____

_____

CHAPTER 3
Section 2 Guide to the Essentials
Spain Builds an Empire

VOCABULARY

conquistador conqueror

plantation large estate farmed by many workers

encomienda land grant given by the Spanish government

SUMMARY

After Columbus, a new wave of Spanish explorers, called **conquistadors,** came to the Americas to secure riches and establish Spanish colonies. Two of these conquistadors, Hernando Cortés and Francisco Pizarro, conquered the Aztecs and the Incas. Not only did Cortés have superior weapons, he joined forces with the Aztecs' enemies. He also took advantage of the Aztecs' belief that the Europeans were gods and of the Aztecs' fear of horses. Likewise, Francisco Pizarro easily overwhelmed the Incas with his advanced weapons.

Soon, Spanish territory spanned from what is now California to Florida. The Spanish king established the Law of the Indies to organize life in the new empire. The law called for three types of settlements—pueblos for farming and trade, presidios for military bases, and missions for converting Native Americans to Christianity. A strict set of social classes emerged in the colonies. Colonists were divided into peninsulares, those people who were born in Spain and had the highest jobs; creoles, who were born to Spanish parents and were often educated and wealthy; mestizos, who were of mixed background and served as skilled workers; and Native Americans, who were often slaves.

Native Americans were the main source of labor, where landowners had **plantations** or

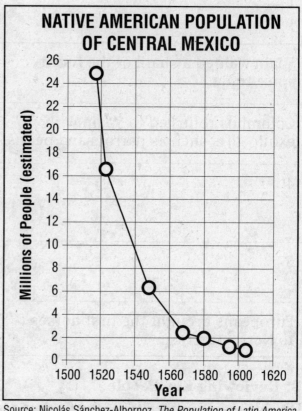

NATIVE AMERICAN POPULATION OF CENTRAL MEXICO

Millions of People (estimated) vs. Year

Source: Nicolás Sánchez-Albornoz, *The Population of Latin America*

encomiendas to be farmed or mines to be excavated. Millions died from overwork, starvation, and disease. (See graph.) Eventually, Africans were imported as slaves. Slavery would remain a key to the economy of the Americas for three centuries.

REVIEW

Answer the following questions on a separate sheet of paper.

1. Why did Spanish conquistadors come to the Americas?

2. **Graph Skills** Describe what happened to the Native American population of Central Mexico between the years 1520 and 1600.

CHAPTER

3 Section 2 Guided Reading and Review

Spain Builds an Empire

A. As You Read

Directions: As you read Section 2 in your textbook, answer each of the following questions.

1. What motivated the Spanish conquistadors to sail to the Americas? _____
   _____

2. How were Cortés and Pizarro able to conquer the Aztecs and Incas? _____
   _____
   _____

3. What became of Álvar Núñez Cabeza de Vaca? _____
   _____

4. Why did Spaniards, such as De Soto and Coronado, fail to settle North America?
   _____
   _____

5. How did the king of Spain arrange for his new lands to be settled? _____
   _____

6. What were the four social classes in the Spanish colonies of North America?
   _____
   _____

7. Why did the Spaniards begin the Atlantic slave trade? _____
   _____

B. Reviewing Key Terms

Directions: Define the following terms.

8. conquistador _____

9. pueblo _____

10. presidio _____

11. mission _____

12. creole _____

13. mestizo _____

14. encomienda _____

CHAPTER

3 Section 3 Guide to the Essentials

Colonizing North America

VOCABULARY

northwest passage a waterway through or around North America
Protestant Reformation Martin Luther's movement of protest against the Catholic Church
coureur de bois French colonists who worked and lived in the woods
missionary a person who goes to another land to win converts for a religion
alliance an agreement between nations to aid and protect one another

SUMMARY

During the 1500s, European nations searched for new ways to reach the riches of Asia. Explorers from England, France, and the Netherlands, including John Cabot, Giovanni da Verrazano, Jacques Cartier, and Henry Hudson, hoped to find a direct route through North America, which they called the **northwest passage.** No such route was ever found, but explorers mapped the territory of North America, leading the way for European settlement.

The competition among European nations for new riches was intensified by religious differences. After the **Protestant Reformation** in 1518, European countries were split between Roman Catholicism and Protestantism. Protestant England and the Netherlands fought against Catholic Spain and France for resources and land, both at home and abroad. Despite religious differences, all European nations wanted colonies in North America.

A rivalry began between the settlements of New France and New Netherland. The first French settlers were **coureurs de bois,** trappers, and Catholic **missionaries.** Led by Native American guides, the French explored and claimed huge areas of land for France. The Dutch meanwhile established trading posts along the Hudson River. Both the Dutch and the French relied on the fur trade for riches, and both sought Native American **alliances.** Fighting between the Dutch and the French and their allies grew intense, but for many years neither side was a clear winner.

FRENCH COLONIES IN NORTH AMERICA

Samuel de Champlain founds the first French colony in 1605, in Nova Scotia.	Champlain builds a trading post known as Quebec in 1608.	French traders and trappers establish friendly relations with Native Americans.	Catholic missionaries seek to convert Native Americans to Christianity.	The French explore the Mississippi River, reaching the Gulf of Mexico in 1682.	The French build forts along the Mississippi, seeking to keep Spain and England out of lands claimed for France.

REVIEW

Answer the following questions on a separate sheet of paper.

1. List the countries that sent explorers to find the northwest passage.

2. **Chart Skills** Why did the French build forts along the Mississippi?

CHAPTER

3 Section 3 Guided Reading and Review
Colonizing North America

A. As You Read

Directions: As you read Section 3 in your textbook, mark each statement true or false. Correct each false statement.

_____ 1. John Cabot and a crew of English sailors thought they had discovered the Northwest Passage. _____

_____ 2. Giovanni da Verrazano sailed up the St. Lawrence River on a voyage sponsored by France. _____

_____ 3. Henry Hudson explored the Hudson River for the Dutch and the Hudson Bay for the English. _____

_____ 4. Supporters of Queen Elizabeth I are called Protestants. _____

_____ 5. French explorer Jacques Cartier founded Port Royal and Quebec in Canada. _____

_____ 6. The French bought Manhattan Island from the local Indians. _____

_____ 7. French and Dutch settlers in North America became rivals over the fur trade. _____

B. Reviewing Key Terms

Directions: Use each term correctly in a sentence about the early French and Dutch settlement of North America.

8. Northwest Passage _____

_____

9. *coureur de bois* _____

_____

10. missionary _____

_____

11. alliance _____

_____

CHAPTER 3

Section 4 Guide to the Essentials

Building the Jamestown Colony

VOCABULARY

charter a legal document giving certain rights to a person or company

representative government a system of government in which voters elect representatives to make laws for them

SUMMARY

Jealous of Spain's American empire, England tried desperately to establish colonies in North America. One, in Roanoke, Virginia, failed when all of the settlers disappeared without a trace. In 1607, a **charter** was granted to establish a colony at Jamestown, Virginia. The colony struggled for years. It did not thrive for several reasons. Early settlers were more interested in searching for gold than in raising food. When food ran out, settlers made enemies of the local Native Americans by taking their supplies by force. Also, the swampy climate and bad water caused outbreaks of disease.

The Jamestown colony began to succeed economically only when settlers learned to plant tobacco. To attract new settlers to the colony, a **representative government** was put in place. Settlers were promised the same rights as any English citizen. **Burgesses,** or representatives, met in an assembly called the **House of Burgesses** to decide matters that affected the colony. The new assembly had roots in the *Magna Carta*—a charter signed by King John in 1215, that limited the power of the monarchy—and Parliament, the representative assembly of England.

After 1619, the Jamestown settlement grew with the addition of women who married, worked, and raised families in the colony. African slaves also arrived at this time. They were brought to Virginia to work in the tobacco fields and on the farms.

REASONS FOR JAMESTOWN'S STRUGGLES	REASONS FOR JAMESTOWN'S SUCCESS
• Swampy climate causes disease.	• A representative government is established.
• Settlers are more interested in gold than in farming.	• Tobacco proves easy to grow and is popular in Europe.
• Settlers have poor relations with local Native Americans.	• Women and African slaves arrive to increase population and to work.

REVIEW

Answer the following questions on a separate sheet of paper.

1. Why was a representative government put into place in Jamestown?

2. **Chart Skills** To what did the Jamestown settlement owe its success?

CHAPTER

3 Section 4 Guided Reading and Review
Building the Jamestown Colony

★

A. As You Read

Directions: As you read Section 4 in your textbook, complete each of the following sentences.

1. When Thomas Gates landed in Virginia in 1610, he found _____
_____

2. Walter Raleigh sent John White to Roanoke in order to _____
_____

3. The Virginia Company charter authorized _____
_____

4. Captain John Smith was an effective leader because he _____
_____

5. Jamestown began to prosper when the colonists _____
_____

6. The Virginia House of Burgesses was important because _____
_____

B. Reviewing Key Terms

Directions: Define the following terms.

7. charter _____
_____

8. burgess _____
_____

9. Magna Carta _____
_____

10. Parliament _____
_____

CHAPTER

3

Section 5 Guide to the Essentials

Seeking Religious Freedom

VOCABULARY

established church the chosen religion of a country

Pilgrims members of a religious sect that wanted to separate from the Church of England in the 1600s

persecution the mistreatment or punishment of people because of their beliefs

Mayflower Compact pledge made by Pilgrims and non-Pilgrims in Plymouth to unite under a government and to uphold laws

SUMMARY

Before the 1600s, European states had **established churches**—either Catholic or Protestant—and all citizens were expected to belong to them. Monarchs believed that uniformity of religious practice was one way to keep people under control.

For years, the **Pilgrims** were victims of **persecution** for their beliefs. Finally, in 1620, more than one hundred Pilgrims boarded the *Mayflower* for North America in search of religious freedom.

The Pilgrims had a charter to settle in the Virginia colonies. The rough voyage, however, sent the *Mayflower* off course, and the Pilgrims landed in what is now Plymouth, Massachusetts. By settling there, the Pilgrims realized that they would be violating the terms of the charter. As a solution, the Pilgrims wrote a framework of self-government called the **Mayflower Compact.**

This spirit of cooperation was crucial to the survival of the colony. The Pilgrims endured hard times and were eventually aided by neighboring Native Americans.

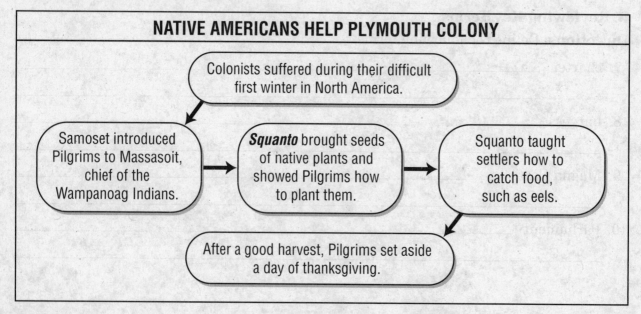

NATIVE AMERICANS HELP PLYMOUTH COLONY

Colonists suffered during their difficult first winter in North America.

Samoset introduced Pilgrims to Massasoit, chief of the Wampanoag Indians.

Squanto brought seeds of native plants and showed Pilgrims how to plant them.

Squanto taught settlers how to catch food, such as eels.

After a good harvest, Pilgrims set aside a day of thanksgiving.

REVIEW

Answer the following questions on a separate sheet of paper.

1. Why did the Pilgrims leave England for North America?

2. **Chart Skills** Identify two ways in which the Pilgrims received help from their Native American neighbors.

CHAPTER

3

Section 5 Guided Reading and Review

Seeking Religious Freedom

A. As You Read

Directions: As you read Section 5 in your textbook, complete the chart below by writing supporting details for each main idea.

Main Idea A: It was not easy for people to practice religion freely in Europe during the 1500s.

1. _____

2. _____

3. _____

Main Idea B: Religious separatists decided to leave Europe and settle in North America.

4. _____

5. _____

6. _____

Main Idea C: The Pilgrims' first years in North America were difficult.

7. _____

8. _____

B. Reviewing Key Terms

Directions: Define the following terms.

9. established church _____

_____

10. persecution _____

_____

11. Mayflower Compact _____

_____

12. precedent _____

_____

CHAPTER
3

TEST
Identifying Main Ideas
Write the letter of the correct answer in the space provided.

____ 1. All of the following groups may have visited North America before 1400 EXCEPT
    A Vikings.
    B Polynesians.
    C Spanish.
    D Asians.

____ 2. The goal of Spanish colonies in North America was to
    A educate Native Americans.
    B enrich Spain.
    C introduce slavery to North America.
    D prevent England from colonizing.

____ 3. One result of Spanish colonization in the Americas was
    A that Native Americans became citizens of Spain.
    B the establishment of strict social classes.
    C that Native American cultures were preserved.
    D that the Native America population of Central Mexico increased.

____ 4. The Europeans looked for new sea routes to Asia in order to
    A increase their profits from trade.
    B find more slaves.
    C reach the Americas more quickly.
    D spread the teachings of the Renaissance.

____ 5. Which of the following caused great rivalry among the European nations?
    A representative government
    B religious differences
    C religious freedom
    D the northwest passage

____ 6. Which of the following was NOT a reason England, France, and the Netherlands set up colonies in North America?
    A jealousy of Spain's colonies
    B seeking riches, such as gold
    C establishing religious freedom
    D competing for the control of land

____ 7. Which is a reason that the Jamestown settlement struggled to survive?
    A Settlers arrived too late in the year to build decent shelter.
    B Settlers planted tobacco instead of food.
    C Diseases caught from Native Americans caused many settlers to die.
    D People were more interested in finding gold than in growing food.

____ 8. What new tradition was created at the English colony at Jamestown?
    A representative government
    B the conversion Native Americans
    C the use of slavery in North America
    D religious freedom

____ 9. One purpose of establishing the House of Burgesses was to
    A keep people from leaving Jamestown.
    B follow the principles of the settlement charter.
    C attract new settlers to Jamestown.
    D encourage women to move to Jamestown.

____ 10. How were the Pilgrims different from other English settlers?
    A They hoped to grow tobacco in their new colony.
    B They sought religious freedom in North America.
    C They wanted to learn about Native American customs.
    D They sought the northwest passage.

CHAPTER

4 The Thirteen English Colonies
(1630–1750)

Vocabulary Development

One way to learn more about words is to study their roots or word origins.

Each of the vocabulary words in the grid below contains a Latin root. For each word listed, use the chart below to explore the root and its meaning. It may be helpful to review how the words are used in Chapter 4. Finally, fill in the column on the right with other forms of the word or words with the same root.

Vocabulary
export
mercantilism
proprietary
triangular

Word	Root	Root meaning	Other words containing root
export	ex-	from, out of	
	portare	to carry	
mercantilism	mercari	to trade	
proprietary	proprietas	property	
triangular	tri-	three	
	angulus	angle	

Directions: *Using the four listed vocabulary words, write a paragraph about the chapter on the lines below. Be sure to use complete sentences and correct spelling in your writing.*

_____

_____

_____

_____

_____

_____

_____

CHAPTER

4 Section 1 Guide to the Essentials

The New England Colonies

VOCABULARY

Puritans a religious group that believed in simple forms of worship

tolerance a willingness to let others practice their own beliefs

town meeting meeting at which New England colonists met to discuss issues and vote on them

SUMMARY

In 1630, the New England colony of Massachusetts Bay was established. It was founded by a religious group known as the **Puritans.** The Puritans wanted to reform the Church of England by introducing simpler forms of worship. In England, some Puritans were punished for their beliefs. The Puritans left England and set up their colony in North America so they could practice their religion in their own way.

Once settled, the Puritans believed that their way of life was the correct one, making life difficult for non-Puritans or Puritans with other ideas. Soon other colonies were founded by Puritans who left Massachusetts Bay. (See chart.) Connecticut was founded by people who felt that the Puritan-based government of Massachusetts had become too powerful. Rhode Island was founded by Roger Williams who thought that the business of church and government should be kept separate. Williams also believed in

tolerance. In Rhode Island, believers of different faiths were allowed to practice their religions.

New England became a land of tightly knit communities. New England colonists worked on small farms, hunted, and fished the oceans. Each village had a meeting house in which people worshipped. At **town meetings,** settlers discussed and voted on many issues. The town meeting helped encourage the growth of democratic ideas in New England.

Colonists took more and more land from Native Americans. As a result, fighting broke out between white settlers and Indian nations of the region. Eventually, the Indians were defeated and forced to move off their homelands. It was a pattern that would eventually be repeated throughout the colonies.

FOUNDING THE NEW ENGLAND COLONIES			
COLONY	**DATE**	**LEADER**	**REASON FOR FOUNDING**
Massachusetts Bay	1630	John Winthrop	to worship freely
Connecticut	1636	Thomas Hooker	to limit power of government
Rhode Island	1636	Roger Williams	to separate church and state

REVIEW

Answer the following questions on a separate sheet of paper.

1. Why did some Puritans found and move to other colonies?

2. **Chart Skills** Why were these three colonies founded?

CHAPTER

4 Section 1 Guided Reading and Review
The New England Colonies

A. As You Read

Directions: As you read Section 1 in your textbook, complete the chart below. Fill in key similarities and differences among the New England colonies of Massachusetts Bay, Connecticut, and Rhode Island.

Similarities
1.
2.
3.
4.
5.
Differences
6.
7.
8.

B. Reviewing Key People

Directions: Identify each of the following people.

9. Charles I _____

10. John Winthrop _____

11. Thomas Hooker _____

12. Roger Williams _____

13. Anne Hutchinson _____

14. Metacom _____

CHAPTER

4

Section 2 Guide to the Essentials

The Middle Colonies

VOCABULARY

patroon owner of a huge estate granted by the Dutch government

proprietary colony land placed by the king into the hands of a person or group of people for personal use or to rent to others

royal colony a colony under control of the English crown

Quakers a group of Protestant reformers who believed that all people are equal under God

cash crop crop that is sold for money at market

SUMMARY

New Netherland was a Dutch colony in which land was held by land owners known as **patroons.** Its main city, New Amsterdam, attracted a wide variety of settlers from all over Europe. Over time, the Dutch owners and leaders became unpopular with these settlers. In 1664, English forces took over New Netherland. The land was given to the king's brother, the Duke of York. Afterward, the colony and its main city became known as New York. The colony, however, proved too large to govern easily, so the king established New Jersey, first as a **proprietary colony** and later as a **royal colony.**

William Penn founded the colony of Pennsylvania as a "holy experiment." He was a **Quaker** who believed that all people were equal in God's sight. Penn wanted his colony to be a model of religious freedom, peace, and Christian living. Protestants from Germany, seeking religious freedom, became known as Pennsylvania Dutch.

The soil in the Middle Colonies was fertile. Farmers in these colonies were able to grow **cash crops.** The Middle Colonies exported so much grain that they became known as the Breadbasket Colonies. The economy of the Middle Colonies also included small manufacturing and the raising of livestock. (See chart.)

THE ECONOMY OF THE MIDDLE COLONIES		
Farming	**Raising Livestock**	**Manufacturing**
Raised cash crops such as wheat, barley, and rye; sold grain to other colonies	Raised cattle and pigs; sold beef, pork, and butter to other colonies and overseas	Made goods such as clocks, glass, and guns; produced iron to make parts for tools and other goods

REVIEW

Answer the following questions on a separate sheet of paper.

1. What goals did William Penn have for his colony?

2. **Chart Skills** Describe the role farming played in the economy of the Middle Colonies.

CHAPTER

Section 2 Guided Reading and Review
The Middle Colonies

A. As You Read

Directions: As you read Section 2 in your textbook, complete the chart below by writing supporting details for each main idea.

Main Idea A: The Dutch colony of New Netherland became the English colony of New York.

1. _____

2. _____

3. _____

Main Idea B: New Jersey attracted settlers from many lands.

4. _____

5. _____

Main Idea C: Pennsylvania was founded as an experiment in religious tolerance.

6. _____

7. _____

8. _____

B. Reviewing Key People and Terms

Directions: Identify each person or define each term below, and note whether it relates to New York, New Jersey, or Pennsylvania.

9. patroon _____

10. Peter Stuyvesant _____

11. proprietary colony _____

12. royal colony _____

13. Quaker _____

14. Pennsylvania Dutch _____

CHAPTER

4 Section 3 Guide to the Essentials
The Southern Colonies

VOCABULARY

debtor a person who owed money but could not pay it back

indigo a plant used to make a valuable blue dye

slave codes laws that controlled the behavior of slaves and denied them basic rights

racism the belief that one race is superior to another

SUMMARY

The border between Pennsylvania and Maryland is known as the Mason-Dixon line. The Southern Colonies lie south of the line.

Maryland was founded as a place where Roman Catholics would be able to worship freely. The *Act of Toleration* ensured that all Christians could practice their beliefs there.

Georgia was founded as a place where **debtors** from England could make a new start in life. The other three colonies in the South—Virginia, South Carolina, and North Carolina—were founded mainly for farming and trade.

Two ways of life developed in the Southern Colonies. (See chart.) Near the coast, large farms, called plantations, developed. Plantation owners, called planters, became rich and powerful.

Backcountry life was very different. In the area of hills and thick forests, settlers had smaller farms and lived a simpler life.

By 1700, slavery had become an important part of plantation life. Enslaved Africans cleared land; raised crops of tobacco, rice, and **indigo;** and tended livestock. They used farming skills they had brought from West Africa. For example, slaves showed English settlers how to grow rice. As the use of slavery increased, planters passed laws that put greater limits on the rights of slaves. Laws called **slave codes** treated Africans not as human beings but as property.

Although some groups in the northern colonies objected to slavery, most colonists' **racism** allowed them to believe that the enslavement of Africans was an acceptable practice.

TWO WAYS OF LIFE IN THE SOUTHERN COLONIES	
Plantation Life	**Backcountry Life**
• Slaves worked on large farms raising rice and tobacco. • Planters gained great wealth from exporting crops.	• Settlers tended small farms and hunted game. • Settlers led a simple life filled with hardship.

REVIEW
Answer the following questions on a separate sheet of paper.

1. How did enslaved Africans contribute to southern plantations?

2. **Chart Skills** How did the practice of farming differ in the two areas of the South?

CHAPTER

Section 3 Guided Reading and Review
The Southern Colonies

A. As You Read

Directions: As you read Section 3 in your textbook, mark each statement true or false. Correct each false statement.

_____ 1. The Mason-Dixon Line marked the border between New England and the Middle Colonies. _____

_____ 2. Maryland was founded as a Catholic colony. _____

_____ 3. During Bacon's Rebellion, the city of Jamestown, Maryland was burned. _____

_____ 4. Slavery quickly become common in North Carolina and South Carolina because of the rice plantations. _____

_____ 5. The first European settlers of Georgia were people who could not pay their debts. _____

_____ 6. Most of the great plantations in the South were located in the backcountry at the base of the Appalachians. _____

_____ 7. Many Africans who became slaves in the colonies were captured and sold into slavery by other Africans. _____

B. Reviewing Key Terms

Directions: Match the terms in Column I with the descriptions in Column II. Write the letter of the correct answer in the space provided.

Column I	Column II
_____ 8. Act of Toleration	a. person who owes money
_____ 9. indigo	b. belief that one race is superior to another
_____ 10. debtor	c. law providing religious freedom to all Christians
_____ 11. slave code	d. plant used to make blue dye
_____ 12. racism	e. laws that set out rules for slaves' behavior and denied their basic rights

CHAPTER

4 Section 4 Guide to the Essentials

Roots of Self-Government

VOCABULARY

mercantilism an economic theory that calls for a country to export more than it imports

export goods that are sent to markets outside a country

import goods that are brought into a country

legislature group of people who make laws

SUMMARY

England, whose economy followed the principle of **mercantilism,** hoped to benefit from the colonies' production of **exports** and their need for **imports.** The purpose of these laws was to ensure that England benefited from colonial trade. *The Navigation Acts* listed certain products that colonial merchants could ship only to England. Many colonists resented these laws.

New England, or Yankee, merchants got around the laws by using triangular trade routes. On these three-legged routes, Yankee traders made illegal stops for valuable goods in ports that belonged to countries other than England.

Although each colony developed its own government, the governments had much in common. In each colony, a governor directed affairs and enforced the laws. Most governors were appointed by the king or by the person to whom the king had given authority over the colony. Each of the colonies also had a **legislature.** Most legislatures had an upper and a lower house. The upper house was made up of advisers appointed by the governor. Members of the lower house of the legislature were elected by voters.

Each colony had its own rules about who could vote. As English subjects, colonists enjoyed certain rights. But by the 1720s, the right to vote was restricted. (See chart.)

THE RIGHT TO VOTE IN THE ENGLISH COLONIES

WHO COULD VOTE?
- White male Christian property owners over 21 years of age

WHO COULD NOT VOTE?
- Women
- Africans
- Native Americans
- Men who did not own property
- Men who were not Christians
- Men who did not belong to a particular church (in some colonies)

REVIEW

Answer the following questions on a separate sheet of paper.

1. What was the purpose of the Navigation Acts?

2. **Chart Skills** Which people in the colonies could not vote?

CHAPTER

Section 4 Guided Reading and Review
Roots of Self-Government

A. As You Read

Directions: As you read Section 4 in your textbook, complete the chart below by writing supporting details under each main idea.

Main Idea A: England regulated trade with the North American colonies.

1. _____

2. _____

3. _____

4. _____

Main Idea B: Governments in all the colonies had certain characteristics in common.

5. _____

6. _____

7. _____

B. Reviewing Key Terms

Directions: Define the following terms.

8. mercantilism _____

_____

9. export _____

_____

10. triangular trade _____

_____

11. legislature _____

_____

12. bill of rights _____

_____

Name_____ Class_____ Date_____

Section 5 Guide to the Essentials

Life in the Colonies

VOCABULARY

indentured servant a person who signed a contract to work without pay for four to seven years for anyone who would pay his or her ocean passage to the Americas

Enlightenment a movement based on belief in reason and scientific methods

SUMMARY

As in England, society in the colonies was divided into classes. Members of the rich gentry and prosperous middle class had more rights and privileges than **indentured servants** or slaves. In addition, white men had more rights than women or African Americans.

Yet, by the mid-1700s, the colonies had developed a culture different from that of England. Inspired by the **Enlightenment,** ideas about reason, science, and democracy became part of this new culture. One factor that contributed to the growth of democratic ideas was a religious movement known as the Great Awakening. This movement spread throughout the colonies in the 1730s and 1740s. Preachers urged people to obey the teachings in the Bible and to repent their sins. The Great Awakening caused the creation of many new churches.

Education was another tradition that grew stronger in the colonies. Different colonies developed different systems of education. (See chart.) New ideas in science and philosophy affected merchants, lawyers, ministers, and the better educated people in the colonies. Benjamin Franklin studied literature, mathematics, and foreign languages and invented a lightning rod, a smokeless fireplace, and bifocal lenses.

EDUCATION IN THE COLONIES		
Region	**Method of Education**	**Who Attended**
New England	Public schools supported by taxes	Boys
Middle Colonies	Private schools	Sons of wealthy families
Southern Colonies	Tutors at home, schools in England	Sons of wealthy planters
New England	Dame Schools	Girls

REVIEW

Answer the following questions on a separate sheet of paper.

1. What was the Great Awakening?
2. **Chart Skills** Describe the type of education found in the Southern Colonies.

CHAPTER

Section 5 Guided Reading and Review

Life in the Colonies

A. As You Read

Directions: As you read Section 5 in your textbook, complete the following sentences.

1. The gentry of colonial society included _____

_____

2. Women in the colonies worked at many jobs, including _____

_____

3. The Gullah language has its roots in _____

_____

4. Two effects of the Great Awakening were _____

_____

5. New Englanders believed in education for all children because _____

_____

6. The basic belief of the Enlightenment era was _____

_____

7. Benjamin Franklin's contributions to the city of Philadelphia included _____

_____

8. The case of John Peter Zenger was important because _____

_____

B. Reviewing Key Terms

Directions: Define the following terms.

9. middle class _____

_____

10. indentured servant _____

_____

11. apprentice _____

_____

12. dame school _____

_____

TEST

Identifying Main Ideas

Write the letter of the correct answer in the space provided.

____ 1. Puritans from Massachusetts founded Connecticut because
A they felt the Massachusetts government was too powerful.
B they felt the Massachusetts government was not powerful enough.
C they practiced a different religion than others in Massachusetts.
D they believed in religious tolerance.

____ 2. New England colonies were characterized by
A county governments.
B plantations.
C tightly knit villages.
D backcountry communities.

____ 3. Which group of people sought religious freedom in William Penn's colony?
A Puritans from Massachusetts
B Protestant Germans
C Native Americans
D Africans

____ 4. Which activity did not contribute to the economy of the Middle Colonies?
A farming
B fishing
C raising livestock
D manufacturing

____ 5. What two ways of life developed in the Southern Colonies?
A Roman Catholic and Protestant
B gentry and middle class
C plantation and backcountry
D Yankee and southerner

____ 6. Which of the following were two key crops grown on southern plantations?
A grain and tobacco
B tobacco and honey
C indigo and grain
D rice and tobacco

____ 7. How did Yankee merchants get around the Navigation Acts?
A They sailed on triangular trade routes.
B They imported slaves to work on southern plantations.
C They exported grain.
D They attended town meetings to protest.

____ 8. Which of the following was NOT true of colonial legislatures?
A Some legislatures had only an upper house.
B All legislatures had an upper and a lower house.
C Lower house members were elected.
D Each colony had a legislature.

____ 9. Which of the following is an idea that influenced the thinking of English colonists in the 1700s?
A legislatures
B tolerance
C the Enlightenment
D mercantilism

____10. What was the impact of the Great Awakening on the colonies?
A Slave codes were established.
B New churches were established.
C Dame schools were started for girls.
D Public schools were opened in the South.

CHAPTER

5 Crisis in the Colonies
(1745–1775)

Vocabulary Development

Vocabulary
boycott
Intolerable
  Acts
militia
minutemen
Proclamation
  of 1763
Stamp Act

Directions: *Choose from the Chapter 5 vocabulary words to the right fill in the blanks in each sentence. Then complete the exercise below.*

1. The _____ were volunteers who were said to keep their muskets ready at all times.

2. To help pay for troops in the American colonies, the _____ taxed newspapers, legal documents, and licenses.

3. To peacefully protest the taxes imposed on them, the colonists organized a _____ on British goods.

4. The _____ denied colonists the right to settle west of the Appalachian Mountains.

5. Parliament passed the _____ in 1774 to punish American colonists.

6. A volunteer army that serves in emergencies is called a _____.

7. In a short paragraph or two, summarize how tensions between the colonists and the British government rose in the years before the American Revolution. Use at least four of the vocabulary words in your answer.

_____

_____

_____

_____

_____

_____

_____

_____

_____

_____

CHAPTER

5 Section 1 Guide to the Essentials

The French and Indian War

VOCABULARY

Plains of Abraham the setting of the Battle of Quebec, the decisive battle of the French and Indian War

SUMMARY

By the mid-1700s, France and Britain were in fierce competition for land and rivers in the Ohio River Valley. They also competed for control of North America's important resources, including the valuable fur trade. France claimed lands west of the English colonies, which prevented the English colonies from expansion.

In addition, the French had firm alliances with several Native American groups. In 1754, when troops under Major George Washington fired on French soldiers near Fort Duquesne, they started the *French and Indian War,* a nine-year war against the French and their Native American allies.

The British suffered many defeats in the course of the war. British troops had little experience fighting in the forests of North America. In addition, the governments of the British colonies could not agree on how to approach the war. *The Albany Plan for Union,* a plan for a unified response proposed by Benjamin Franklin, was rejected by the colonies, who feared giving up too much power.

The tide of the war did not turn until the government in Britain gave the war its full support. In 1758, British-trained troops captured Louisbourg, a key French fort, and Fort Duquesne. In 1759, the British staged a daring attack. They scaled the cliffs below the **Plains of Abraham** and captured the key French city of Quebec. The fall of Quebec led to the collapse of French power in North America. The 1763 *Treaty of Paris* ended the war, and France gave up nearly all its lands on the continent.

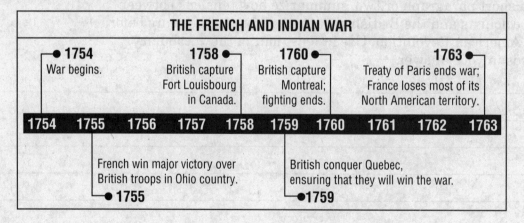

THE FRENCH AND INDIAN WAR

1754	1758	1760	1763
War begins.	British capture Fort Louisbourg in Canada.	British capture Montreal; fighting ends.	Treaty of Paris ends war; France loses most of its North American territory.

| 1754 | 1755 | 1756 | 1757 | 1758 | 1759 | 1760 | 1761 | 1762 | 1763 |

French win major victory over British troops in Ohio country.
● 1755

British conquer Quebec, ensuring that they will win the war.
●1759

REVIEW

Answer the following questions on a separate sheet of paper.

1. What did the British colonies hope to gain by going to war with the French?

2. **Time Line Skills** What event ensured that Britain would win the French and Indian War?

Name_____ Class_____ Date_____

5 Section 1 Guided Reading and Review
The French and Indian War

A. As You Read

Directions: Write the missing cause or effect as you read Section 1 in your textbook.

1. Cause: French trappers and traders in North America adopted Native American Ways.	1. Effect _____ _____
2. Cause _____ _____	2. Effect: Washington attacked the French but later surrendered.
3. Cause: General Braddock ignored warnings of Indian scouts near Fort Duquesne.	3. Effect _____ _____
4. Cause _____ _____	4. Effect: The best British generals were sent to North America.
5. Cause: The British won the Battle of Quebec.	5. Effect _____ _____

B. Reviewing Key Places

Directions: Explain how each of the following places relates to the French and Indian War.

6. Ohio River _____
   _____

7. Fort Duquesne _____
   _____

8. Louisbourg _____
   _____

9. Quebec _____
   _____

CHAPTER

5

Section 2 Guide to the Essentials

Turmoil Over Taxation

VOCABULARY

petition a formal written request to someone in authority, signed by a group of people

committee of correspondence a group whose members regularly wrote letters and pamphlets, reporting on events

boycott to refuse to buy certain goods and services

SUMMARY

After the French and Indian War, the British faced new problems in North America. With the French gone, British colonists began to move west in larger numbers. On this frontier, settlers clashed with Native Americans. A series of clashes led by an Ottawa chief named Pontiac became known as *Pontiac's War.* In response, the British government issued the *Proclamation of 1763,* which said that colonists could not move west of the Appalachian Mountains. Many colonists ignored this law and moved west anyway.

The French and Indian War had cost a great deal of money. The British government wanted the American colonists to contribute to these costs, so it placed new taxes on them. The colonists argued that the taxes were unfair. They claimed that since they did not elect representatives to the British government, it did not have the right to tax

them. Colonists protested by holding demonstrations, writing **petitions,** forming **committees of correspondence,** and attacking tax collectors. They also joined together to **boycott** certain British goods. A number of leaders played key roles in the protests. (See chart.)

Although Parliament canceled some taxes in response to colonial protests, others stayed in place. The British sent soldiers to the colonies to remind the colonists that the government still had the power to tax them.

In Boston, where many citizens felt they were being bullied into paying unjust taxes, tensions between colonists and soldiers led to the *Boston Massacre* in 1770. Facing a large and angry crowd, British soldiers panicked and opened fire. Five colonists died. The Boston Massacre outraged the colonists, stirring up more anti-British feelings.

COLONIAL LEADERS IN PROTEST AGAINST BRITISH POLICIES	
Samuel Adams	Worked behind the scenes to organize protests.
John Adams	Used skills as a lawyer to argue for justice.
Mercy Otis Warren	Wrote plays criticizing British officials.
Patrick Henry	Delivered fiery speeches that criticized British policies.

REVIEW

Answer the following questions on a separate sheet of paper.

1. What was a result of the Boston Massacre?

2. **Chart Skills** What role did Samuel Adams play in colonial protests against the British?

CHAPTER

5 Section 2 Guided Reading and Review

Turmoil Over Taxation

A. As You Read

Directions: As you read Section 2 in your textbook, answer the following questions:

1. What was the cause of Pontiac's War? _____

_____

2. What did the Proclamation of 1763 state? _____

_____

3. How did colonists react to the Proclamation of 1763? Why? _____

_____

4. Why did Parliament pass the Sugar Act? _____

_____

5. What reason did the colonists have for protesting the Stamp Act? _____

_____

6. What did the Townshend Acts create besides new taxes? _____

_____

7. What activities did the Sons of Liberty and the Daughters of Liberty organize?

_____

_____

8. In what way did the Boston Massacre differ from earlier protests? _____

_____

B. Reviewing Key People

Directions: Briefly identify each of the following people, and explain how each relates to the protests over taxes.

9. Samuel Adams _____

10. Mercy Otis Warren _____

11. Patrick Henry _____

12. Crispus Attucks _____

13. Paul Revere _____

CHAPTER

5 Section 3 Guide to the Essentials

From Protest to Revolution

VOCABULARY

First Continental Congress the meeting in Philadelphia of delegates from 12 of the 13 colonies

militia army of citizens who serve as soldiers during an emergency

minutemen volunteer soldiers ready to fight at a minute's notice

SUMMARY

In 1773, the British passed the *Tea Act,* a law that taxed tea shipped to the American colonies. The colonists believed that even though the law actually made tea less expensive, it was a trick to make them accept taxes passed by the British government. Colonists protested the tax with a boycott on tea and other actions.

On the night of December 16, 1773, a group of colonists boarded British ships in Boston harbor. Working quickly, they dumped valuable tea into the bay. This act, the *Boston Tea Party,* outraged the British. Britain responded by passing the *Quebec Act,* which set aside valuable western land for French Canadians. The

British Parliament also handed down a set of extremely harsh laws meant to punish the colonists for their protests. Colonists called these laws the *Intolerable Acts.*

In response to the Intolerable Acts, colonial leaders formed the **First Continental Congress.** The colonies united and began to organize **militias.** Early in 1775, the British learned that Massachusetts colonists had been storing weapons. On April 18, British soldiers marched to capture the weapons. In the villages outside Boston, the British fought groups of colonial **minutemen.** The *Battles of Lexington and Concord* were the beginning of the American Revolution.

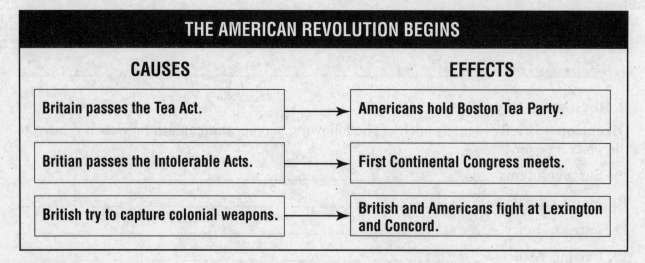

THE AMERICAN REVOLUTION BEGINS

CAUSES	EFFECTS
Britain passes the Tea Act.	Americans hold Boston Tea Party.
Britian passes the Intolerable Acts.	First Continental Congress meets.
British try to capture colonial weapons.	British and Americans fight at Lexington and Concord.

REVIEW

Answer the following questions on a separate sheet of paper.

1. Why did colonists protest the tax on tea?

2. **Chart Skills** What occurred as a result of the Intolerable Acts?

CHAPTER 5

Section 3 Guided Reading and Review

From Protest to Revolution

A. As You Read

Directions: Each of the following statements is either true or false. As you read Section 3 in your textbook, mark each statement true or false. If a statement is false, correct the statement.

	True or False	Correct Statement
1. Sons of Liberty supported the tea boycott by throwing British tea overboard.		
2. The British passed the Intolerable Acts in response to the Boston Massacre.		
3. Other colonies could not agree whether or not to support Boston after the passage of the Intolerable Acts.		
4. The British marched on Concord to seize arms and ammunition.		
5. A professional colonial army opened fire on the British on Lexington Green.		

B. Reviewing Key Terms

Directions: Match the description in Column I with the terms in Column II. Write the letter of the correct answer in the space provided.

Column I

_____ 6. dumping of three shiploads of tea into Boston Harbor

_____ 7. meeting of representatives of all the colonies to decide on response to British policies

_____ 8. made lands between Ohio and Missouri Rivers part of Quebec

Column II

a. First Continental Congress

b. Quebec Act

c. Boston Tea Party

CHAPTER

5 TEST

Identifying Main Ideas

Write the letter of the correct answer in the space provided.

____ 1. In the mid–1700s, France and Britain were competing for land and rivers in
A Quebec.
B Massachusetts.
C the Ohio River Valley.
D Canada.

____ 2. Which of the following is true of French rule in North America?
A It ended with the capture of Quebec.
B It was strengthened by the Quebec Act.
C It ended when Native American allies joined the British.
D It began with the Treaty of Paris.

____ 3. Which of the following did NOT happen after the British victory in the French and Indian War?
A Many British colonists decided to move westward.
B Colonists clashed with Native Americans in western territories.
C The Albany Plan of Union was adopted.
D British taxation of colonists increased greatly.

____ 4. The French and Indian War resulted in
A Britain gaining French lands in North America.
B the end of British power in North America.
C the defeat of all Indians.
D the Albany Plan of Union.

____ 5. What happened as a result of the Intolerable Acts?
A The colonists went to war with the French and Native Americans.
B Colonists were banned from moving westward.
C Colonial leaders formed the First Continental Congress.
D Five colonists were killed in the Boston Massacre.

____ 6. The colonies united and began to form militias in response to
A taxation on tea and other goods.
B the end of French rule in North America.
C the Intolerable Acts.
D the formation of colonial militia.

____ 7. One way colonists demonstrated their opposition to British actions was to
A pass the Proclamation of 1763.
B vote out their representatives in Parliament.
C boycott British goods.
D leave the colonies and move westward.

____ 8. Why did Massachusetts colonists hold the Boston Tea Party?
A to protest the British tax on tea
B to support the Boston Massacre
C to protest the repeal of taxes
D to force leaders to hold a Continental Congress

____ 9. Which of the following did NOT happen after the Boston Tea Party?
A The First Continental Congress met.
B Colonists organized militias.
C The British passed laws to punish the colonists.
D The British passed a tax on tea.

____ 10. The first battles of the American Revolutionary War were fought in
A Boston.
B Fort Duquesne.
C Lexington and Concord
D Louisbourg.

CHAPTER

6 The American Revolution
(1775–1783)

Vocabulary Development

Some words change forms when their part of speech changes. For example, the noun *siege* changes form when it changes into a verb, *besiege*. Other words keep the same form even when changing from a noun to an adjective or verb. For example, *sail*, the noun, is spelled the same as *sail*, the verb.

Directions: *Complete the following sentences with the form each word takes when it is used in different parts of speech. One form of each word is done for you as an example.*

Noun form:

British warships imposed a *blockade* of colonial ports.

Verb form:

1. British warships were ordered to _____ all colonial ports.

Adjective form:

2. Goods could not be shipped into or out of the _____ ports.

Verb form:

It was the task of Congress to *ratify* the Treaty of Paris.

Adjective form:

3. The Treaty of Paris was _____ by Congress in 1783.

Noun form:

4. A soldier who fights for no cause but money is considered to be a _____.

Adjective form:

The man's *mercenary* behavior showed that he had no loyalty to his country.

Noun form:

To be successful, a *guerrilla* must make use of surprise and deception.

Adjective form:

5. The _____ fighters fired from behind trees and stone walls.

CHAPTER

6 Section 1 Guide to the Essentials

Fighting Begins in the North

VOCABULARY

Patriot a colonist who favored war and independence from Britain

Loyalist a colonist who was loyal to Britain

blockade shutting of a port to keep people and supplies from moving in or out

SUMMARY

After the battles of Lexington and Concord, American colonists still hoped to avoid war with Britain. In 1775, the *Second Continental Congress* met to decide the colonies' future. The delegates sent the *Olive Branch Petition* to King George III. They declared their loyalty but asked the king to repeal the Intolerable Acts. At the same time, the Congress formed the first *Continental Army* and appointed George Washington to lead it.

Altough only a third of the colonists claimed to be **Patriots** (another third were **Loyalists;** the final third were neutral), war with Britain was likely.

At the beginning of the war, the British appeared to have many advantages. However, the colonists also had factors in their favor. (See chart.) The main disadvantage for the British troops was their distance from home. The colonists' lack of training put them at a disadvantage, too.

During the first year of the war, the two sides fought over Boston. British troops controlled the city, but Americans held the surrounding area, keeping the British from marching out. In January 1776, Americans set up cannons on the heights overlooking Boston harbor. The British commander, General Howe, realized he could no longer hold the city. He withdrew his troops to Halifax, Canada. After Howe's retreat, however, the British navy used its powerful fleet to set up a **blockade** of all colonial ports. The blockade eventually cut the colonies off from the world.

| ADVANTAGES OF EACH SIDE IN THE AMERICAN REVOLUTION ||
THE BRITISH	THE COLONISTS
• well-trained, experienced troops • powerful navy • mercenary troops	• George Washington, a strong leader • fighting to defend their own land • many experienced rifle users

REVIEW

Answer the following questions on a separate sheet of paper.

1. How did the Americans gain control of Boston?
2. **Chart Skills** Identify two advantages the British had as the war began.

Name_____ Class_____ Date_____

Section 1 Guided Reading and Review
Fighting Begins in the North

A. As You Read

Directions: As you read Section 1 in your textbook, use the letters A–D to label the following events in correct chronological order. Write a sentence or two explaining the importance of each event.

_____1. the blockade of all colonial ports

_____

_____

_____2. the appointment of George Washington as Commander of the Continental Army

_____

_____

_____3. the Battle of Bunker Hill

_____

_____

_____4. the American victory at Fort Ticonderoga

_____

_____

B. Reviewing Key Terms

Directions: Complete the sentences in Column I with the terms in Column II. Write the letter of the correct term in the space provided.

Column I

_____ 5. The request of Congress that King George repeal the Intolerable Acts was called the _____.

_____ 6. The _____ was made up entirely of volunteers, most of whom had no military training or experience.

_____ 7. A/An _____ was a colonist who supported Britain.

_____ 8. When a/an _____ is set up, people and supplies cannot pass through a port.

Column II

a. Loyalist

b. Olive Branch Petition

c. blockade

d. Continental Army

Section 2 Guide to the Essentials

The Colonies Declare Independence

VOCABULARY

Declaration of Independence a document that declared the 13 colonies to be free from British rule

natural rights rights that belong to all people at birth

SUMMARY

Although the colonists had begun fighting the British, many still felt loyal to the king. Then, in early 1776, Thomas Paine published a pamphlet called *Common Sense*. Paine argued the case for American independence. He wrote that the colonists owed nothing to Britain, which had only helped colonists for its own profit. Paine stated that having a king or queen was wrong. *Common Sense* persuaded many colonists to support independence.

The members of the Continental Congress asked Thomas Jefferson to write a document declaring that the United States was now an independent country. On July 4, 1776, the Continental Congress passed the **Declaration of Independence.** Copies of the Declaration were sent all around the colonies. Many Patriots supported independence. They cheered the Declaration, firing guns in celebration and pulling down statues of the king. Loyalists did not support independence. They wanted to remain loyal to Britain.

The Declaration has three main parts. (See chart.) The first part stresses the idea that people are born with **natural rights** given to them by God. These rights include "life, liberty, and the pursuit of happiness." The document states that if a government fails to respect these rights, then the people have the right to rebel against it.

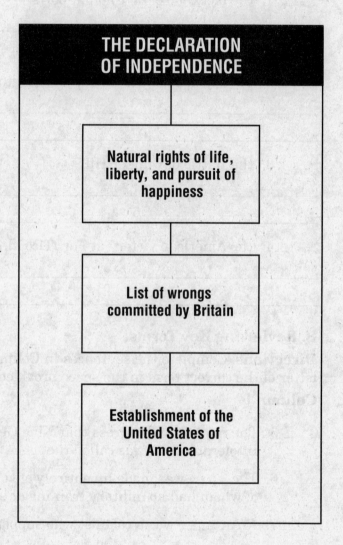

THE DECLARATION OF INDEPENDENCE

Natural rights of life, liberty, and pursuit of happiness

List of wrongs committed by Britain

Establishment of the United States of America

REVIEW

Answer the following questions on a separate sheet of paper.

1. What arguments did *Common Sense* make in favor of independence?

2. **Chart Skills** What are the three main parts of the Declaration of Independence?

CHAPTER

Section 2 Guided Reading and Review
The Colonies Declare Independence

A. As You Read

Directions: As you read Section 2 in your textbook, complete the chart below by writing three supporting details under each main idea.

Main Idea A: Certain natural rights belong to all people from birth.

1. _____

2. _____

3. _____

Main Idea B: Great Britain committed many wrongs against the colonies.

4. _____

5. _____

6. _____

Main Idea C: The British colonies are now the United States of America.

7. _____

8. _____

9. _____

B. Reviewing Key Terms

Directions: Explain how each of the following relates to the American Revolution.

10. *Common Sense* _____

_____

_____

11. traitor _____

_____

_____

12. Declaration of Independence _____

_____

_____

CHAPTER
6 Section 3 Guide to the Essentials
Struggles in the Middle States

VOCABULARY

ally a nation that works with another nation to reach a common goal

cavalry troops on horseback

SUMMARY

After British attempts to conquer New England failed, fighting shifted to the Middle States. There, the Patriots suffered many defeats and hardships. In August 1776, the British clashed with Washington and his troops in the *Battle of Long Island.* Washington was forced to retreat to Manhattan. There Washington fought a series of battles with the British army. The British captured New York.

Eventually, the Continental Army was forced to retreat across the Hudson River into New Jersey, then into Pennsylvania. In December and January, Washington boldly attacked the British and fought the *Battles of Trenton and Princeton.* These victories gave Americans new hope.

Good news also came for Americans in October 1777. Patriot troops defeated the British in the *Battle of Saratoga* in New York. This American victory was a major turning point in the war. (See chart.) The victory ended British threats to New England and raised American spirits. It also convinced France to become an **ally** of the United States.

Other countries and individual volunteers also gave help to the Americans. Foreign military officers, such as the Marquis de Lafayette from France, helped train American troops and **cavalry.**

Washington's troops still suffered hardships through the long winter of 1777–1778 at *Valley Forge,* Pennsylvania. Lacking food and supplies, many soldiers fell ill or victim to frostbite. Eventually, Patriots around the colonies sent supplies and ammunition to the troops, who still faced months of fighting.

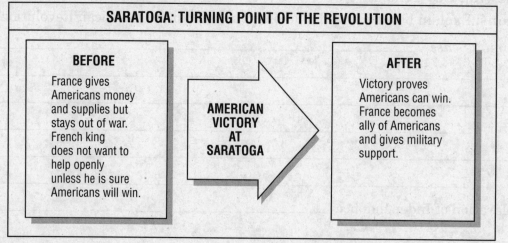

SARATOGA: TURNING POINT OF THE REVOLUTION

BEFORE
France gives Americans money and supplies but stays out of war. French king does not want to help openly unless he is sure Americans will win.

AMERICAN VICTORY AT SARATOGA

AFTER
Victory proves Americans can win. France becomes ally of Americans and gives military support.

REVIEW

Answer the following questions on a separate sheet of paper.

1. What happened after the British troops captured New York?

2. **Chart Skills** What did France decide to do as a result of the American victory at Saratoga?

CHAPTER

6 Section 3 Guided Reading and Review
Struggles in the Middle States

★

A. As You Read

Directions: As you read Section 3 in your textbook, answer the following questions:

1. What happened during the Battle of Long Island? _____

   _____

2. Who was Nathan Hale? _____

   _____

3. What was the result of the American attack on Trenton? _____

   _____

4. How did the Americans defeat Cornwallis at Princeton? _____

   _____

5. What was General Burgoyne's plan of attack? _____

   _____

6. Why was the British defeat at Saratoga important? _____

   _____

7. Name two Europeans who contributed to the American cause, and explain their

   contributions. _____

   _____

   _____

8. Describe conditions at Valley Forge in the winter of 1777–1778. _____

   _____

B. Reviewing Key Places and Terms

Directions: Identify each place, and define each term.

9. Battle of Long Island _____

10. Battle of Trenton _____

11. Battle of Saratoga _____

12. allies _____

13. cavalry _____

14. Valley Forge _____

CHAPTER

6 Section 4 Guide to the Essentials

Fighting for Liberty on Many Fronts

VOCABULARY

front a line of battle or zone of conflict between two armies

SUMMARY

The American Revolution took place on many **fronts.** Fighting occurred not only in New England and the Middle States but also in the West and the South. Important battles were fought on the frontier and at sea. (See chart.)

In the West, many Native Americans became allies of the British. The British were able to persuade Native Americans that a Patriot victory would mean more white settlers moving onto Native Americans lands.

Although the American navy was poorly funded, it still managed to do some damage to British fleets. The most famous battle was won by American John Paul Jones, who captured a British ship off the coast of England.

Women played important roles during the American Revolution. When men joined the army, women took on the added work of tending farms and businesses. Women also helped supply the troops, making shoes and weaving cloth for blankets and uniforms. Some traveled with the army, caring for the wounded, washing clothes, and cooking. A few women took part in battle.

African Americans fought on both sides during the war. The British promised freedom to any male slave who fought for the king. About 5,000 African Americans fought on the Patriot side, serving as soldiers, sailors, drummers, spies, and guides.

Enslaved African Americans faced difficult choices. They could fight for the colonists—who had no plans for granting the slaves freedom—and risk being captured and sold by the British, or they could try to escape to the British. By doing so, they risked being hanged by angry Patriots.

THE WAR IN THE WEST

- Cherokee and other southern Native Americans become British allies and fight against settlers.

- Fierce fighting takes place between settlers and Iroquois forces in Pennsylvania and New York.

- Patriots under George Rogers Clark capture British forts in the Ohio Valley.

- Spain provides military help to the Patriots on the southwestern frontier.

REVIEW

Answer the following questions on a separate sheet of paper.

1. How did women take part in the war?

2. **Chart Skills** Which allies did each side have in the war in the West?

CHAPTER

6 Section 4 Guided Reading and Review

Fighting for Liberty on Many Fronts

A. As You Read

Directions: As you read Section 4 in your textbook, complete the chart below by writing key supporting details under each main idea.

Main Idea A: American women played important roles in the war.

1. _____

2. _____

Main Idea B: Many African Americans served in the war.

3. _____

4. _____

Main Idea C: Fierce battles were fought in the West.

5. _____

6. _____

Main Idea D: American ships struck some important blows for the Patriot cause.

7. _____

B. Reviewing Key People

Directions: Briefly identify the following people.

8. Mary Ludwig Hays _____

_____

9. Peter Salem _____

_____

10. Joseph Brant _____

_____

11. George Rogers Clark _____

_____

12. John Paul Jones _____

_____

6 Section 5 Guide to the Essentials

Winning the War in the South

★

VOCABULARY

guerrilla hit-and-run tactics of fighting

siege a strategy of surrounding, blockading, and bombarding an enemy position in order to capture it

ratify to approve

SUMMARY

The South became the main battle-ground of the war after British plans to conquer New England and New York failed. The British won a number of early victories in Georgia and South Carolina. The tide turned, however, by late 1780 when the Patriots began to win victories in the South.

Nathaniel Greene and Daniel Morgan used clever tactics to wear down the British army at the ***Battle of Cowpens.*** Another American, Francis Marion—the "Swamp Fox"—led a group of soldiers who slept by day and traveled by night. They used **guerrilla** tactics, attacking and then retreating quickly into the swamps of South Carolina.

The British commander in the South, Charles Cornwallis, had planned to capture the Carolinas. After Patriot victories there, however, Cornwallis moved his troops north to Virginia. In 1781, the British army occupied the Yorktown peninsula. Seeing an opportunity to trap the British, Washington marched his army south from New York. The French navy closed off the possibility of escape by sea. After weeks under **siege,** the British surrendered.

The British defeat at the Battle of Yorktown forced them to agree to peace talks. The war was officially over with the ***Treaty of Paris,*** which was **ratified** by Congress in April 1783. The British recognized the United States as an independent nation. The treaty also established the borders of the United States: east and west, the border extended from the Atlantic Ocean to the Mississippi River; to the north, the border stopped at the Great Lakes; and to the south, the border stopped at Florida. The United States also agreed to pay Loyalists for property they had lost in the war; however, most states never made those payments.

WHY THE AMERICANS WON

GEOGRAPHY	FOREIGN HELP	PATRIOTISM
• The British were far from home and fighting in unfamiliar territory.	• France provided money, supplies, and military support.	• The Americans grew proud of their country and their achievements.
• The Americans knew the landscape, the best routes, and the best places to fight.	• Spanish forces attacked the British along the Gulf of Mexico.	• British cruelty in the South turned many Loyalists into Patriots.

REVIEW

Answer the following questions on a separate sheet of paper.

1. What battle led to the end of the American Revolution?

2. **Chart Skills** How did geography play a role in the American victory over the British?

CHAPTER

6 Section 5 Guided Reading and Review
Winning the War in the South

A. As You Read

Directions: As you read Section 5 in your textbook, write the missing information under each heading.

Fighting in the South	Victory at Yorktown	The Peace Treaty
1. The British decided to try to win the war in the South because many _____ lived in the southern colonies.	5. General Cornwallis thought that if he conquered _____, he would cut off American supply routes to the South.	8. The Treaty of Paris stated that the _____ formed the western border of the United States.
2. The Americans' greater knowledge of _____ put the British at a disadvantage in the South.	6. _____ was a skilled American general, but his name became a synonym for "traitor" when he agreed to turn over West Point to the British.	
3. Two American generals who helped turn the tide in the southern battles were _____ and _____.	7. Retreating to Yorktown was a serious mistake for the British because Yorktown was on a/an _____, and they were trapped with no means of retreat.	
4. Francis Marion was called the _____ because of his surprise appearances, sudden attacks, and quick retreats.		

B. Reviewing Key Terms

Directions: Match the descriptions in Column I with the terms in Column II. Write the letter of the correct answer in the space provided.

Column I

_____ 9. army surrounds and blockades an enemy position

_____ 10. approve

_____ 11. hit-and-run tactics

Column II

a. guerrilla

b. siege

c. ratify

CHAPTER 6

TEST

Identifying Main Ideas

Write the letter of the correct answer in the space provided.

____ 1. How did the Second Continental Congress attempt to make peace with the British?

A It sent the Olive Branch Petition to the king.

B It asked George Washington to lead the Continental Army.

C It asked the colonists to stop fighting back.

D It withdrew to Canada.

____ 2. *Common Sense* called for

A peace with Britain.

B colonists to support independence from Britain.

C colonists to remain loyal to Britain.

D people to pursue their natural rights.

____ 3. Which is NOT a natural right mentioned in the Declaration of Independence?

A loyalty to the United States

B the pursuit of happiness

C life

D liberty

____ 4. Which was NOT a result of the Battle of Saratoga?

A Washington retreated into Pennsylvania.

B The British no longer threatened New England.

C American spirits were raised.

D France became an American ally.

____ 5. Women played an important role during the American Revolution by

A spying on the British.

B providing entertainment.

C tending farms and businesses.

D collecting taxes.

____ 6. By fighting for the colonists, enslaved African Americans

A knew they would be freed by the colonists after the war.

B planned to escape to Canada.

C wanted to be Loyalists.

D risked being captured and sold by the British.

____ 7. Which of the following was an ally of the colonies in the West?

A France

B Spain

C Native Americans

D Canada

____ 8. The South became the main battlefield in the Revolution because

A the British were more familiar with the southern landscape.

B Francis Marion used guerrilla tactics against British troops.

C the French navy had blocked off the Yorktown peninsula.

D British attempts to conquer the northern colonies had failed.

____ 9. The battle that brought an end to the American Revolution was at

A Long Island.

B Trenton.

C Yorktown.

D Saratoga.

____10. After the Treaty of Paris

A the British surrendered at the battle of Yorktown.

B the French supported the American war effort.

C the United States declared its independence from Britain.

D Britain recognized the independence of the United States.

CHAPTER

7 Creating a Republic
(1776–1790)

Vocabulary
monarchy
dictatorship
democracy

Vocabulary Development

After the American Revolution, the new nation struggled to establish a strong republic in which the citizens would rule themselves by electing representatives to run the government. A government in which the people rule themselves is called a democracy. What other types of government existed throughout the world?

monarchy: a government in which a king or queen has ruling power

dictatorship: a government with a ruler who has the power to give orders that must be obeyed

Directions: *On the following word grid, place an X in the boxes of the features that describe each type of government.*

	ruler has absolute power	voters elect officials	people who are governed have equal rights	ruler inherits position	ruler is elected
monarchy					
democracy					
dictatorship					

Directions: *Answer the following questions on the lines provided.*

1. How would a dictatorship respond to the concerns of the citizens?

_____

_____

2. Describe two characteristics of a dictatorship.

_____

3. Which government could be described as representing its citizens?

_____

4. How would a democracy respond to the concerns of the citizens?

_____

_____

5. Describe two characteristics of a monarchy.

_____

CHAPTER

7 Section 1 Guide to the Essentials
A Loose Confederation

VOCABULARY

constitution a document that sets out the laws, principles, organization, and processes of a government

bill of rights list of freedoms that a government promises to protect

currency money

depression a period in which business activity slows, prices and wages fall, and unemployment rises

SUMMARY

The Declaration of Independence created a nation made up of 13 independent states. Most states wrote **constitutions** that stated the rights of citizens and set limits on the power of government. States divided power between executive and legislative branches. Some included a **bill of rights** in their constitutions.

While states formed their governments, the Continental Congress developed a plan for the nation. In 1777, it completed the *Articles of Confederation,* the first American constitution. Under the Articles, the national government was weak. (See graphic organizer.) There was no president to carry out laws passed by Congress. There was no court system to settle disputes between states.

The weakness of the Confederation was a problem as the nation faced an economic crisis. The national **currency** was valueless after the war, and states refused to share taxes with the national government. As a result, the country fell into a **depression** as it struggled to pay its bills.

The depression hurt farmers, and many of them lost their land. Some Massachusetts farmers resisted the seizure of their property in an uprising called *Shays' Rebellion.* Many Americans saw the rebellion as a sign that the Articles of Confederation did not work and needed to be revised.

In 1787, Congress passed the *Northwest Ordinance.* It set up a government for the Northwest Territory, the lands lying north of the Ohio River and east of the Mississippi River. It outlawed slavery in the territory and said that the area could be divided into smaller territories. Once a territory had a population of 60,000, it could apply for statehood. Each new state received the same privileges as the original 13 states.

THE ARTICLES OF CONFEDERATION
Weaknesses of the National Government
Each state has one vote in Congress.
Laws must be approved by 9 of 13 states.
Congress cannot control trade between states or with foreign countries.
Congress has to ask states for money.
There is no executive branch and no judicial branch.

REVIEW
Answer the following questions on a separate sheet of paper.

1. How did the Northwest Ordinance provide for the growth of the United States?

2. **Graphic Organizer Skills** Under the Articles of Confederation, how many states must approve a law?

CHAPTER

7 Section 1 Guided Reading and Review
A Loose Confederation

A. As You Read

Directions: Complete the following sentences as you read Section 1 in your textbook.

1. Each state's constitution sets out _____

   _____

2. In 1777, the Continental Congress approved _____

3. Compared with the states, under the Articles Congress had _____

   _____

4. Maryland demanded that other states cede their claims to western lands because

   _____

5. Disputes continued to arise among states because _____

   _____

6. Without the power to tax, Congress _____

7. Britain refused to withdraw its troops from the Ohio Valley, and Spain

   _____

8. Under the Land Ordinance of 1785, the Northwest Territory would be

   _____

9. The Northwest Ordinance allowed a territory to request statehood if

   _____

10. Many Americans saw Shays' Rebellion as _____

    _____

B. Reviewing Key Terms

Directions: Complete each sentence by writing the correct term in the blank.

11. _____ is a list of freedoms that the government promises to protect.

12. The _____ set up a loose alliance of the 13 states.

13. The _____ set up rules for settling the Northwest Territory.

14. The _____ set up a government for the Northwest Territory.

15. In an uprising known as _____, farmers attacked the Massachusetts government for raising taxes.

CHAPTER

7 Section 2 Guide to the Essentials
The Constitutional Convention

VOCABULARY

compromise agreement in which each side gives up something

SUMMARY

The ***Constitutional Convention*** opened on May 25, 1787. It was a meeting of delegates from each state. The leading delegates included Benjamin Franklin, George Washington, Alexander Hamilton, and James Madison. Their goal was to revise the Articles of Confederation. After some discussion, the delegates decided to write a new constitution. However, the delegates disagreed about the form of the new government. Two groups proposed two different plans, the ***Virginia Plan*** and the ***New Jersey Plan.*** (See chart.)

States with large populations supported the Virginia Plan. It would give them more members in Congress. Small states did not like the Virginia Plan because they feared that large states could outvote them. They favored the New Jersey Plan because it would let each state have the same number of members. Finally, delegates agreed on a **compromise.** According to this ***Great Compromise,*** there would be two houses of Congress. In the Senate, each state would have two members. In the House of Representatives, the number of members would be based on each state's population.

The Convention also made compromises about slavery. Southern states wanted slaves included in their population count. If slaves were not counted, northern states would have more members in the House of Representatives. Delegates finally agreed to let the South count three-fifths, or three out of every five, of the slaves. Delegates also agreed to not outlaw the slave trade for at least 20 years.

VIRGINIA AND NEW JERSEY PLANS

VIRGINIA PLAN	NEW JERSEY PLAN
• Legislative branch has two houses.	• Legislative branch has one house.
• Number of members is based on number of people in each state.	• Each state has one member.

REVIEW

Answer the following questions on a separate sheet of paper.

1. What was the original goal of the Constitutional Convention?

2. **Chart Skills** What were two differences between the Virginia and the New Jersey plans?

CHAPTER

7 Section 2 Guided Reading and Review
The Constitutional Convention

A. As You Read

Directions: As you read Section 2 in your textbook, answer the following questions:

1. What was the original goal of the Constitutional Convention? _____
_____

2. Why is James Madison called "the Father of the Constitution"? _____
_____

3. Why did the delegates keep their debates secret? _____
_____

4. How would the legislature differ under the Virginia Plan and the New Jersey Plan?
_____
_____

5. What was Roger Sherman's main contribution to the Convention? _____
_____
_____

6. How was the dispute between states over the question of the slave population resolved?
_____
_____

7. What were the Northern and Southern positions on outlawing the slave trade?
_____
_____

8. How was this disagreement resolved? _____
_____

9. How would the Constitution be approved and go into effect? _____
_____

B. Reviewing Key Terms

Directions: Briefly describe the responsibilities of each branch of government.

10. legislative branch _____

11. executive branch _____

12. judicial branch _____

CHAPTER

7 Section 3 Guide to the Essentials
Ideas Behind the Constitution

VOCABULARY

dictatorship a government in which one person or small group holds complete authority

SUMMARY

The ideas in the United States Constitution came from many sources. First, the founders were inspired by the example of the Roman republic, a system in which Roman citizens governed themselves by electing representatives. The Founding Fathers were impressed by the willingness of Roman citizens to serve in public office out of devotion to self-government. At the same time, the founders saw the collapse of Rome's republic and its shift to **dictatorship** as a warning to the United States.

The English tradition was centuries old. At the heart of the English system of government was the **Magna Carta** and the **English Bill of Rights,** documents in which rulers recognized certain rights of citizens. These rights included the right not to be jailed without being charged and the right not to be taxed unfairly.

Beginning in the 1600s, Americans enjoyed a tradition of representative government. In Virginia, colonists had established the **House of Burgesses.** In Massachusetts, the Pilgrims set the limits and powers of government in the **Mayflower Compact.**

Enlightenment thinkers were another source. John Locke wrote that people have natural rights and that rulers must protect those rights. Baron de Montesquieu urged that the power of government be clearly defined and divided among three branches of government.

Above all, the founders considered their own experiences as colonists fighting for independence. They remembered the struggle to put together a national government and the failures of the Articles of the Confederation.

SOURCES OF IDEAS BEHIND THE CONSTITUTION

ROMAN REPUBLIC	ENGLISH TRADITION	ENLIGHTENMENT	AMERICAN EXPERIENCE
• representational government • citizen's involvement in government	• written declaration of citizen's rights	• recognition that people have natural rights • division and separation of the powers of government	• experience of claiming independence • struggle to create strong national government

REVIEW

Answer the following questions on a separate sheet of paper.

1. What ideas of the Enlightenment helped the founders?

2. **Chart Skills** Identify the four sources of ideas for the Constitution.

CHAPTER

7 Section 3 Guided Reading and Review
Ideas Behind the Constitution

★

A. As You Read

Directions: As you read Section 3 in your textbook, fill in the graphic organizer with the ideas that influenced the Constitution of the United States.

The Roman Republic	The American Experience
1. _____ _____ 2. _____ _____	6. _____ _____ 7. _____ _____
Great Britain	**The Enlightenment**
3. _____ _____ 4. _____ _____ 5. _____ _____	8. _____ _____ 9. _____ _____ 10. _____ _____

B. Reviewing Key Terms

Directions: Define the following terms.

11. republic _____

12. dictatorship _____

13. Magna Carta _____

14. habeas corpus _____

CHAPTER

7 Section 4 Guide to the Essentials

Ratification and the Bill of Rights

VOCABULARY

amend change

SUMMARY

The Constitution had to be approved by 9 of the 13 states before it could go into effect. In 1787 and 1788, delegates from every state debated the Constitution. Supporters of the Constitution called themselves *Federalists.* The Federalists favored a strong national government. The *Antifederalists* thought the Constitution weakened the powers of the states too much. They also thought it gave the President too much power.

Some Antifederalists agreed to accept the Constitution if a citizens' bill of rights were added to it. One by one, the states finally voted to accept the Constitution.

The framers of the Constitution had established a way to **amend** the document. By 1789, James Madison had prepared a list of 12 amendments that would serve as a bill of rights.

By December 1791, the states had approved the first 10 amendments to the Constitution. These amendments became known as the *Bill of Rights.* Some of these rights include freedom of religion, freedom of the press, and freedom of speech.

The Bill of Rights protects citizens' rights. The government cannot take away these rights.

THE BILL OF RIGHTS	
Amendment 1	Freedom of religion, speech, press, assembly (to meet in groups), and petition
Amendment 2	Right to keep weapons
Amendment 3	Protection against being forced to house and feed soldiers
Amendment 4	Freedom from unreasonable searches of homes and property
Amendments 5–8	Rights of citizens accused of crimes to have a fair trial
Amendments 9–10	Limit the powers of the federal government to those granted in the Constitution

REVIEW

Answer the following questions on a separate sheet of paper.

1. What were the concerns of the Antifederalists?

2. **Chart Skills** What is the Bill of Rights?

CHAPTER

7 Section 4 Guided Reading and Review
Ratification and the Bill of Rights

★

A. As You Read

Directions: Complete the crossword puzzle below as you read Section 4 in your textbook.

Across

1. To approve the Constitution

4. Needed to protect basic liberties

5. Amendment that protects freedom of religion, speech, and the press

7. Assembly that proposed the first 10 amendments

Down

2. Believed in a strong national government

3. Last state to approve the Constitution

6. What Antifederalists thought states would be

B. Reviewing Key Terms

Directions: Define the following terms.

8. The *Federalist Papers* _____

9. amend _____

CHAPTER

7 TEST

Identifying Main Ideas

Write the letter of the correct answer in the space provided.

____ 1. The Articles of Confederation
   A formed a weak national government.
   B created strong federal courts.
   C planned for an executive branch.
   D included many state laws.

____ 2. Eventually, the Articles of the Confederation failed because the new national government
   A spent all its time resolving disputes between states.
   B had too much power.
   C did not have the power to deal with an economic crisis.
   D outlawed slavery in the Northwest territories.

____ 3. Which was NOT part of the Articles of Confederation?
   A a bill of rights
   B each state had one vote
   C no executive branch
   D no judicial branch

____ 4. The Great Compromise was an agreement on which of the following?
   A the way in which slaves in southern states would be counted
   B the number of state representatives in Congress
   C the separation of powers into three distinct branches
   D the order of the amendments in the Bill of Rights

____ 5. The writers of the Constitution had to compromise on all of the following issues EXCEPT
   A the rules a territory would follow in order to become a state.
   B the way in which slaves in southern states would be counted.
   C the number of legislative representatives for each state.
   D the addition of a bill of rights.

____ 6. What idea did the writers of the Constitution borrow from the Romans?
   A the division of power
   B declaration of citizens' rights
   C limitations of a ruler's power
   D self-government

____ 7. The idea of an American bill of rights has historical roots in
   A the British Parliament.
   B the Revolutionary era.
   C Roman law.
   D the Magna Carta.

____ 8. From what source did the writers of the Constitution get the idea of natural human rights?
   A the Roman tradition
   B the American experience
   C the Enlightenment
   D the English tradition

____ 9. Antifederalists objected to the Constitution on the grounds that it
   A failed to provide smaller states with equal representation.
   B did not abolish slavery in the United States.
   C gave the president too little power.
   D gave too much power to the national government.

____10. Which was the key issue in the process of ratifying the Constitution?
   A statehood for new territories
   B the Bill of Rights
   C the number of legislative representatives for each state
   D fear of a dictatorship

CHAPTER

8 Government, Citizenship, and the Constitution (1787–Present)

Vocabulary Development

Vocabulary
immigrant
impeach
incriminate
independence
infrastructure
initiative

The prefix *in-* (or *im-*, which is used before the letters *b*, *m*, or *p*) has more than one meaning. It can change the meaning of a root word to mean "not," as in *impossible* and *informal*. It also can mean "in or into, part of" as in words such as *input* or *implant*. But there are other words that begin with *in-* that don't follow either of those rules.

Directions: *Draw a line to match each word to its definition.*

1. immigrant

2. impeach

3. incriminate

4. independence

5. infrastructure

6. initiative

a. process by which voters can put a bill directly before the state legislature

b. to give evidence against

c. free from the control of any outside government

d. system of roads, bridges, and tunnels

e. to bring charges of serious wrongdoing against a public official

f. a person who enters another country in order to settle there

Directions: *Using at least four of the listed vocabulary words, write a paragraph about the chapter on the lines below. Be sure to use complete sentences and correct spelling in your writing.*

_____

_____

_____

_____

_____

_____

_____

_____

_____

Section 1 Guide to the Essentials

Goals and Principles of the Constitution

VOCABULARY

Preamble the opening statement of the United States Constitution

Articles the sections of the Constitution

SUMMARY

The goals and principles of the Constitution have guided the United States for more than 200 years. The **Preamble** of the Constitution introduces its six goals. They are to unite the nation, to establish justice, to keep peace at home, to protect the freedom of the people, to promote the well-being of the people, and to provide for the nation's defense. One of the most important goals of the Constitution when it was written was to unite the states into a single nation. To achieve this goal, the Constitution gives broad powers to the federal government.

The main body of the Constitution is made up of **Articles,** which establish the framework for our government. The first three Articles describe the three branches of government—legislative, executive, and judicial. Article 4 deals with relations between the states, and Article 5 explains how the Constitution may be amended. Article 6 declares that the Constitution is the highest law in the land, and Article 7 explains the procedures for ratifying the Constitution.

The Constitution rests on seven basic principles, or ideas. (See chart.) These principles make sure that the citizens of the United States enjoy a careful balance of power and freedom.

PRINCIPLES OF THE CONSTITUTION	
Popular sovereignty	All government power belongs to the people.
Limited government	Government can do only what the people say it can do.
Separation of powers	Power is also divided between three branches of the national government.
Checks and balances	Each branch of the national government is able to check the power of the other branches.
Federalism	Power is divided between the national government and the state governments.
Republicanism	Citizens elect representatives to carry out the will of the people.
Individual rights	Individual rights are protected.

REVIEW

Answer the following questions on a separate sheet of paper.

1. What was the most important goal of the Constitution when it was written?

2. **Graphic Organizer Skills** What are the seven principles of the Constitution?

CHAPTER

8 Section 1 Guided Reading and Review

Goals and Principles of the Constitution

A. As You Read

Directions: As you read Section 1 in your textbook, complete the graphic organizer by writing in the goals and principles of the Constitution.

The Constitution

Goals

1.

2.

3.

4.

5.

6.

Principles

7.

8.

9.

10.

11.

12.

13.

B. Reviewing Key Terms

Directions: Define the following terms.

14. Preamble _____

15. Articles _____

16. general welfare _____

CHAPTER

8 Section 2 Guide to the Essentials

How the Federal Government Works

VOCABULARY

appeal to ask that a court decision be reviewed by a higher court

unconstitutional not allowed under the Constitution

impeach to bring charges of serious wrongdoing against the President

SUMMARY

The United States' government is divided into three branches with separate roles and responsibilities. (See chart.) The legislative branch is made up of two houses—the **Senate**—with two senators from each state—and the **House of Representatives,** whose membership is based on the population of each state. (For example, California, with its large population, has more than 10 times as many representatives as New Mexico does.) Together the House and Senate form **Congress.** The chief job of Congress is to make the nation's laws. Congress is also responsible for controlling federal monies.

The President is the head of the executive branch. The main role of the President is to carry out the nation's laws. The President also directs the nation's foreign policy and commands the armed forces.

In the judicial branch, the highest court is the **Supreme Court,** which settles issues concerning the Constitution and federal law. Most federal cases are heard in lower courts, or district courts. People can **appeal** a district court decision. The final court of appeal is the Supreme Court.

In a system of checks and balances, each branch of the government may limit the power of the other two. For example, if the President vetoes, or rejects, a bill, it returns to Congress, where members may overrule, or cancel, the veto. The Supreme Court can check both the President and Congress by declaring laws **unconstitutional.** Congress may check the President—the House of Representatives has the power to **impeach** the President, and the Senate decides whether the President is guilty.

THE THREE BRANCHES OF AMERICAN GOVERNMENT

LEGISLATIVE BRANCH	EXECUTIVE BRANCH	JUDICIAL BRANCH
Passes laws	Carries out laws	Interprets laws
• Can override President's veto • Can impeach and remove President • Deals with money	• Can veto laws • Negotiates foreign treaties • Serves as commander in chief of armed forces	• Can try federal cases • Can review appealed cases • Can decide what the Constitution means • Can declare laws or executive actions unconstitutional

REVIEW

Answer the following questions on a separate sheet of paper.

1. Describe how the system of checks and balances might work in the federal government.

2. **Chart Skills** What is the role of the executive branch of the government?

CHAPTER

8 Section 2 Guided Reading and Review

How the Federal Government Works

A. As You Read

Directions: As you read Section 2 in your textbook, complete the chart below by listing key facts that describe each branch of government.

	Legislative	Executive	Judicial (Supreme Court)
Officer(s)	1. 2.	8. 9.	12.
Primary Duty	3.	10.	13.
Checks on other branches	4. 5. 6. 7.	11.	14.

B. Reviewing Key Terms

Directions: Define the following terms.

15. bill _____

16. electoral college _____

17. appeal _____

18. veto _____

19. override _____

20. impeach _____

CHAPTER

8 Section 3 Guide to the Essentials
Changing the Constitution

VOCABULARY

civil rights a citizen's privileges, rights, and freedoms

SUMMARY

The writers, or framers, of the Constitution knew that the world might change and that the Constitution should change with it. But the framers did not want the process to be an easy one. Written changes to the Constitution are called amendments. The process of amending the Constitution is complex and may take months or years to complete.

An amendment may be proposed using two methods. It may be proposed by two thirds of both the House and the Senate or by a national convention called by Congress at the request of two thirds of the state legislatures. The second method has never been used.

An amendment may be ratified in two ways. It may be approved by the legislatures of three fourths of the states, or it may be approved by special conventions in three fourths of the states.

The first 10 amendments to the Constitution are called the Bill of Rights. The purpose of the Bill of Rights is to list the **civil rights** that may not be taken away by the government. More amendments were added over the years to expand the rights of citizens. (See chart.)

Later amendments—the Thirteenth, Fourteenth, and Fifteenth, also known as the Civil War Amendments—expanded democratic rights. These amendments abolished slavery, gave citizenship to former slaves, and guaranteed African American men the right to vote.

CONSTITUTIONAL AMENDMENTS AND WHAT THEY GUARANTEE	
First Amendment	Individual freedoms, such as speech
Second Amendment	Right to bear arms and form militias
Third Amendment	Freedom from having troops housed in one's home
Fourth Amendment	Protection from unlawful searches
Fifth Amendment	Freedom from self-incrimination
Sixth Amendment	Right to speedy public trial by impartial judge and jury
Seventh Amendment	Right to jury at civil trial
Eighth Amendment	Freedom from excessive punishments from judges
Ninth Amendment	Citizens' freedoms not limited to those covered in the Constitution
Tenth Amendment	People's right of a limited government (all power not belonging to the nation or the state belongs to the people)
Fourteenth Amendment	Right of citizenship for former slaves
Fifteenth Amendment	Right to vote not based on race, color, or "previous condition of servitude"
Nineteenth Amendment	Right of women to vote
Twenty-sixth Amendment	Right to vote for anyone 18 years old or older

REVIEW
Answer the following questions on a separate sheet of paper.

1. How may an amendment to the Constitution be proposed?

2. **Chart Skills** What freedom does the Fifth Amendment protect?

CHAPTER

8 Section 3 Guided Reading and Review
Changing the Constitution

★

A. As You Read

Directions: As you read Section 3 in your textbook, answer the following questions:

1. Why did the framers provide for changes to the Constitution? _____

_____

2. What are the two ways in which an amendment to the Constitution can be ratified?

_____

_____

3. What is the overall purpose of the Bill of Rights? _____

_____

List the provisions of each of the 10 amendments in the Bill of Rights.

4. First: _____

5. Second: _____

6. Third: _____

7. Fourth: _____

8. Fifth: _____

9. Sixth: _____

10. Seventh: _____

11. Eighth: _____

12. Ninth: _____

13. Tenth: _____

B. Reviewing Key Terms

Directions: Explain what each of the following added to the Constitution.

14. Civil War Amendments _____

_____

15. Nineteenth Amendment _____

_____

16. Twenty-sixth Amendment _____

_____

CHAPTER

8 Section 4 Guide to the Essentials

State and Local Governments

VOCABULARY

constitutional initiative a process in which sponsors of an amendment gather signatures on a petition that is sent to the legislature or voters for approval

local government government on the county, city, town, village, or district level

SUMMARY

Although the federal government plays a role in every citizen's life, state and local governments have a more regular and direct impact. The Constitution divides power between the federal government and the states. Every state has its own constitution that is similar in purpose and content to the national Constitution.

State constitutions have a preamble and a bill of rights, but they tend to be longer and include details about finances, education, and other local matters. State constitutions may be changed more easily than the national one. In many states, citizens may use the process of **constitutional initiative** to introduce changes to the state constitution.

State governments provide a wide range of services, including law enforcement,

education, property protection, health and welfare programs, auto and professional licensing, and maintenance of highways and park and recreation areas. In addition, each state must build and care for its own infrastructure—highways, bridges, and tunnels.

Local governments are created by the states and have only as much power as the state allows, yet they have the most direct impact on people. Local governments provide schooling, as well as day-to-day services, such as fire protection, waste collection, law enforcement, water management, and health code inspections.

Local governments often operate facilities such as libraries, arenas and playing fields, airports, museums, and zoos.

THE RESPONSIBILITIES OF STATE AND LOCAL GOVERNMENTS

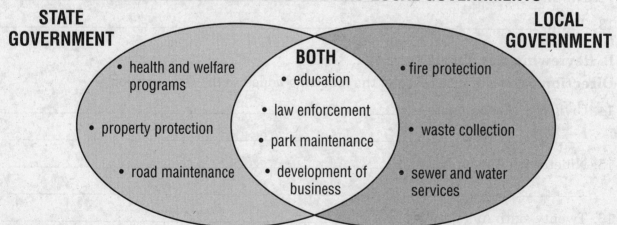

STATE GOVERNMENT

- health and welfare programs
- property protection
- road maintenance

BOTH
- education
- law enforcement
- park maintenance
- development of business

LOCAL GOVERNMENT

- fire protection
- waste collection
- sewer and water services

REVIEW

Answer the following questions on a separate sheet of paper.

1. How are state constitutions similar to the United States Constitution?

2. **Chart Skills** What are the services provided by both state and local governments?

CHAPTER

8 Section 4 Guided Reading and Review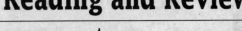
State and Local Governments

A. As You Read

Directions: As you read Section 4 in your textbook, complete the graphic organizer by listing the powers and services of state and local governments.

State Governments	Local Governments
Power determined by:	Power determined by:
1. _____	11. _____
Services	Services
2. _____	12. _____
3. _____	13. _____
4. _____	14. _____
5. _____	15. _____
6. _____	16. _____
7. _____	
8. _____	
9. _____	
10. _____	

B. Reviewing Key Terms

Directions: Define the following terms.

17. constitutional initiative _____

18. infrastructure _____

19. local government _____

CHAPTER

8 Section 5 Guide to the Essentials

Rights and Responsibilities of Citizens

VOCABULARY

citizen a person who owes loyalty to a particular nation and is entitled to all its rights and protections

naturalize to complete the legal process of becoming a citizen

immigrant a person who enters another country in order to settle there

SUMMARY

Being a **citizen** of the United States brings both rights and responsibilities. In order to be considered a citizen of the United States, one must be born in the United States; be born to at least one parent who is a United States citizen; have completed the process of naturalization; or be 16 or younger when an individual's parents were **naturalized. Immigrants** may become United States citizens by completing the long legal process of naturalization.

Civic virtue—a willingness to contribute to one's nation or community—was important to the founders of the United States. They valued the men and women who served democracy, putting their country ahead of their own interests. Today there is still a place for such democratic values. These values include honesty, compassion, patriotism, respect for others, responsibility, and courage. American citizens can develop these values at home, in school, or in the community.

Along with the basic rights they enjoy, American citizens have responsibilities. (See chart.) The responsibilities of citizenship are part of living in a free and democratic society. Citizens have the responsibilities of obeying the law and respecting the rights of others. Some other important responsibilities are voting and appearing for jury duty.

WHAT ARE THE RESPONSIBILITIES OF CITIZENSHIP?					
Serving on a jury	Voting	Keeping informed about national and community issues	Obeying the laws and respecting the rights of others	Volunteering your time and talents to help others and improve your community	Helping to defend the nation

REVIEW

Answer the following questions on a separate sheet of paper.

1. What conditions must one meet in order to be considered a United States citizen?
2. **Chart Skills** If you help clean up a local park, which responsibility of citizenship would you be exercising?

CHAPTER

8 Section 5 Guided Reading and Review

Rights and Responsibilities of Citizens

A. As You Read

Directions: As you read Section 5 in your textbook, answer the following questions:

1. In what two ways can a person be considered a citizen of the United States by birth?

_____

_____

2. How does an adult become a naturalized citizen? _____

_____

3. What are some basic rights United States citizens enjoy? _____

_____

List six basic responsibilities of a citizen, and give one reason for fulfilling each.

4. _____

5. _____

6. _____

7. _____

8. _____

9. _____

B. Reviewing Key Terms

Directions: Complete the sentences in Column I with the terms in Column II. Write the letter of the correct answer in the space provided.

Column I

_____ 10. A feeling of love and devotion toward one's country is called _____.

_____ 11. A/An _____ is a person who enters another country in order to settle there.

_____ 12. A/An _____ is a noncitizen living in the country.

_____ 13. Every citizen has a responsibility to serve when called for _____.

_____ 14. A/An _____ citizen is one who has completed the official legal process for becoming a citizen.

Column II

a. jury duty

b. immigrant

c. naturalized

d. patriotism

e. resident alien

CHAPTER

8 TEST

Identifying Main Ideas

Write the letter of the correct answer in the space provided.

____ 1. Which of the following is NOT a goal of the United States Constitution?

A to establish justice

B to provide public schooling

C to promote general well-being

D to unite the states

____ 2. The Constitutional principle that says each branch of the government can limit the power of the other two is called

A checks and balances.

B popular sovereignty.

C separation of powers.

D federalism.

____ 3. Which of the following is NOT a power of Congress?

A to make the nation's laws

B to control how much money government spends

C to decide whether a law is constitutional

D to impeach the President

____ 4. The Supreme Court can check the power of the legislative branch by

A overriding a veto.

B passing a bill.

C impeaching the president.

D declaring a law unconstitutional.

____ 5. How may the United States Constitution be amended?

A The President may make changes to it.

B The Supreme Court may call for changes to it.

C Congress may suggest amendments.

D The people may sign a petition for changes to it.

____ 6. The process of proposing an amendment to the Constitution

A takes one year to complete.

B requires support of two thirds of both the House and the Senate.

C requires full support of both the House and the Senate.

D requires approval of three fourths of the states.

____ 7. The Fourteenth, Fifteenth, Nineteenth, and Twenty-third Amendments all expanded the rights of citizens to

A speak freely.

B stand trial.

C own guns.

D vote.

____ 8. Both state and local governments

A have constitutions.

B have a bill of rights.

C provide law enforcement and education services.

D can change their constitutions with a petition from citizens.

____ 9. State constitutions are different from the United States Constitution because they

A state their goals in a preamble.

B are longer and contain more details.

C can be amended.

D have a bill of rights.

____ 10. Which of the following is NOT a responsibility of citizenship?

A owning land

B voting

C volunteering

D staying informed

Name_____ Class_____ Date_____

9 Launching the New Government
(1789–1800)

Vocabulary Development

Vocabulary
faction
inauguration
neutral
precedent
sedition
speculators

Directions: *Using what you learned in Chapter 9, read each sentence below, and decide whether the underlined word is being used correctly. Indicate your answer by circling either* Correct *or* Incorrect. *If the sentence is incorrect, write your own sentence that uses the word properly.*

1. Maria wanted to watch the play, so she joined the other <u>speculators</u> in the theater.

   Correct   Incorrect

   _____

2. George Washington wanted the United States to remain <u>neutral</u> in European wars.

   Correct   Incorrect

   _____

3. The book was rare and valuable since it was a first <u>sedition</u>.

   Correct   Incorrect

   _____

4. We were excited to be invited to the <u>inauguration</u> of our next president.

   Correct   Incorrect

   _____

5. The man did not want the whole sandwich, so he took only a <u>faction</u> of what was offered to him.

   Correct   Incorrect

   _____

Name_____ Class_____ Date_____

Section 1 Guide to the Essentials
Washington Takes Office

VOCABULARY

precedent an act or decision that sets an example for others to follow

national debt the total amount of money that a government owes to others

bond a certificate that promises to repay money loaned, plus interest, on a certain date

SUMMARY

After George Washington's inauguration, it became clear that there were no **precedents** for the office of President. It was up to Washington to make the new government work and to set a good example for future Presidents. First, Washington asked people to call him "President of the United States" instead of "His Highness the President of the United States and Protector of the Rights of the Same" as a few members of Congress urged him to do.

Then, Washington set up a Cabinet of advisors to help him run the country. Together they set about making the new government work. (See chart.) Washington also left the Presidency after two terms.

Alexander Hamilton was the first Secretary of the Treasury. His biggest challenge was the **national debt.** After the Revolutionary War, the United States owed money to many people and other nations. Hamilton introduced a plan to improve the economy. The nation would buy up all **bonds** that had been issued by the nation and the states during the war and issue

new ones to pay off the debt. He faced opposition from Southern states, which had already repaid their debts from the war. In the end, a compromise was reached when Hamilton agreed to build the nation's capital in the South.

Hamilton also called for a high tariff—a tax—on imported goods. This move was designed to help Northerners who imported less than Southerners. Southerners objected to the plan. Again, a compromise was reached when Congress passed a tariff that was lower than Hamilton wanted. To raise more money, Hamilton got Congress to pass a liquor tax. This tax affected Pennsylvania farmers who grew corn and made whiskey. In 1794, the farmers staged an uprising against the tax that became known as the ***Whiskey Rebellion.*** But President Washington quickly put down the rebellion with federal troops. However, he did not punish the farmers; he pardoned them. By doing so, he demonstrated the new government's strength and mercy.

ACHIEVEMENTS OF THE NEW GOVERNMENT	
Judiciary Act	Set up federal court system.
Washington, D. C.	Leaders chose new site for nation's capital.
Debts paid off	Federal government repaid the debts of states and the nation.
Bank of the United States	Hamilton got Congress to create a national bank to hold government money and help pay bills.

REVIEW
Answer the following questions on a separate sheet of paper.

1. List two ways that Washington set an example for future Presidents.

2. **Chart Skills** Why did Hamilton set up the Bank of the United States?

CHAPTER
9 Section 1 Guided Reading and Review
Washington Takes Office

A. As You Read

Directions: As you read Section 1 in your textbook, answer the following questions.

1. What were the first five executive departments of the federal government? _____
   _____
   _____

2. Who are members of the President's Cabinet, and what is their function? _____
   _____

3. What did the Judiciary Act establish? _____
   _____

4. How did Hamilton propose to repay the national debt, and what was the response of
   the opposition? _____
   _____

5. What steps did the government take to strengthen the economy? _____
   _____

6. What was the purpose of the tax on whiskey? _____
   _____

7. Who rebelled during the Whiskey Rebellion, and what was the outcome? _____
   _____

B. Reviewing Key People

Directions: Match each description in Column I with the correct name in Column II.
Write the letter of the answer in the space provided.

Column I

_____ 8. first President of the United States; served
   two terms

_____ 9. first Secretary of State

_____ 10. first Secretary of the Treasury; set up the
   Bank of the United States

_____ 11. led the opposition to the government's plan
   for repaying the national debt

_____ 12. first Chief Justice of the Supreme Court

Column II

a. John Jay

b. Alexander Hamilton

c. George Washington

d. James Madison

e. Thomas Jefferson

CHAPTER

9 Section 2 Guide to the Essentials

Creating a Foreign Policy

VOCABULARY

French Revolution a war waged by common people against the monarchs of France

foreign policy the actions that a nation takes in relation to other nations

neutral choosing not to support either side in a war

SUMMARY

In 1789, the French people rebelled against King Louis XVI. They fought for liberty and equality. At first, the United States supported the **French Revolution.** When the revolution leaders turned more violent and killed the king, some Americans withdrew their support.

In Europe, other countries opposed the French Revolution. War soon broke out between France and Britain. France asked the United States to help. Some Americans wanted to say yes. France had supported the American Revolution. Faced with the possibility of a war that the United States could not afford, President Washington had to decide on a **foreign policy.** After much debate, he issued the **Neutrality Proclamation.** It said that the United States would stay **neutral,** supporting neither France nor Britain.

American businesses depended on foreign trade. As a result, some Americans continued trading with both Britain and France. Britain seized more than 250 American ships trading with the French. Again, many Americans wanted to go to war with Britain. President Washington knew that the United States was too weak to fight. He sent Chief Justice John Jay to Britain for talks. Congress approved **Jay's Treaty.** Washington had again avoided war.

Before leaving office, President Washington published his **Farewell Address.** He urged Americans to avoid becoming involved in the quarrels among European countries. Neutrality remained an important American goal. (See time line.)

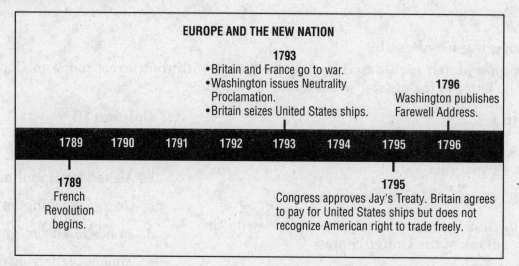

EUROPE AND THE NEW NATION

1793
• Britain and France go to war.
• Washington issues Neutrality Proclamation.
• Britain seizes United States ships.

1796
Washington publishes Farewell Address.

1789 1790 1791 1792 1793 1794 1795 1796

1789
French Revolution begins.

1795
Congress approves Jay's Treaty. Britain agrees to pay for United States ships but does not recognize American right to trade freely.

REVIEW

Answer the following questions on a separate sheet of paper.

1. What policy did the United States adopt when war broke out in Europe?

2. **Time Line Skills** What was Jay's Treaty? When was it approved by Congress?

CHAPTER

9 Section 2 Guided Reading and Review
Creating a Foreign Policy

A. As You Read

Directions: As you read Section 2 in your textbook, complete the following sentences.

1. American responses to the French Revolution were _____

_____

2. Washington's Cabinet members had the following opinions on the French

Revolution: _____

_____

3. The main foreign policy issue facing President Washington was _____

_____

4. The Neutrality Proclamation stated that _____

_____

5. Jay's Treaty provided that _____

_____

6. In his Farewell Address, George Washington advised the nation _____

_____

B. Reviewing Key Terms

Directions: Define the following terms.

7. French Revolution _____

_____

8. foreign policy _____

_____

9. neutral _____

_____

10. Farewell Address _____

_____

CHAPTER

9 Section 3 Guide to the Essentials
Political Parties Emerge

★

VOCABULARY

faction opposing groups within political parties

unconstitutional not permitted by the Constitution

Federalist the party of Alexander Hamilton

Democratic Republican the party of Jefferson, called Republicans

SUMMARY

Americans had reason to distrust political parties. They remembered how **factions** within British political parties had upset the working relations among politicians. Factions, American thought, led politicians to seek political favors and to act for personal gain rather than for public good.

Alexander Hamilton and Thomas Jefferson were both members of President Washington's Cabinet. They disagreed about what was best for the new country. For example, Jefferson thought that the law creating the Bank of the United States was **unconstitutional.** He believed that the federal government should only have powers specifically mentioned in the Constitution. However, Hamilton interpreted the Constitution more loosely.

As Congress passed many of Hamilton's programs, Jefferson and his supporters decided to organize. Eventually, the followers of Hamilton and Jefferson started two political parties. The two parties were the **Federalists** and the **Democratic Republicans.** (See chart.)

In the 1796 election, the results were unexpected. The President and Vice President did not belong to the same party. John Adams, a Federalist, was President. Thomas Jefferson, a Republican, was Vice President. The election of two men with opposing views caused tensions within the government.

FEDERALISTS VS. DEMOCRATIC REPUBLICANS	
Federalists	**Democratic Republicans**
Led by Alexander Hamilton	Led by Thomas Jefferson
Thought rich, educated people should lead nation	Thought more people should have political power
Wanted strong federal government	Wanted strong state governments
Wanted to encourage manufacturing and trade	Wanted to encourage farming
Supported loose interpretation of the Constitution	Supported strict interpretation of the Constitution

REVIEW

Answer the following questions on a separate sheet of paper.

1. What was unexpected about the results of the 1796 election?

2. **Chart Skills** List two differences between Federalists and Democratic Republicans.

CHAPTER

9 Section 3 Guided Reading and Review
Political Parties Emerge

★

A. As You Read

Directions: Complete the chart below as you read Section 3 in your textbook. Fill in details about the differences between the Federalists and the Democratic Republicans.

	Federalists	Democratic Republicans
Basis of economy	1.	5.
Federal or state powers	2.	6.
Interpretation of the Constitution	3.	7.
Foreign policy	4.	8.

B. Reviewing Key People

Directions: Briefly identify the following people. Mark Federalists with an *F* and Democratic Republicans with a *DR*.

_____ 9. Alexander Hamilton _____

_____ 10. Thomas Jefferson _____

_____ 11. George Clinton _____

_____ 12. Aaron Burr _____

_____ 13. John Fenno _____

_____ 14. Philip Freneau _____

CHAPTER

9

Section 4 Guided Reading and Review

The Second President

VOCABULARY

frigate fast sailing ships with guns

alien a foreign born resident who is the subject of another country

sedition act of causing rebellion against a government

nullify to cancel

SUMMARY

Conflict with France arose after John Adams became President in 1797. France began to seize American ships. Many Americans called for war. In an incident that became known as the *XYZ Affair,* France demanded bribes, but Adams refused. Instead he called for strengthening the U.S. navy by building a fleet of **frigates.** He was able to avoid war.

Adams's party, the Federalists, split over his peace policy with France. Alexander Hamilton had hoped for war with France because it would hurt Thomas Jefferson and the Republicans.

In 1798, Congress passed the *Alien and Sedition Acts.* The Alien Act allowed the President to force any **alien** to leave the country if that person was considered dangerous to the government. Under the Sedition Act, citizens could be punished for criticizing the government or its officials. These laws angered many people, especially the Republicans. They believed the Sedition Act threatened citizens' rights to free speech. Jefferson believed states should have more power and he helped pass the *Kentucky and Virginia Resolutions.* These resolutions allowed the states to **nullify** the Sedition Act.

The race for President in 1800 was extremely close. When Thomas Jefferson and Aaron Burr, both Republicans, received the same number of votes, it took Congress four days to decide the election. Jefferson became President.

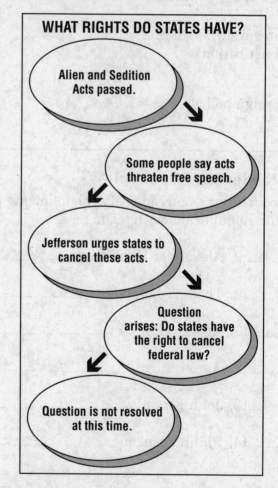

WHAT RIGHTS DO STATES HAVE?

Alien and Sedition Acts passed.

Some people say acts threaten free speech.

Jefferson urges states to cancel these acts.

Question arises: Do states have the right to cancel federal law?

Question is not resolved at this time.

REVIEW

Answer the following questions on a separate sheet of paper.

1. Why did the Federalist party split in two?

2. **Diagram Skills** What did Jefferson say the states should do about the Alien and Sedition Acts?

CHAPTER

9 Section 4 Guided Reading and Review
The Second President

A. As You Read

Directions: As you read Section 4 in your textbook, fill in supporting details for each of the main ideas listed below.

Main Idea A: As President Adams took office, the United States faced a crisis with France.

1. _____

2. _____

3. _____

Main Idea B: The Federalist Party split during the Adams administration.

4. _____

5. _____

Main Idea C: The Alien and Sedition acts raised the issue of states' rights.

6. _____

7. _____

8. _____

B. Reviewing Key Terms

Directions: Complete each sentence below by writing the correct term in the blank.

9. The _____ involved discussions between French agents and American diplomats.

10. President Adams did not want war, but he strengthened the navy by building

_____.

11. _____ is the act of stirring up rebellion against a government.

12. Kentucky and Virginia wanted to be able to _____ federal laws.

13. The _____ claimed that each state had the power to judge whether a law was unconstitutional.

Name_____ Class_____ Date_____

TEST
Identifying Main Ideas
Write the letter of the correct choice in the answer space.

___ 1. Which of the following actions was NOT an example set by President George Washington?
A asking people to call him "President of the United States"
B choosing the first Cabinet
C leaving office after two terms
D importing goods from overseas

___ 2. Which item was NOT part of Hamilton's plan?
A high tariff
B repaying state debts
C the Bank of the United States
D starting political parties

___ 3. The rebellion of Pennsylvania farmers during Washington's presidency was a reaction to
A a tax placed on whiskey.
B attacks by Native Americans.
C Jay's Treaty.
D a tariff.

___ 4. Washington's Neutrality Proclamation kept the United States out of war with
A Spain.
B France.
C Britain.
D Britain and France.

___ 5. What was one result of Jay's Treaty?
A The United States went to war with France.
B The United States went to war with Britain.
C President Washington decided not to run for President again.
D The United States avoided war with Britain.

___ 6. Which idea was supported by Thomas Jefferson?
A State governments should be stronger than the federal government.
B Only educated people should lead the nation.
C The Constitution should be interpreted loosely.
D The government should encourage manufacturing over farming.

___ 7. The results of the election of 1796 were unexpected because
A it led to war with France.
B George Washington was elected for a third term.
C the President and Vice President were not from the same party.
D it showed that the United States would stay neutral.

___ 8. A foreign born resident and subject of another country is called a(an)
A citizen.
B alien.
C Federalist.
D Republican.

___ 9. The Federalist party split in two because
A Hamilton wanted war with France.
B Jefferson joined the Federalists.
C Adams declared war on France.
D Hamilton opposed the Alien and Sedition Acts.

___ 10. Which event took place first?
A Alien and Sedition Acts pass.
B Congress approves Jay's Treaty.
C Washington becomes President.
D First political parties are formed.

CHAPTER

10 The Age of Jefferson
(1801–1816)

Vocabulary Development

Key information about a word may include its part of speech, its definition, other meanings of the word, and its root. This information may be organized graphically. Look at the finished graphic organizer below. Then complete the next two organizers.

<u>Vocabulary</u>
confederation
democratic
nationalism

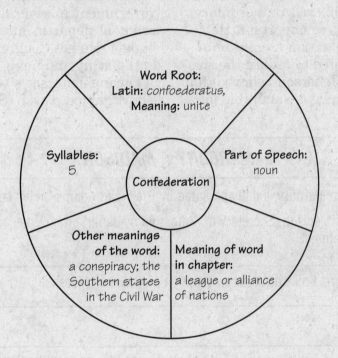

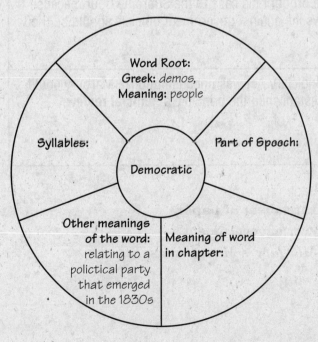

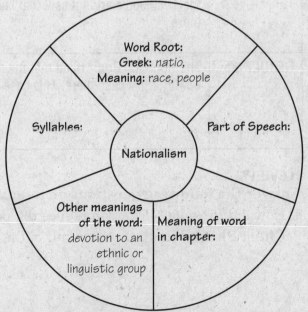

CHAPTER 10

Section 1 Guide to the Essentials

A Republican Takes Office

VOCABULARY

democratic making sure that all people have the same rights

judicial review power of the Supreme Court to decide whether laws passed by Congress are constitutional

SUMMARY

President Thomas Jefferson took office in 1801. Jefferson believed that ordinary American citizens were important. He wanted to make the nation more **democratic.** He also wanted to reduce the size of the government. Jefferson believed that government should play a small role in economic matters.

President Jefferson reduced the power of government in several ways. He made government departments smaller. He cut the budget. He got Congress to reduce the size of the army and navy.

During Jefferson's term, the Supreme Court gained power. (See chart.)

MARBURY v. MADISON	
WHO	William Marbury, judge appointed by President Adams on his last night as President James Madison, Secretary of State, told by Jefferson not to accept Marbury's appointment
WHAT	Supreme Court decision written by Chief Justice Marshall
WHEN	1803
WHY	Marbury wanted to keep his job. He brought his case to the Supreme Court because the 1789 Judiciary Act said that lawsuits against government officials should be tried there.
RESULT	The Supreme Court ruled that the Judiciary Act was unconstitutional. Marbury could *not* bring his case there. This case established the principle of **judicial review.**

REVIEW

Answer the following questions on a separate sheet of paper.

1. How did President Jefferson reduce the power of government?

2. **Chart Skills** What was the result of the *Marbury* v. *Madison* case?

CHAPTER

10 Section 1 Guided Reading and Review
A Republican Takes Office

A. As You Read

Directions: As you read Section 1, answer the following questions.

1. Why did Thomas Jefferson want to make the government more democratic?

_____

_____

2. How did Federalists feel about Jefferson's election?

_____

_____

3. What goals did Jefferson achieve in reducing the size of government?

_____

_____

_____

4. What action did Jefferson take when the Sedition Act expired?

_____

_____

5. What was the major difference in the philosophies of Jefferson and John Marshall?

_____

6. What was the outcome of *Marbury* v. *Madison*?

_____

_____

B. Reviewing Key Terms

Directions: Match the definitions in Column I with the terms in Column II.

Column I	Column II
_____ 7. idea that government should play as small a role as possible in economic affairs	a. free market
_____ 8. an economy with little regulation	b. judicial review
_____ 9. Supreme Court decides whether laws are constitutional	c. laissez faire

CHAPTER

10 Section 2 Guide to the Essentials

The Louisiana Purchase

VOCABULARY

expedition a long journey or voyage of exploration

SUMMARY

The Mississippi River was very important to farmers in the West. They shipped their products down the river to New Orleans, Louisiana. From New Orleans, ships took the products to other cities. First Spain, then France controlled the vast territory of Louisiana. The **Pinckney Treaty** with Spain kept New Orleans open to American shipping. Then, Spain gave Louisiana to France. President Jefferson worried that France might one day close the port of New Orleans to Americans.

President Jefferson sent officials to buy New Orleans from France. The French offered to sell all of Louisiana

for $15 million. Jefferson agreed to the **Louisiana Purchase** in 1803. The United States took control of a huge area west of the Mississippi River.

President Jefferson asked Meriwether Lewis and William Clark to explore the Louisiana Purchase and to map a route to the Pacific Ocean. The Lewis and Clark **expedition** reached the Pacific Ocean in 1805. The explorers learned a great deal about climate, wildlife, and Native American nations in the area. (See diagram.) At the same time, **Zebulon Pike** explored the Southwest. These expeditions made further exploration and settlement possible.

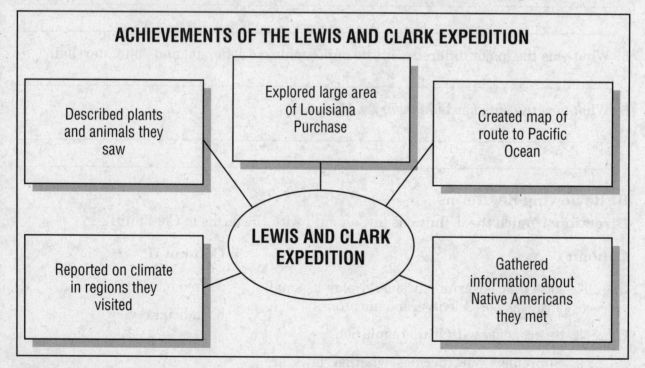

ACHIEVEMENTS OF THE LEWIS AND CLARK EXPEDITION

Described plants and animals they saw

Explored large area of Louisiana Purchase

Created map of route to Pacific Ocean

LEWIS AND CLARK EXPEDITION

Reported on climate in regions they visited

Gathered information about Native Americans they met

REVIEW

Answer the following questions on a separate sheet of paper.

1. Why was the Mississippi River important to western farmers?

2. **Diagram Skills** List three achievements of the Lewis and Clark expedition.

CHAPTER

10 Section 2 Guided Reading and Review
The Louisiana Purchase

A. As You Read

Directions: As you read Section 2, complete the following sentences.

1. Settlers west of the Appalachians relied on the Mississippi River for

_____

2. The United States wanted to purchase New Orleans and West Florida because

_____

_____

3. The French offered to sell all of Louisiana because

_____

4. Jefferson sent Lewis and Clark to explore the Louisiana territory because

_____

_____

_____

5. Sacagawea's contribution to the Lewis and Clark expedition was

_____

_____

6. The expedition had peaceful dealings with the Indians because

_____

7. Zebulon Pike explored

_____

_____

B. Reviewing Key Terms

Directions: Define each of the following terms.

8. Pinckney Treaty _____

_____

9. Louisiana Purchase _____

_____

10. continental divide _____

_____

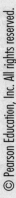

CHAPTER

10 Section 3 Guide to the Essentials
New Threats From Overseas

VOCABULARY

impressment practice of forcing sailors to work on a ship

SUMMARY

During the late 1700s and early 1800s, the United States began to trade with many nations. American ships sailed to India and China. In India, Americans traded ice for silks and spices. United States traders also sailed to the Pacific Northwest of North America to trade for furs.

United States trading expanded at first when war broke out in Europe in 1803. As in the 1790s, Britain and France ignored American neutrality and seized American trading ships. The British also forced American sailors to work on their ships. This was called **impressment.**

The United States was very angry with Britain and France for interfering with trade. In 1807, President Jefferson convinced Congress to pass the ***Embargo Act.*** It banned trade with other countries. Jefferson thought this would hurt France and Britain by cutting off their supplies. However, it also hurt Americans by reducing trade. (See graph.) The ***Nonintercourse Act*** replaced the embargo. It allowed Americans to trade with all nations except France and Britain.

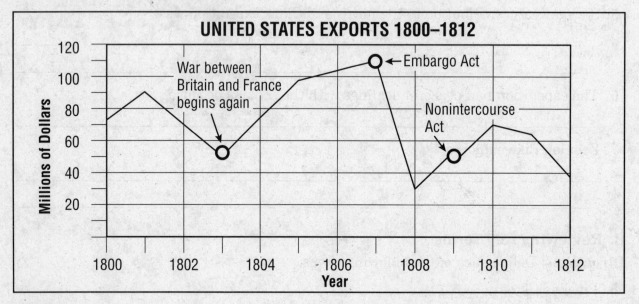

UNITED STATES EXPORTS 1800–1812

REVIEW

Answer the following questions on a separate sheet of paper.

1. What actions of the British angered Americans?

2. **Graph Skills** By how much did United States exports go down the year after the passage of the Embargo Act?

CHAPTER

10 Section 3 Guided Reading and Review
New Threats From Overseas ★

A. As You Read

Directions: As you read Section 3, complete the chart below by writing supporting details under each main idea.

Main Idea A: After the Revolution, American overseas trade grew rapidly.

1. _____

2. _____

3. _____

4. _____

Main Idea B: Britain and France violated American neutrality.

5. _____

6. _____

Main Idea C: Jefferson hoped that an American embargo would hurt Britain and France.

7. _____

8. _____

9. _____

B. Reviewing Key Terms

Directions: Complete each sentence by writing the correct term in the blank.

10. To protect its ships from attack, the United States paid a _____ to Tripoli.

11. British _____ gangs kidnapped young men and forced them into service in the British navy.

12. A law banning trade is called an _____.

13. From 1807 to 1809, many American merchants violated trade laws by _____.

CHAPTER

10

Section 4 Guide to the Essentials
The Road to War

VOCABULARY

confederation a league or alliance

nationalism devotion to one's country

SUMMARY

The United States faced conflicts with Native Americans on the western frontier. Many white settlers moved west into Ohio and Indian territory. The settlers broke treaties with Indians and built their farms on Indian lands. Two Shawnees worked to unite Native Americans. Tecumseh and his brother, a religious leader called "the Prophet," organized an Indian **confederation** to save their lands. In 1811, Indian forces fought American soldiers at the **Battle of Tippecanoe.** The Americans were led by William Henry Harrison. Harrison's troops defeated the Shawnees.

Problems between the United States and Britain grew worse. The British were giving guns to the Native Americans. The **War Hawks** were a group in Congress who wanted a war with Britain. The War Hawks had a strong sense of **nationalism.** They thought that Britain was treating the United States like a colony. They favored war for other reasons, too. (See diagram.) They urged President Madison to ask Congress to declare war on Britain. In 1812, Congress declared war.

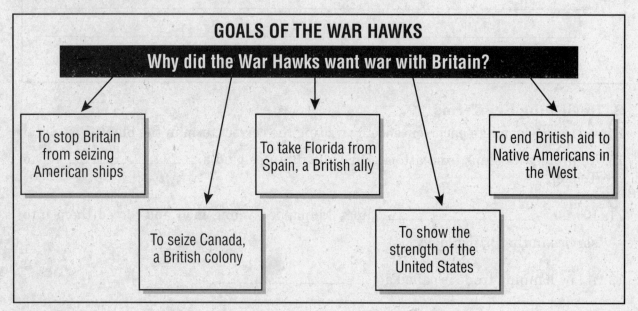

GOALS OF THE WAR HAWKS

Why did the War Hawks want war with Britain?

To stop Britain from seizing American ships

To take Florida from Spain, a British ally

To end British aid to Native Americans in the West

To seize Canada, a British colony

To show the strength of the United States

REVIEW

Answer the following questions on a separate sheet of paper.

1. Why did Tecumseh want to unite Native Americans?

2. **Diagram Skills** What were three goals of the War Hawks?

CHAPTER

10 Section 4 Guided Reading and Review
The Road to War

A. As You Read

Directions: As you read Section 4, fill in the graphic organizer with the reasons why the United States and Britain went to war.

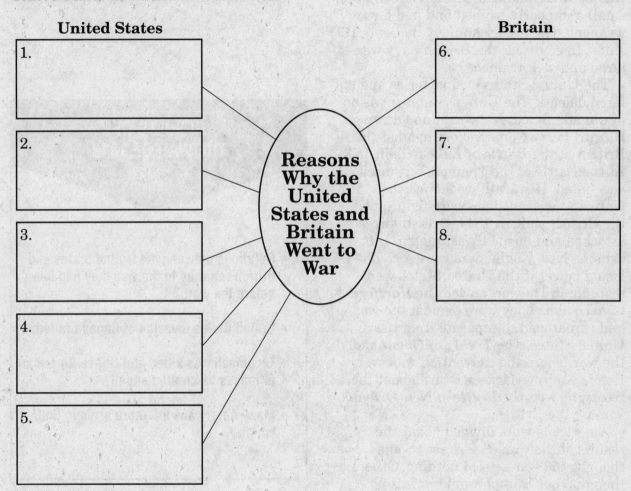

United States

1.

2.

3.

4.

5.

Britain

6.

7.

8.

Reasons Why the United States and Britain Went to War

B. Reviewing Key Terms

Directions: Identify each person listed below, and describe his role in the conflict between white settlers and Native Americans.

9. Tecumseh _____

_____

10. Tenskwatawa "The Prophet" _____

_____

11. William Henry Harrison _____

_____

CHAPTER 10

Section 5 Guide to the Essentials

The War of 1812

SUMMARY

The United States was not ready for the *War of 1812*. The United States Army was small and poorly trained and had few weapons. The American navy had only 16 ships. In contrast, the British navy was large and well trained.

The United States won victories and suffered defeats. The United States invasion of Canada failed. Navy captain Oliver Hazard Perry won a victory against the British at the *Battle of Lake Erie* in 1813. At the Battle of the Thames, Tecumseh was killed. His death weakened the Native Americans who were fighting on the British side. In 1814, British forces attacked and burned Washington, D.C.

Some New Englanders were afraid of losing power if the United States won more land. They organized the *Hartford Convention*. They were against the war and threatened to separate from the United States. The *Treaty of Ghent* ended the war before the convention was over. Before Andrew Jackson heard about the treaty, he won the *Battle of New Orleans* against the British.

Americans were divided about the results of the war. (See chart.) Some thought the war settled nothing. Others thought that Europe would now treat the United States with more respect.

RESULTS OF THE WAR OF 1812

- Relations between the United States and Britain returned to the way they had been before the war.

- United States invasion of Canada failed.

- Tecumseh was killed and Native American alliances he created ended.

- Many Americans felt more pride in their country.

REVIEW

Answer the following questions on a separate sheet of paper.

1. What disadvantages did the United States face at the beginning of the War of 1812?

2. **Chart Skills** How did the War of 1812 affect relations between the United States and Britain?

CHAPTER
10 Section 5 Guided Reading and Review
The War of 1812

A. As You Read

Directions: As you read Section 5, answer the following questions.

1. What difficulties did the United States face as the War of 1812 began?

   _____

   _____

2. What happened in the battle between the USS *Constitution* and the HMS *Guerrière?*

   _____

   _____

3. How did General Brock defeat the American invasion of Canada?

   _____

   _____

4. How did the battles at the Thames and Horseshoe Bend affect Native Americans?

   _____

5. What did Dolley Madison do when the British invaded Washington, D.C.?

   _____

6. What happened at Fort McHenry?

   _____

   _____

7. What role did Andrew Jackson play in the Battle of New Orleans?

   _____

   _____

8. What did the United States and Britain agree to after the war ended?

   _____

B. Reviewing Key Terms

Directions: Identify the significance of the following terms.

9. Battle of Lake Erie _____

10. Battle of New Orleans _____

11. Hartford Convention _____

12. Treaty of Ghent _____

CHAPTER 10 TEST

Identifying Main Ideas

Write the letter of the correct answer in the space provided.

____ 1. One of Thomas Jefferson's goals as President was to

A increase the size of the army.

B stop paying off state debts.

C reduce the power of the federal government.

D increase the size of government departments.

____ 2. As a result of the Louisiana Purchase, the United States

A bought land from Spain.

B went to war with France.

C lost control of New Orleans.

D doubled in size.

____ 3. Lewis and Clark were sent to

A remove Native Americans from Louisiana.

B explore and map the Louisiana Purchase.

C defeat the Spanish in Mexico.

D Europe to buy Louisiana from France.

____ 4. When Britain and France seized American ships, they

A impressed American sailors into their navies.

B used the captured ships against the American navy.

C forced American sailors to become British subjects.

D returned the American sailors unharmed.

____ 5. Which of the following laws allowed the United States to trade with all nations except Britain and France?

A Nonintercourse Act

B Embargo Act

C Stamp Act

D Pinckney Act

____ 6. The War Hawks wanted all of the following EXCEPT

A to seize Canada, a British colony.

B to stop from seizing American ships.

C to give aid to Native Americans in the West.

D to take Florida from Spain.

____ 7. The War of 1812 was a result of American conflicts with both the

A French and the British.

B British and the Native Americans.

C British and the Spanish.

D French and the Native Americans.

____ 8. The meeting of the Hartford Convention was a clear sign that

A not everyone supported the war.

B the feeling of nationalism was strong in New England.

C the end of the War of 1812 was near.

D New Englanders supported the war.

____ 9. During which battle of the War of 1812 were American forces led by Andrew Jackson?

A Battle of New Orleans

B Battle of Lake Erie

C Battle of Thames

D Battle of Washington, D.C.

____ 10. One result of the War of 1812 was

A a United States victory.

B increased American pride.

C a British victory.

D a blockade of American ports.

CHAPTER

11 The Nation Grows and Prospers
(1790–1825)

Vocabulary Development

To understand the meaning and context of a new word, it is helpful to explore the word in a word-map diagram. A word map asks three questions: "What is it?"; "What is it like?"; and "What are some examples?" Complete a word map for the Chapter 11 words on the right. One is started for you.

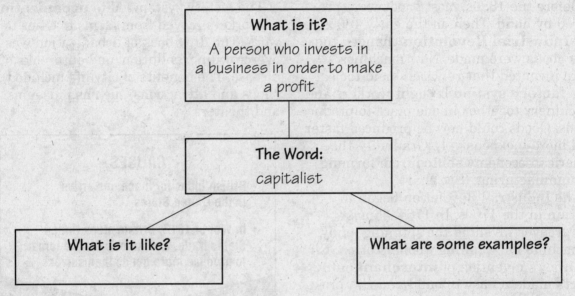

What is it?
A person who invests in a business in order to make a profit

The Word:
capitalist

What is it like?   **What are some examples?**

What is it?

The Word:
urbanization

What is it like?   **What are some examples?**

CHAPTER
11 Section 1 Guide to the Essentials
The Industrial Revolution

VOCABULARY

Industrial Revolution the widespread use of machines to manufacture goods

factory system a system that brought workers and machines together in one place to produce goods

interchangeable parts machine-made parts that would be identical

urbanization the movement of population from farms to cities

SUMMARY

Before the 1880s, most goods were produced by hand. Then, in the early 1800s, the **Industrial Revolution** changed the way goods were made. New machines were invented that replaced hand tools. The **factory system** brought workers and machinery together in one place to produce goods. Goods could now be produced faster and more inexpensively. Gradually, the American economy shifted from farming to manufacturing. (See chart.)

The Industrial Revolution began in Britain in the 1700s. In 1764, James Hargreaves invented the spinning jenny, a machine for spinning wool or cotton. Eli Whitney's invention of **interchangeable parts** made it easy to build and run productive machines and factories. Samuel Slater, a British mechanic, memorized designs of the machines in a British factory. He then came to the United States. In 1790, Slater and Moses Brown opened a mill in Rhode Island.

Other factories soon followed. Lowell, Massachusetts, became the first factory town. The towns were small communities where workers lived in attractive houses near the factories. Working hours in the new factories were long. Workers toiled 12 hours a day, 6 days a week. Most workers were women and children. As factories grew, conditions worsened and wages dropped.

The factory system led to **urbanization,** as workers moved from farms to cities to work. The drawback of urbanization was overcrowding, pollution, and outbreaks of disease. The benefits of city life included shops and attractions, such as museums and theaters.

CAUSES

- British ideas for machines arrive in the United States.

- In War of 1812, Britain stops United States trade, and Americans are forced to produce more goods themselves.

THE INDUSTRIAL REVOLUTION OF THE UNITED STATES

EFFECTS

- Factory system spreads throughout northeastern United States.

- As people move close to factories, cities grow.

- Growing cities have problems of crowding and disease.

REVIEW
Answer the following questions on a separate sheet of paper.

1. How did working conditions change as factories grew?

2. **Chart Skills** What were the effects of the Industrial Revolution in the United States?

CHAPTER
11 Section 1 Guided Reading and Review
The Industrial Revolution

A. As You Read

Directions: As you read Section 1 in your textbook, write one cause and one effect for each of the following events.

1. The Industrial Revolution began in Britain in the mid-1700s.

   Cause: _____

   Effect: _____

2. Samuel Slater memorized the design of the machines in British textile mills.

   Cause: _____

   Effect: _____

3. Eli Whitney invented machines that could manufacture identical parts.

   Cause: _____

   Effect: _____

4. Francis Cabot Lowell's partners built a factory town named for him.

   Cause: _____

   Effect: _____

5. Textile mills hired young women.

   Cause: _____

   Effect: _____

B. Reviewing Key Terms

Directions: Define the following terms.

6. spinning jenny _____

   _____

7. capitalist _____

   _____

8. factory system _____

   _____

9. urbanization _____

   _____

CHAPTER

11 Section 2 Guide to the Essentials
Americans Move Westward

VOCABULARY

flatboat a barge used for river travel

toll money charged to use a road or bridge

turnpike toll road on which a pole, or "pike," was lifted after toll was paid

canal waterway built by people that allows boats to cross a stretch of land

SUMMARY

In the early 1800s, many people began moving west to the land between the Appalachian Mountains and the Mississippi River. Settlers took several routes. Some traveled the Great Wagon Road across Pennsylvania. Others followed the Wilderness Road into Kentucky. Some went west to Pittsburgh. Then they took **flatboats** down the Ohio River into Indiana, Kentucky, and Illinois. Some northern pioneers traveled across New York State into Ohio. Southern pioneers followed trails into Alabama and Mississippi.

Settlers traveling west needed better roads. To pay for roads, road builders collected **tolls.** These toll roads were called **turnpikes.** In 1806, Congress set aside money for a **National Road** leading from Cumberland, Maryland, to Wheeling, in western Virginia. The National Road was later extended to Illinois.

Water travel was cheaper, faster, and more comfortable than road travel. In 1807, Robert Fulton launched a successful steamboat called the **Clermont.** It set new records in travel time. Steamboats began to carry people and goods quickly and cheaply. Americans also began to build **canals.** The **Erie Canal** let western farmers ship their goods to New York City. Steamboats and canals linked western farmers with eastern cities. (See diagram.)

TRANSPORTATION IN THE UNITED STATES, 1790–1830

PROBLEM

- People wanted to move west but travel was difficult.
- Settlers in the West needed ways to transport goods to eastern markets.

→

SOLUTION

Americans developed new methods of transportation.

- BETTER ROADS
- CANALS
- STEAMBOATS

REVIEW

Answer the following questions on a separate sheet of paper.

1. What were the advantages of travel by water?

2. **Diagram Skills** Which three new forms of transportation did Americans develop in the early 1800s?

CHAPTER

11 Section 2 Guided Reading and Review

Americans Move Westward

A. As You Read

Directions: As you read Section 2 in your textbook, fill in the supporting details for each main idea.

Main Idea A: Many settlers traveled westward during the early 1800s.

1. _____

2. _____

3. _____

4. _____

Main Idea B: In the early 1800s, Americans found faster and better ways to travel or move goods by water.

5. _____

6. _____

7. _____

B. Reviewing Key Terms

Directions: Match the terms in Column I with the definitions in Column II. Write the letter of the correct answer in the space provided.

Column I	Column II
_____ 8. turnpike	a. road paved with logs
_____ 9. corduroy road	b. road on which tolls were collected
_____ 10. *Clermont*	c. linked the Great Lakes with the Mohawk and Hudson rivers
_____ 11. Erie Canal	d. began the age of steamboats

CHAPTER

11 Section 3 Guide to the Essentials
Unity and Division

VOCABULARY

tariff duties imposed by a government on imported goods

sectionalism loyalty to one's state or section, rather than to the nation as a whole

interstate commerce trade between different states

SUMMARY

After the War of 1812, tensions between political parties decreased and Americans enjoyed a new sense of unity. A newspaper wrote that the country was in an *"Era of Good Feelings."* When President James Monroe ran for a second term in 1820, no one ran against him.

Congress worked to build the economy. The charter for the first national bank had run out. Congress created a *second Bank of the United States.* The bank helped American businesses grow. Congress also passed the *Tariff of 1816,* which raised **tariffs** on imports. (See diagram.) People bought American goods rather than British imports. The tariff helped manufacturers in New England. However, southerners did not like the tariff. It made goods expensive for them. The conflict over the tariff showed that Americans in different sections of the country had different interests. **Sectionalism** would play an increasing role in American politics.

Henry Clay, a Congress member from Kentucky, wanted all sections of the country to prosper. He proposed a plan called the *American System.* One of its goals was to keep tariffs high to help northern factories. With more wealth, northerners would buy goods from the South and West. Another goal was to use money from the tariffs to build roads and canals. Many people opposed Clay's plan, and it was never carried out.

The Supreme Court helped strengthen the federal government. Court decisions made it easier for the government to promote economic growth and regulate **interstate commerce,** while ruling that states could not interfere with federal institutions within their borders.

EFFECT OF A PROTECTIVE TARIFF

In the United States

American-made cloth sells for $6 per roll.

In Britain

British-made cloth sells for $5 per roll.

Shipped to the United States

British-made cloth sells for $6.25 per roll.

Add 25% tariff of $1.25 per roll.

REVIEW

Answer the following questions on a separate sheet of paper.

1. What did Congress do to make the economy strong after the War of 1812?
2. **Diagram Skills** What is the effect of a protective tariff?

CHAPTER
11 Section 3 Guided Reading and Review
Unity and Division

A. As You Read

Directions: Complete the chart below as you read Section 3 in your textbook. Fill in information to compare and contrast the ideas and political positions of three sectional leaders.

John C. Calhoun (South)	Daniel Webster (North)	Henry Clay (West)
1.	4.	7.
2.	5.	8.
3.	6.	9.

B. Reviewing Key Terms

Directions: Briefly define or identify each term.

10. Era of Good Feelings _____

_____

11. sectionalism _____

_____

12. American System _____

_____

13. internal improvements _____

_____

14. *McCulloch* v. *Maryland* _____

_____

15. *Gibbons* v. *Ogden* _____

_____

16. interstate commerce _____

_____

CHAPTER

11 Section 4 Guide to the Essentials

New Nations in the Americas

★

VOCABULARY

intervention direct involvement

SUMMARY

In the early 1800s, Spanish colonies in Latin America fought for independence. In Mexico, Miguel Hidalgo began a revolution. After a long struggle, Mexico became independent in 1821. Simón Bolívar led a war for independence in South America. In 1819, he defeated Spanish forces and formed the *Republic of Great Colombia.* José de San Martín led Argentina to freedom in 1816. In 1821, the people of Central America declared their independence, forming the *United Provinces of Central America.* In Brazil, independence was gained in 1822 without a battle. (See chart.)

General Andrew Jackson led United States forces into Spanish-owned Florida in 1818. Many Americans wanted to add Florida to the United States. Southerners were concerned about Creek and Seminole Indians who sometimes attacked Georgia settlements from Florida. Spanish Florida also offered protection to African Americans who escaped from slavery. Because Spain was fighting in Latin America, it could not risk war with the United States. In 1821, under the *Adams-Onis Treaty,* Spain sold Florida to the United States for $5 million.

The United States supported the independence of Latin American countries. However, some European countries seemed ready to help Spain regain its colonies. President Monroe issued the *Monroe Doctrine* in

1823. It said the United States would not interfere with European nations or colonies. It also warned European nations to leave the newly independent nations of Latin America alone. Over the years, an increasingly strong United States would oppose European **intervention** in Latin America.

LATIN AMERICAN NATIONS GAIN INDEPENDENCE

NATION	DATE
Haiti	1804
Paraguay	1811
Argentina	1816
Chile	1818
Republic of Great Colombia*	1819
Dominican Republic	1821
Mexico	1821
Brazil	1822
United Provinces of Central America▲	1823
Peru	1824
Bolivia	1825
Uruguay	1825

*included present-day Venezuela, Colombia, Equador, Panama

▲included present-day Nicaragua, Costa Rica, El Salvador, Honduras, Guatemala

REVIEW

Answer the following questions on a separate sheet of paper.

1. Why did the United States want to gain control of Florida?

2. **Chart Skills** Which Latin American nation gained independence first?

CHAPTER

11 Section 4 Guided Reading and Review

New Nations in the Americas

A. As You Read

Directions: Complete the following sentences as you read Section 4 in your textbook.

1. Latin American nations were eager for independence because _____
_____

2. Mexico gained its independence when _____
_____

3. The United Provinces of Central America included _____
_____

4. Latin American republics did not unite as a single country because _____
_____

5. Spain gave up its rights to Florida in exchange for _____
_____

6. The Monroe Doctrine stated that _____
_____

B. Reviewing Key People

Directions: Explain the role that each of the following people played in achieving Latin American independence.

7. Miguel Hidalgo _____
_____

8. José Morelos _____
_____

9. Simón Bolívar _____
_____

10. José de San Martín _____
_____

11. Prince Pedro of Portugal _____
_____

CHAPTER

11 TEST

Identifying Main Ideas

Write the letter of the correct choice in the answer space.

____ 1. The Industrial Revolution began in the
   A shipping industry.
   B textile industry.
   C mining industry.
   D farming industry.

____ 2. Which of the following changes was NOT a result of the Industrial Revolution?
   A Goods were produced faster and more cheaply.
   B The American economy shifted from manufacturing to farming.
   C The factory system spread.
   D Machines were invented that replaced hand tools.

____ 3. Most workers in the early factories were
   A women and children.
   B men from England.
   C trained cloth spinners.
   D southern farmers.

____ 4. Which of the following is NOT an example of an early road leading west?
   A Great Wagon Road
   B Coastal Turnpike
   C Wilderness Road
   D National Road

____ 5. Which of the following enabled western farmers to ship goods to New York City?
   A Ohio River
   B National Road
   C Erie Canal
   D Illinois Railroad

____ 6. Which invention improved travel by water in the early 1800s?
   A steamboat
   B turnpike
   C spinning jenny
   D water frame

____ 7. James Monroe was President during the
   A founding of First Bank of the United States.
   B "Era of Good Feelings."
   C War of 1812.
   D Embargo Act.

____ 8. What was one goal of the American System proposed by Henry Clay?
   A to use money from the tariffs to build roads and canals
   B to help southerners by keeping tariffs high
   C to help northerners by lowering tariffs
   D to use money from the tariffs to buy more goods from the North

____ 9. Which country did José de San Martín lead toward independence?
   A Argentina
   B Mexico
   C Brazil
   D Haiti

____ 10. European nations were warned to leave Latin American countries alone in the
   A Dominion of Canada.
   B American System.
   C Bolívar Treaty.
   D Monroe Doctrine.

CHAPTER

12 The Jacksonian Era
(1824–1840)

Vocabulary Development

You have read about the political parties in the United States in the 1830s and how each came to be. Write a brief paragraph that explains the differences between the two parties. Some questions to ask yourself are:

- What issues did the party support?
- What kinds of people voted for that party?
- What issues separated the parties?

Write your paragraph on the lines below. Be sure to use complete sentences and correct spelling in your writing.

_____

_____

_____

_____

_____

_____

_____

_____

_____

_____

_____

_____

_____

_____

_____

_____

_____

_____

CHAPTER

12 Section 1 Guide to the Essentials
A New Era in Politics

VOCABULARY

majority more than half of the votes

suffrage the right to vote

Whigs supporters of John Quincy Adams

Democrats supporters of Andrew Jackson

SUMMARY

John Quincy Adams was not a popular President. Adams became President after a very close election in 1824. Andrew Jackson received more votes that Adams, but no candidate won a **majority** of electoral votes. Congress then chose Adams to be President. Many of Jackson's supporters were very angry. Adams also angered many people because he believed that government should pay for new roads and canals and a national university. Most of his plans did not pass. Adams lost the election of 1828 to Jackson. Jackson's victory was viewed by his supporters as a victory for the common people and a sign of a new, more democratic era.

In the 1820s and the 1830s, more people gained **suffrage.** In the new western states, any white man over 21 could vote. In the East, by the 1830s, most states no longer required voters to own land. (See graphs.) Still, women, Native Americans, and most African Americans could not vote.

In the 1830s, political parties became more democratic. Two new parties, the **Whigs** and **Democrats,** began. These parties held nominating conventions to choose their candidates for President. More people now had a more direct role in choosing their leaders.

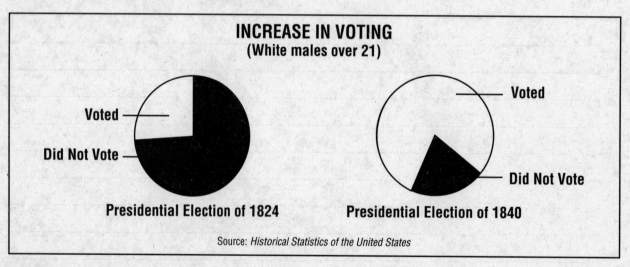

INCREASE IN VOTING
(White males over 21)

Voted — / Did Not Vote —

Presidential Election of 1824

Voted / Did Not Vote

Presidential Election of 1840

Source: *Historical Statistics of the United States*

REVIEW

Answer the following questions on a separate sheet of paper.

1. Why was John Quincy Adams an unpopular President?

2. **Graph Skills** Make a statement about the change in the percentage of white males over 21 who voted in 1824 and in 1840.

CHAPTER

12 Section 1 Guided Reading and Review

A New Era in Politics

A. As You Read

Directions: As you read Section 1 in your textbook, fill in the chart to compare and contrast John Quincy Adams and Andrew Jackson.

	John Quincy Adams	Andrew Jackson
1. home state		
2. family background		
3. professional background		
4. political party		
5. political philosophy		

B. Reviewing Key Terms

Directions: Define each term.

6. suffrage _____

7. majority _____

8. Whig _____

9. Democrat _____

10. caucus _____

11. nominating convention _____

CHAPTER
12 Section 2 Guide to the Essentials
Jackson in the White House

VOCABULARY

spoils system the practice of rewarding political supporters with government jobs

"kitchen cabinet" Democratic leaders and newspaper writers who served as President Jackson's unofficial advisors

SUMMARY

Andrew Jackson was a powerful President. His life experiences helped make him a successful leader. (See chart.) His parents died before he was 15, and he had to grow up quickly. He began his military career in the American Revolution. After the Revolution, he became a lawyer in Tennessee. Then, Jackson became a hero in the War of 1812.

Jackson was elected President in 1828. He fired many government employees and replaced them with his supporters. Critics complained that Jackson's new appointments were not qualified. Jackson said he was letting more people take part in government. Jackson's practice of rewarding supporters with jobs became known as the **spoils system.** Jackson even ignored his official Cabinet of advisors, relying instead on advice from Democratic leaders and

newspaper writers who were his friends. Because their informal meetings were often held in the White House kitchen, the advisors became known as the **"kitchen cabinet."**

Jackson believed that the national Bank of the United States was too powerful. The national Bank controlled loans made by state banks and limited the amount of money state banks could loan. This practice hurt farmers and merchants who needed to borrow money. When Jackson ran for reelection in 1832, the Whigs made the Bank an issue. Jackson told the American people that he thought only states had the right to charter banks. He also said that the Bank helped rich people at the expense of common people. Jackson won the election. The Bank closed when its charter ran out in 1836, leading to an economic downturn.

JACKSON'S RISE TO THE PRESIDENCY

Background	Military Experience	Political Experience
• Studied law	• Gained fame as hero in War of 1812	• Senator
• Lived on the frontier	• Defeated Creek Indians	• Judge
• Born the son of immigrants	• Fought in American Revolution	• Lawyer

---

REVIEW

Answer the following questions on a separate sheet of paper.

1. Why did Andrew Jackson oppose the Bank of the United States?

2. **Diagram Skills** List three facts that help explain Jackson's rise to the presidency.

CHAPTER

12 Section 2 Guided Reading and Review
Jackson in the White House

A. As You Read

Directions: As you read Section 2 in your textbook, answer the following questions.

1. What was Andrew Jackson's early professional experience? _____

_____

_____

2. How did President Jackson plan to reform the government? _____

_____

_____

3. Why did Jackson oppose the existence of the National Bank? _____

_____

_____

4. What powers did the National Bank have? _____

_____

_____

5. How did Clay and Webster try to save the National Bank? _____

_____

_____

6. How did Jackson eventually destroy the National Bank? _____

_____

_____

B. Reviewing Key Terms

Directions: Use each term correctly in a sentence about the Jackson administration.

7. spoils system _____

_____

8. kitchen cabinet _____

_____

CHAPTER 12

Section 3 Guide to the Essentials
A New Crisis

VOCABULARY

states' rights the right of states to limit the power of the federal government

nullification the idea that a state could cancel a federal law that it considered unconstitutional

depression an economic period in which business declines and many people lose their jobs

mudslinging the use of insults to attack a political opponent's reputation

SUMMARY

President Jackson faced a crisis. In 1828, Congress passed a high tariff on imports. Southerners hated the tariff and called it the *Tariff of Abominations* because they imported many goods from Europe. Vice President John C. Calhoun of South Carolina agreed with the southerners. He supported **states' rights** and believed South Carolina had the right to nullify the tariff. Senator Daniel Webster of Massachusetts disagreed. Webster said that the Constitution united the American people, not the states. When Jackson spoke out against **nullification,** Calhoun resigned as Vice President.

In 1832, Congress passed a lower tariff. However, South Carolina passed the *Nullification Act,* declaring the new tariff illegal. President Jackson asked Congress to pass the *Force Bill.* The bill allowed the President to use the army to enforce the tariff. Henry Clay proposed a lower compromise tariff. After fierce debate, South Carolina finally agreed to the compromise tariff.

Jackson also influenced how the United States dealt with Native Americans. In 1830, Jackson's supporters in Congress passed the *Indian Removal Act.* This act forced Native Americans to move west. In this case, Jackson now supported the rights of the Southern states to expel Indians from their lands.

Vice President Martin Van Buren became President after Jackson left office. Van Buren faced a terrible economic crisis, a **depression** caused by state banks printing too much money that had little value. Another problem was a sudden downturn in the price of cotton. Banks failed, and farmers lost their land.

The campaign of 1840 was a wild one, with candidates from both parties attending parades, holding rallies, and engaging in **mudslinging.** Whig candidate William Henry Harrison won but died within weeks. Vice President John Tyler became President.

TRAIL OF TEARS	
Who	Creek, Chickasaw, Cherokee, Choctaw, and Seminole nations
What	The United States government forced Native Americans to resettle in the West, and thousands died on forced marches.
When	1830s
Where	Moved from Southeast to Indian territory in what is now Oklahoma
Why	White settlers wanted Native American land.

REVIEW

Answer the following questions on a separate sheet of paper.

1. How did Jackson respond to the nullification crisis?

2. **Chart Skills** What happened on the Trail of Tears?

CHAPTER

12

Section 3 Guided Reading and Review
A New Crisis

A. As You Read

Directions: Complete the following sentences as you read Section 3 in your textbook.

1. Southerners hated the 1828 tariff because _____

_____

_____

2. Daniel Webster argued against nullification on the grounds that _____

_____

_____

3. The Indian Removal Act forced Indians to _____

_____

_____

4. Causes of the Panic of 1837 included _____

_____

_____

_____

5. To ease the economic depression, President Van Buren _____

_____

_____

6. Changes in political campaigns that started in 1840 included _____

_____

_____

B. Reviewing Key Terms

Directions: Match each term in Column I with the correct definition in Column II. Write the letter of the correct answer in the space provided.

Column I

_____ 7. nullification

_____ 8. depression

_____ 9. mudslinging

Column II

a. a period in which business declines and many people lose their jobs

b. the use of insults to attack an opponent's reputation

c. cancellation

CHAPTER 12 TEST

Identifying Main Ideas

Write the letter of the correct choice in the answer space.

____ 1. Why did John Quincy Adams become President after the election of 1824?

A Adams was more popular.

B Adams received the majority of electoral votes.

C Congress chose Adams to be President.

D Jackson received fewer popular votes than Adams.

____ 2. President John Quincy Adams favored all of the following EXCEPT

A the vote for women.

B a national university.

C building roads.

D building canals.

____ 3. The practice of rewarding supporters with political jobs is known as

A nullification.

B the spoils system.

C states' rights.

D secession.

____ 4. President Jackson opposed the Bank of the United States because he believed it

A helped farmers and merchants.

B helped only the poor.

C was too powerful.

D made state banks too powerful.

____ 5. The belief that a state has the right to cancel a federal law it considers unconstitutional is known as

A secession.

B judicial review.

C a tariff.

D nullification.

____ 6. Senator Daniel Webster of Massachusetts did not believe in states' rights because he believed that

A the Constitution united the American people, not the states.

B states had the right to cancel federal laws.

C the liberty of a state was more important than the Union.

D nullification was right.

____ 7. The Nullification Act passed in

A Georgia.

B South Carolina.

C New York.

D Rhode Island.

____ 8. President Jackson's supporters wanted Native Americans to

A start their own state.

B take their case to court.

C get rich lands in the Southeast.

D move west.

____ 9. By calling for the Indian Removal Act, President Jackson was now supporting

A states' rights.

B a strong federal government.

C Native Americans' rights.

D the Bank of the United States.

____ 10. The Vice President who became President when William Henry Harrison died was

A Martin Van Buren.

B John Tyler.

C Daniel Webster.

D John C. Calhoun.

CHAPTER 13 Westward Expansion (1820–1860)

Vocabulary Development

> **Vocabulary**
> annex
> cede
> Manifest Destiny
> refuge
> rendezvous
> vigilante

Directions: *Using what you have learned about westward expansion, fill in the blank in each sentence with one of the vocabulary words on the right.*

1. Some people believed it was the _____ of the United States to expand westward to the Pacific Ocean.

2. The pioneers took _____ in an abandoned miner's cabin.

3. In places without a sheriff or other lawman, a _____ sometimes took over the job of punishing criminals.

4. The trappers met at the _____ to sell their furs and to purchase supplies.

5. The treaty that ended the Mexican War called for Mexico to _____ land to the United States.

6. The United States was glad to _____ the land that eventually formed several western states.

Directions: *Using at least four of the listed vocabulary words, write a paragraph about the chapter on the lines below. Be sure to use complete sentences and correct spelling in your writing.*

_____

_____

_____

_____

_____

_____

_____

_____

_____

_____

CHAPTER

13 Section 1 Guide to the Essentials

Oregon Country

VOCABULARY

mountain men adventurous people who lived off the land in Oregon Country

Oregon Trail a route followed by wagon trains from the East to Oregon

SUMMARY

Oregon Country was an area in the Far West, between the Rocky Mountains and the Pacific Ocean. That part of the country has fertile soil and plenty of water for growing crops. It also has forests full of animals for hunting and trapping. In the early 1800s, it was a land full of promise for settlers and trappers. At that time, four countries claimed Oregon. They were the United States, Great Britain, Russia, and Spain. Russia and Spain had few settlers there and gave up their claims. In 1818, the United States and Britain agreed to control Oregon Country together.

The first white settlers in Oregon Country were fur trappers. Known as **mountain men,** the trappers followed old Indian trails as they trapped animals. They sold the furs of these animals to traders. Later, the mountain men would guide pioneers along the same trails.

The first white Americans to make permanent homes in Oregon Country were missionaries, such as Marcus and Narcissa Whitman. They hoped to convert Native Americans to Christianity. The presence of the missionaries was not appreciated by all Native Americans. In 1847, the Cayuse Indians attacked the Whitmans' mission and killed 14 people. Still, settlers back East had heard enough about the Oregon Country to believe that moving west was worth the risk.

Many of the settlers went west on wagon trains. (See diagram.) Life on the **Oregon Trail** was difficult. Settlers faced many hardships. They had to deal with raging rivers, fierce weather, lack of food, attacks from wild animals, and disease. In spite of the hardships, more than 50,000 people reached the Oregon Country between 1840 and 1860.

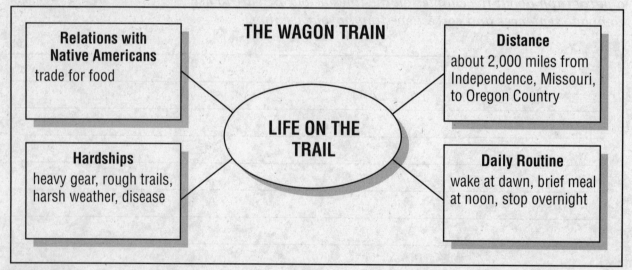

THE WAGON TRAIN

Relations with Native Americans
trade for food

Distance
about 2,000 miles from Independence, Missouri, to Oregon Country

LIFE ON THE TRAIL

Hardships
heavy gear, rough trails, harsh weather, disease

Daily Routine
wake at dawn, brief meal at noon, stop overnight

REVIEW

Answer the following questions on a separate sheet of paper.

1. Name two groups who helped open up the Far West for settlement.

2. **Diagram Skills** What were three hardships that the settlers faced on the trail?

CHAPTER

13 Section 1 Guided Reading and Review
Oregon Country

A. As You Read

Directions: As you read Section 1 in your textbook, write details about Oregon Country in the following chart.

Oregon Country	
Land	1.
	2.
	3.
Climate	4.
	5.
Journey to Oregon	6.
	7.
	8.
Who Traveled There	9.
	10.
	11.
	12.
Occupations in Oregon	13.
	14.
	15.

B. Reviewing Key People

Directions: Briefly identify each of the following people.

16. Jedediah Smith _____

17. Manuel Lisa _____

18. James Beckwourth _____

19. Marcus and Narcissa Whitman _____

_____

CHAPTER

13

Section 2 Guide to the Essentials
The Republic of Texas

VOCABULARY

dictator a ruler with absolute power and authority

siege a strategy in which enemy forces try to capture a fort or city by surrounding and bombarding it

Alamo an old Spanish mission in San Antonio, Texas

annex to take control of a territory or country

SUMMARY

The new independent country of Mexico wanted Americans to settle in Texas. It offered each settler a large piece of land. Stephen Austin led the first American settlers. By 1830, about 20,000 Americans lived in Texas.

As American settlers moved in, problems between the Mexicans and the Americans grew. Mexico feared that the United States wanted to take over Texas. Also, American settlers did not like certain Mexican laws. One law required Texans to worship in the Catholic church. Another law banned slavery.

Texans declared independence from Mexico in 1836. A large Mexican army, led by **dictator** General Santa Anna, entered Texas. In San Antonio, about 180 Texans

and almost 1,500 Mexicans died during the **siege** at the **Alamo** mission. Shortly afterward, Mexican forces killed hundreds of Texas soldiers who had surrendered at Goliad. Now Texans wanted revenge for both the Alamo and Goliad. At the *Battle of San Jacinto,* an army of Texans defeated the Mexicans. (See time line.) Texas was now an independent country that was also called the *Lone Star Republic.*

The war left Texas with many problems. Many Mexicans did not want to accept the treaty that granted Texas independence. Also, Texas had little money because of the cost of the war. Many people in the United States and in Texas felt it would be best for the United States to **annex** Texas.

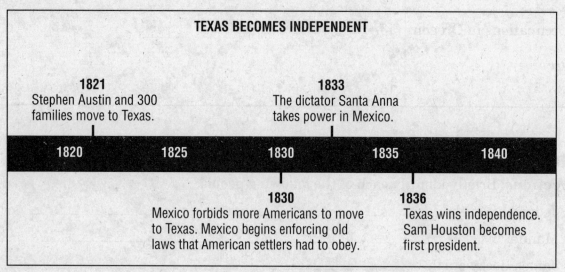

TEXAS BECOMES INDEPENDENT

1821
Stephen Austin and 300 families move to Texas.

1833
The dictator Santa Anna takes power in Mexico.

1820   1825   1830   1835   1840

1830
Mexico forbids more Americans to move to Texas. Mexico begins enforcing old laws that American settlers had to obey.

1836
Texas wins independence. Sam Houston becomes first president.

REVIEW
Answer the following questions on a separate sheet of paper.

1. What were two problems that led Texans to declare independence from Mexico?

2. **Time Line Skills** Who was the first president of Texas?

CHAPTER

13 Section 2 Guided Reading and Review
The Republic of Texas

A. As You Read

Directions: Use the letters A through E to put the following events into chronological order as you read Section 2 in your textbook. Write the letter in the space provided. Then, write a sentence about the importance of each event.

_____ 1. The Mexican army began the siege of the Alamo.

_____

_____

_____ 2. Mexico barred any more Americans from settling in Texas.

_____

_____

_____ 3. Sam Houston led his troops to victory at the Battle of San Jacinto.

_____

_____

_____ 4. The Republic of Texas declared its independence from Mexico.

_____

_____

_____ 5. Spain gave American Moses Austin permission to establish a colony in Texas.

_____

_____

B. Reviewing Key People and Terms

Directions: Complete the following sentences by writing the correct person or term in the space provided.

6. Mexicans who lived in Texas were called _____.

7. During the _____ no food or water could reach the Texans defending the Alamo.

8. The _____ resulted in the capture of General Santa Anna.

9. Texas was called the _____ Republic because of the design on its flag.

10. _____ became the first president of the Republic of Texas.

CHAPTER

13 Section 3 Guide to the Essentials
California and the Southwest

VOCABULARY

New Mexico Territory the huge region in the southwest United States

found to start or set up

SUMMARY

The first white settlers to New Mexico and California were explorers and missionaries from Spain. The Spanish founded Santa Fe as the capital of the **New Mexico Territory** in the early 1600s. It became a busy trading town. When Mexico gained its independence from Spain, it welcomed Americans to New Mexico territory. After 1821, American traders and settlers began to follow the Santa Fe Trail to New Mexico.

In the late 1700s, Spanish soldiers and priests built the first white settlements in California. Father Junipero Serra **founded** missions at San Diego, Monterey, and other places along the Pacific Coast.

Many Native Americans in California lived in the missions and ranches that the Spanish founded. They tended sheep and cattle and grew crops. In return, they learned about the Roman Catholic religion. Mission and ranch life was very difficult for the Native Americans. Thousands died from diseases, mistreatment, and overwork. (See graph.)

By the late 1840s, many Americans began to think that the West should belong to the United States. They began to believe in *Manifest Destiny,* a belief that the United States had a clear right and duty to expand all the way to the Pacific Ocean. Many Americans believed that their system of

democratic government was the best in the world. The idea of Manifest Destiny also grew because some Americans felt superior to Native Americans and Mexicans. In 1844, Americans elected President James K. Polk, a man who would make Manifest Destiny a reality.

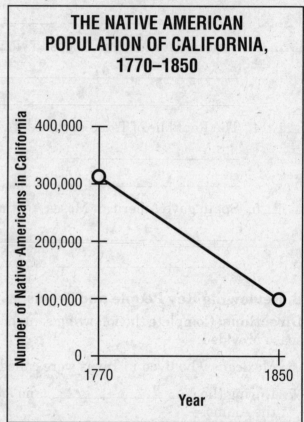

THE NATIVE AMERICAN POPULATION OF CALIFORNIA, 1770–1850

REVIEW

Answer the following questions on a separate sheet of paper.

1. Define the idea of Manifest Destiny. Why did many Americans believe in it?

2. **Graph Skills** About how much did the Native American population in California change from 1770 to 1850?

CHAPTER

13 Section 3 Guided Reading and Review
California and the Southwest

A. As You Read

Directions: Below are three main ideas from Section 3 in your textbook. As you read, fill in the supporting details for each main idea.

Main Idea A: New Mexico Territory was home to three cultures.

1. _____

2. _____

3. _____

Main Idea B: Settlements in California included missions and ranches.

4. _____

5. _____

6. _____

7. _____

Main Idea C: Many Americans supported the idea of western expansion.

8. _____

9. _____

10. _____

B. Reviewing Key Terms

Directions: Briefly explain the relevance of each term to the westward expansion of the United States.

11. New Mexico Territory _____

12. Santa Fe Trail _____

13. Manifest Destiny _____

CHAPTER

13 Section 4 Guide to the Essentials
The Mexican War

VOCABULARY

Bear Flag Republic the nickname for the nation of California

SUMMARY

James K. Polk became President in 1845. He wanted to expand United States lands. In 1846, Polk made an agreement with Great Britain. The two nations would divide the Oregon Country between them. The American part of the Oregon Territory later became the states of Oregon, Washington, and Idaho.

In 1845, the United States admitted Texas as a state. Mexico was angry at the move. Many Mexicans believed that Texas was still part of Mexico. War soon broke out.

The *Mexican War* between the United States and Mexico lasted from 1846 to 1848. It started over a disagreement about the exact location of the border between Texas and Mexico. During the course of the war, Americans took over New Mexico. California declared itself independent. It called itself the **Bear Flag Republic.**

In 1847, United States troops occupied Mexico City, Mexico's capital. Then the Mexicans agreed to a peace treaty. Under the *Treaty of Guadalupe-Hidalgo,* Mexico agreed to cede all of California and New Mexico to the United States. These lands were called the *Mexican Cession.* The United States paid Mexico $15 million for this land. It also agreed to respect the rights of Spanish-speaking people in the territories. Now the United States had expanded to reach the Pacific Ocean.

People of different cultures continued to live in the Southwest. They learned from each other. (See diagram.) Some Mexican laws remained in place. For example, landowners could not cut off water to their neighbors. However, many Mexicans lost their lands to American settlers.

CULTURES MIX IN NEW MEXICO AND CALIFORNIA

AMERICAN NEWCOMERS
- English words
- Democratic government

MIX OF CULTURES

NATIVE AMERICANS
- Native American words
- Art and architecture styles

MEXICAN AMERICANS
- Spanish words
- Irrigation and mining techniques

REVIEW

Answer the following questions on a separate sheet of paper.

1. How did the United States gain Oregon, New Mexico, and California?

2. **Diagram Skills** Name two ways that cultures mixed in the Southwest.

CHAPTER

13 Section 4 Guided Reading and Review
The Mexican War

A. As You Read

Directions: Write in the missing cause or effect as you read Section 4 in your textbook.

1. Cause: President Polk did not want to fight Britain for control of Oregon.	1. Effect: _____ _____
2. Cause: _____ _____	2. Effect: Congress admitted Texas to the Union.
3. Cause: Mexico refused to sell California and New Mexico to the United States.	3. Effect: _____ _____
4. Cause: _____ _____	4. Effect: Congress declared war on Mexico.
5. Cause: _____ _____	5. Effect: The Mexican government moved to make peace.
6. Cause: The United States needed a strip of Mexican land to complete a railroad.	6. Effect: _____ _____

B. Reviewing Key Terms

Directions: Match each term in Column I with the correct description in Column II. Write the letter of the correct answer in the space provided.

Column I

_____ 7. Bear Flag Republic

_____ 8. Treaty of Guadalupe-Hidalgo

_____ 9. Mexican Cession

_____10. Gadsden Purchase

Column II

a. land in present-day Arizona and New Mexico that Mexico sold to the United States for $10 million

b. stated that Mexico would cede California and New Mexico to the United States for $15 million

c. nickname given to California

d. lands Mexico sold to the United States at the end of the war

Section 5 Guide to the Essentials
Americans Rush West

VOCABULARY

vigilante person who decides to help keep law and order

SUMMARY

In the middle 1800s, American pioneers headed into the new lands of the Mexican Cession. One of the largest groups to move west was the **Mormons,** members of the Church of Jesus Christ of Latter-Day Saints. The Mormons had been driven away from their settlements in New York and Illinois because their teachings and beliefs upset many people. The Mormons hoped to find refuge in Utah.

In 1847, Mormons led by **Brigham Young** settled in the desert in Utah, near the Great Salt Lake. About 15,000 Mormon men, women, and children moved there. In time, the settlement grew and prospered.

Other pioneers headed to California, inspired by the discovery of gold in 1848. More than 80,000 people joined the "Gold Rush" to California. These newcomers became known as "forty-niners" because many arrived in the year 1849.

The Gold Rush attracted people from all over the world. Immigrants from China and Europe joined both black and white newcomers from other parts of the United States. San Francisco grew into a bustling city with a diverse, or varied, population. Few people became rich, but many people decided to stay in California.

The large growth in population led to problems. Native Americans and Mexican Americans lost more lands. Some of the mining towns were wild, lawless places. Sometimes **vigilantes** tried to keep order even though they had no legal right to do so. Despite these problems, California grew steadily. It became a state in 1850.

CAUSES

- **Gold is discovered.**
- **Thousands of forty-niners arrive.**

GROWTH OF CALIFORNIA

EFFECTS

- **California becomes a state.**
- **Rights of some Californians ignored.**
- **California has a diverse culture.**

REVIEW

Answer the following questions on a separate sheet of paper.

1. Where did the Mormons settle?
2. **Chart Skills** Name two ways that the discovery of gold changed California.

CHAPTER
13 Section 5 Guided Reading and Review
Americans Rush West

A. As You Read

Directions: As you read Section 5 in your textbook, answer the following questions.

1. Why did Joseph Smith and his followers move west? _____

_____

_____

2. Why did many Americans go to California? _____

_____

_____

3. Why were the people who joined the gold rush called "forty-niners"? _____

_____

_____

4. How did a miner get gold from the earth? _____

_____

_____

5. What effect did the gold rush have on California? _____

_____

_____

6. What did the gold rush mean for Mexican Americans and Indians? _____

_____

_____

B. Reviewing Key Places

Directions: Briefly explain the importance of the following places to westward expansion or the gold rush.

7. Salt Lake City _____

_____

8. Sutter's Mill _____

_____

9. San Francisco _____

_____

CHAPTER

13 TEST

Identifying Main Ideas
Write the letter of the correct choice in the answer space.

___ 1. In 1818, the United States and Great Britain agreed to
   A control Oregon Country together.
   B leave Oregon Country.
   C give Oregon Country to Spain.
   D let the people in Oregon Country decide who would rule.

___ 2. The first white Americans to make permanent homes in Oregon Country were
   A fur trappers.
   B missionaries.
   C Lewis and Clark.
   D forty-niners.

___ 3. Mexico encouraged Americans to settle in Texas by
   A building missions.
   B banning slavery.
   C giving them land.
   D giving them independence.

___ 4. Which of the following events happened immediately after Texans declared independence from Mexico in 1836?
   A The United States annexed Texas.
   B Texans fought the Mexican army.
   C Stephen Austin led the first American settlers into Texas.
   D Mexico enforced old laws that American settlers had to obey.

___ 5. In the Spanish missions in California, Native Americans
   A tended sheep and cattle and grew crops.
   B served the Spanish as soldiers.
   C grew in number.
   D worked in gold mines.

___ 6. The idea of Manifest Destiny meant that
   A American democracy needed improvement.
   B slavery should be allowed in the West.
   C Native Americans had equal claims to lands in the West.
   D the United States should expand to the Pacific Ocean.

___ 7. The Mexican War began a year after
   A Texas joined the United States.
   B California declared independence.
   C Texas became independent.
   D the United States and Britain agreed to share Oregon Country.

___ 8. Which territory did the United States gain as a result of the Mexican War?
   A Louisiana
   B California and New Mexico
   C Texas
   D Oregon Country

___ 9. Where did the Mormons led by Brigham Young settle in the late 1840s?
   A Utah
   B California
   C Mexico
   D Oregon

___ 10. Which word best describes the population of California after the Gold Rush?
   A rich
   B unchanged
   C small
   D growing

CHAPTER

14 North and South
(1820–1860)

Vocabulary Development

The prefixes *ex-* and *tele-* help to create many words. The prefix *ex-* comes from Latin and means "out of, from" or "former." The prefix *tele-* comes from Greek and means "far off, distant."

Below are a list of prefixes and root words, along with the meanings of the root words. On the lines next to each one, write the vocabulary word that most closely matches the meaning of the prefix combined with the root word.

1. _____ ex + tendere (to stretch)

2. _____ tele + skopein (to look)

3. _____ ex + cambiare (to change)

4. _____ tele + graphos (written)

5. _____ ex + portare (to carry)

6. _____ tele + videre (to see)

Directions: *Using at least four of the listed vocabulary words, write a paragraph about the chapter on the lines below. Be sure to use complete sentences and correct spelling in your writing.*

_____

_____

_____

_____

_____

_____

_____

_____

_____

_____

_____

_____

CHAPTER
14

Section 1 Guide to the Essentials
Industry in the North

VOCABULARY

telegraph communication device that works by sending electrical signals along a wire

locomotive a steam-powered train engine

clipper ship narrow, speedy sailing vessel designed to make best use of wind

SUMMARY

In the middle 1800s, a number of inventions helped manufacturing and farming grow in the North. The sewing machine allowed a worker to make dozens of shirts in the same amount of time that it took to sew one shirt by hand. Farmers could now use lightweight steel plow pulled by a horse. (Older iron or wooden plows were heavy and had to be pulled by slow-moving oxen.) A mechanical reaper could harvest as much as five people using hand tools.

New means of communication helped business. Samuel F.B. Morse invented the **telegraph** in the 1840s. The telegraph allowed news to travel rapidly. Businesses in different parts of the country could now exchange information quickly.

New transportation methods also helped northern businesses grow. Steam-powered **locomotives** moved people and freight at amazing speeds. Early trains had many troubles. They broke down often and were unsafe. They caused fires. It took years for railroad builders to build strong, safe tracks. Yet, by the 1850s, railroads linked cities from the East to the Midwest. (See graph.)

The **clipper ship** moved very fast through the water. These ships helped American merchants win a large share of the world's sea trade by the 1840s and 1850s. However, ships powered by steam soon replaced the clipper ships.

Steam was also used in other ways. By the 1830s, machines in factories began to use steam power. In earlier times, factories used water power and had to be built near swift rivers. Now, however, factories could be built anywhere.

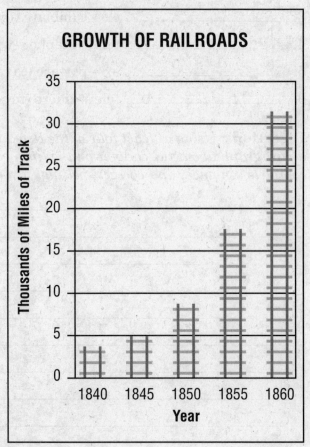

GROWTH OF RAILROADS

REVIEW

Answer the following questions on a separate sheet of paper.

1. What are three inventions that helped change farming and manufacturing in the North?

2. **Graph Skills** By about how many miles of track did the railroads grow between 1840 and 1860?

CHAPTER 14

Section 1 Guided Reading and Review

Industry in the North

A. As You Read

Directions: As you read Section 1 in your textbook, answer the following questions.

1. What could a sewing machine do that a tailor could not? _____
_____

2. How was John Deere's plow an improvement over earlier plows? _____
_____

3. What effect did Morse's telegraph have on American businesses? _____
_____

4. What were some of the problems with the first railroads? _____
_____

5. Why were clipper ships able to sail faster than other types of ships? _____
_____

6. What effects did factories, new machines, and railroads have on the northern economy in the mid-1800s? _____
_____

B. Reviewing Key Terms

Directions: Briefly explain the function of the following inventions.

7. reaper _____
_____

8. thresher _____
_____

9. telegraph _____
_____

10. locomotive _____
_____

11. clipper ship _____
_____

CHAPTER 14

Section 2 Guide to the Essentials
Life in the North

VOCABULARY

artisan a skilled worker who has learned a trade, such as carpentry

trade union organized group of skilled workers trying to improve pay and working conditions

strike the refusal of union workers to work

immigrant a person who comes to a country to take up permanent residence

discrimination policy or attitude that denies equal rights to a group of people

SUMMARY

By the 1840s, the number of factories in the North had grown. Now, more laborers worked longer hours for lower wages. Factories were unhealthy places to work. In summer, they were very hot. In winter, they were very cold. Factory machines had no safety devices and accidents were common. Many workers lived in run-down houses near the factories.

The low wages and poor working conditions led workers to join together. The first people to do so were **artisans.** They began to form **trade unions** in the 1820s and 1830s. By going on **strike,** workers tried to make factory owners improve working conditions.

Many of the workers in factories were **immigrants** from Europe. About 4 million immigrants arrived in the 1840s and 1850s. Many were from Ireland and Germany. Immigrants brought their own traditions to the United States, making American culture richer. Some people did not welcome immigrants. They blamed immigrants for the problems of the country. One group, who called themselves nativists, wanted to preserve the country for native-born, white citizens. The nativists formed a political party called the ***Know-Nothing party.*** In 1856, the party won 21 percent of the vote. (See chart.)

Thousands of free African Americans lived in the North. Slavery was against the law in the northern states. However, free African Americans faced **discrimination.** Even skilled African Americans had trouble finding good jobs. Despite these difficulties, many African Americans were able to achieve success.

CAUSES

- **Famines develop in Ireland.**

- **Revolutions erupt in Germany.**

- **Number of factory jobs in United States grows.**

IMMIGRATION

EFFECTS

- **American industry continues to grow.**

- **Immigrant traditions become part of American culture.**

- **Some Americans want to limit immigration.**

REVIEW

Answer the following questions on a separate sheet of paper.

1. Why did northern workers begin to form unions?

2. **Chart Skills** What was one cause and one effect of immigration?

CHAPTER

14 Section 2 Guided Reading and Review

Life in the North

A. As You Read

Directions: Below are three main ideas from Section 2 in your textbook. As you read, fill in the supporting details for each main idea.

Main Idea A: Factory conditions in the North grew worse as the century advanced.

1. _____

2. _____

Main Idea B: Workers began organizing to improve conditions.

3. _____

4. _____

Main Idea C: Immigrants faced both opportunity and hardship in the United States in the 1840s.

5. _____

6. _____

7. _____

B. Reviewing Key Terms

Directions: Match each term in Column I with its definition in Column II. Write the letter of the correct answer in the space provided.

Column I	Column II
_____ 8. artisan	a. severe food shortage
_____ 9. trade union	b. workers' refusal to do their jobs
_____ 10. strike	c. one who wants to limit immigration and immigrants' rights
_____ 11. famine	d. organized group of skilled workers who do the same types of jobs
_____ 12. nativist	e. policy or attitude that denies equal rights
_____ 13. discrimination	f. skilled worker

CHAPTER

14 Section 3 Guide to the Essentials

Cotton Kingdom in the South

SUMMARY

During the early years of the Industrial Revolution, the demand for cotton increased. Textile mills needed cotton to make cloth. Cotton grew well in parts of the South. Southern planters, however, had difficulty meeting the demand for cotton. Removing seeds from cotton was a slow process that had to be done by hand.

Then in 1793, Eli Whitney invented the cotton gin. This machine led to a large increase in cotton production. One worker using a cotton gin could do the work of 50 people cleaning cotton by hand.

As southern planters grew more cotton, they began moving west to start more plantations. By the 1850s, cotton was grown in a wide area of land from South Carolina to Texas. This area came to be called the Cotton Kingdom. As the cotton kingdom grew, so did the need for slaves to work on the plantations. (See graph.)

Unlike the economy of the industrial North, the economy in the South depended on farming. In areas where cotton did not grow well, farmers grew rice, sugar cane, or tobacco. Some southerners wanted the South to build factories. However, most planters were more interested in buying land and slaves than they were in building factories. Despite having rich resources, such as iron, wood, and stone, the South relied on farming. Because slaves could not afford to buy goods, there was little demand

for southern manufactured goods. Southerners relied on the North and Europe for most of the factory products they used. They also borrowed money from northern banks to buy more land and slaves.

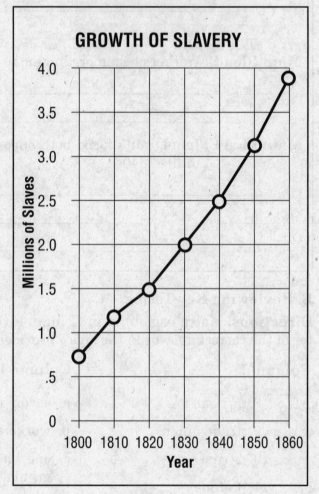

REVIEW

Answer the following questions on a separate sheet of paper.

1. How did the cotton gin affect the production of cotton in the South?

2. **Graph Skills** About how many slaves were there in 1820? In 1860?

CHAPTER 14

Section 3 Guided Reading and Review

Cotton Kingdom in the South

A. As You Read

Directions: Write in the missing cause or effect as you read Section 4 in your textbook.

1. Cause: Eli Whitney invented a machine that could separate cotton seeds from fibers.	1. Effect: _____ _____
2. Cause: _____ _____	2. Effect: Slavery spread further throughout the South.
3. Cause: Conditions for growing cotton were limited to certain areas of the South.	3. Effect: _____ _____
4. Cause: _____ _____	4. Effect: Southern industry remained small-scale.
5. Cause: The South depended on the North for almost all of its manufactured goods.	5. Effect: _____ _____

B. Reviewing Key Terms

Directions: Define or identify each term.

6. cotton gin _____

7. Cotton Kingdom _____

CHAPTER

14 Section 4 Guide to the Essentials
Life in the South

VOCABULARY

"cottonocracy" the wealthy families in the South whose money came from the production of cotton

slave codes laws meant to keep enslaved African Americans from running away or rebelling

extended family a family unit in which several generations live together

SUMMARY

Southern society was made up of five main groups. (See diagram.) Planters were the smallest group in number, but they had the most influence. They were called the **"cottonocracy,"** and they made large fortunes growing cotton and other crops with slave labor. Small farmers were the largest group. Some small farmers owned a few slaves. Poor whites owned neither land nor slaves.

Free African Americans lived under harsh laws. For example, they were not allowed to vote or travel. Enslaved African Americans made up one third of the population in the South. Most worked in the fields, clearing land and planting and harvesting crops. Some slaves worked at skilled jobs such as carpentry. Others worked as house servants.

Slaves worked long hours, usually under harsh conditions. Sometimes families were separated. Strict laws, called **slave codes,** made it illegal for slaves to learn to read and write or to own guns.

Enslaved people tried to ease the hardships of slavery. They struggled to keep their families together. On large plantations, **extended families** could stay together. They also kept some African traditions. Many drew hope from Christianity.

African Americans resisted slavery in many ways. Many attempted to escape. Only a few succeeded. Some people, like Nat Turner in 1831, organized violent rebellions against slavery. However, rebellions were not common. White planters were so powerful that slave revolts had almost no chance of success.

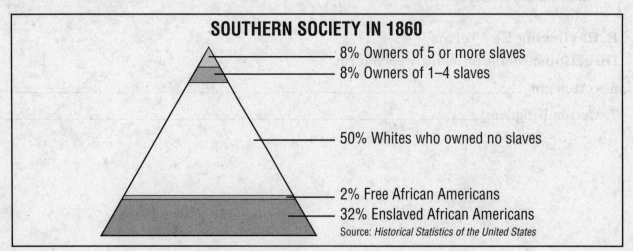

SOUTHERN SOCIETY IN 1860

- 8% Owners of 5 or more slaves
- 8% Owners of 1–4 slaves
- 50% Whites who owned no slaves
- 2% Free African Americans
- 32% Enslaved African Americans

Source: *Historical Statistics of the United States*

REVIEW

Answer the following questions on a separate sheet of paper.

1. What were some ways African Americans struggled against slavery?

2. **Diagram Skills** What percentage of people in the South were enslaved? What percentage were whites who owned no slaves?

Name_____ Class_____ Date_____

CHAPTER

14 Section 4 Guided Reading and Review
Life in the South

A. As You Read

Directions: As you read Section 4 in your textbook, complete the following sentences.

1. Planters dominated southern society because _____
_____

2. Slave owners created difficulties for free African Americans because _____
_____

3. Rights that were denied to slaves included _____
_____

4. African American families were often separated because _____
_____

5. Christianity contributed to African American culture by _____
_____

6. Slave revolts during the 1830s resulted in _____
_____

B. Reviewing Key People and Terms

Directions: Define or identify the following people and terms.

7. cottonocracy _____
_____

8. Denmark Vesey _____
_____

9. slave codes _____
_____

10. Nat Turner _____
_____

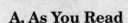

14 TEST

Identifying Main Ideas

Write the letter of the correct choice in the answer space.

___ 1. The telegraph allowed businesses in different parts of the country to
A exchange information quickly.
B share workers.
C compete more equally.
D keep their work secret.

___ 2. How did new transportation methods help business grow in the mid-1800s?
A Workers could get to factories more quickly.
B Factories could use water power.
C Owners did not need to go to their factories.
D Raw materials and factory goods could be transported more cheaply and quickly.

___ 3. Steam power was important because it
A made the best use of rivers.
B allowed factories to use water power.
C allowed factories to be built almost anywhere.
D made machines expensive to run.

___ 4. Workers began to organize because of
A help from the government.
B higher pay, but longer hours.
C new educational opportunities.
D low wages and poor conditions.

___ 5. Many of the workers in northern factories were
A cotton planters.
B immigrants from Ireland and Germany.
C African American slaves.
D people who moved from the South.

___ 6. Cotton planters needed new land because
A the demand for cotton increased.
B they wished to raise different crops.
C factory owners were buying up older lands.
D they sold the older lands to their slaves.

___ 7. How did the cotton gin change cotton production?
A It had little effect on cotton production.
B It led to a decrease in cotton production.
C It led to a large increase in cotton production.
D It led to a small increase in cotton production.

___ 8. In the South, the small group that had the most influence was
A poor whites.
B merchants and factory owners.
C free African Americans.
D planters.

___ 9. The largest group of southern whites was
A planters.
B small farmers.
C factory workers.
D slave owners.

___ 10. Most enslaved African Americans worked
A in small factories.
B in the fields.
C as house servants.
D at skilled jobs such as carpentry.

CHAPTER

15 Reform and a New American Culture (1820–1860)

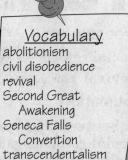

Vocabulary
abolitionism
civil disobedience
revival
Second Great
    Awakening
Seneca Falls
    Convention
transcendentalism
Underground Railroad
women's suffrage

Vocabulary Development

The mid-1800s were filled with new ideas and reforms. Look at the list of historical terms in the grid below. Mark an *X* in the boxes that are related to each term. Then answer the questions below.

	Ending Slavery	Religious/Spiritual Movement	Women's Rights
Second Great Awakening			
Abolitionism			
Women's Suffrage			
Transcendentalism			
Revival			
Underground Railroad			
Seneca Falls Convention			
Civil Disobedience			

1. What was the significance of the Seneca Falls Convention?

_____

_____

_____

2. Why did many transcendentalists become involved in social reform?

_____

_____

_____

3. What groups were opposed to the growing abolitionist movement?

_____

_____

_____

CHAPTER 15
Section 1 Guide to the Essentials
The Reforming Spirit

VOCABULARY

social reform an organized attempt to improve what is unjust or imperfect in society

revival a huge religious meeting, usually held outdoors

SUMMARY

Between 1820 and 1860, a variety of **social reforms** gained support in the United States. The reform movements had both political and religious roots.

The political roots of reform went back to the ideals expressed in the Declaration of Independence. These ideals included liberty and equality. Some reformers pointed out that slaves had no liberty. Others argued that women had few rights.

The religious roots of reform included the ***Second Great Awakening,*** a religious movement that swept the country in the early 1800s. People attended **revivals** and were taught that they could choose to save their own souls. As a result of this movement, many people decided to reform their personal lives. Some felt that they should also reform society. Dorothea Dix, an important social reformer, dedicated

herself to improving conditions for women confined in prisons and mental hospitals.

Reformers had a number of goals. (See chart.) One of the most important areas in which the reformers worked was education. Before the 1820s, few American children attended school. Public schools were rare and teachers were poorly trained and paid. Education reformers urged that more money be spent on education. By the 1850s, most northern states had set up public elementary schools. Education in the South was slower to improve. In most parts of the country, African Americans had little chance to go to school.

In the late 1820s, some women reformers organized the temperance movement. This movement was a campaign against alcohol abuse.

REFORM MOVEMENTS IN THE MID-1800s

Problem	Solution
Mistreatment of the mentally ill	New mental hospitals built.
Poor prison conditions	Better prisons built; cruel punishments outlawed; debtors no longer treated as criminals.
Alcohol abuse	Temperance movement; sale of alcohol banned by some states.
Limited educational opportunities	More public schools built; colleges opened for teacher training; schools opened for the deaf and blind.

REVIEW
Answer the following questions on a separate sheet of paper.

1. What were the roots of the reform movements of the mid-1800s?
2. **Chart Skills** Identify two problems and describe the responses of the reformers.

CHAPTER
15
Section 1 Guided Reading and Review
The Reforming Spirit

A. As You Read

Directions: As you read Section 1 in your textbook, fill in the chart below by writing in details of each reform movement.

hospital reform	1.
	2.
prison reform	3.
	4.
temperance movement	5.
	6.
education reform	7.
	8.
	9.

B. Reviewing Key Terms

Directions: Complete the following sentences by writing the correct term in the space provided.

10. In the mid-1800s, people became involved in _____ to improve

   unjust or imperfect conditions in society.

11. Many Protestants believed in _____, which held that God decided

   in advance which people would attain salvation after death.

12. A huge outdoor meeting intended to stir up or renew religious feeling is called

   a _____.

Name_____ Class_____ Date_____

Section 2 Guide to the Essentials
Opposing Slavery

VOCABULARY

American Colonization Society a group that hoped to end slavery by setting up an independent colony in Africa for freed slaves

abolitionist person who wanted to end slavery

Underground Railroad a network of abolitionists who secretly helped slaves escape to freedom

SUMMARY

By 1804, all the northern states had outlawed slavery. Many people in the North were concerned about the issue. Certain religious groups like the Quakers taught that it was a sin for one person to own another. Some people formed the **American Colonization Society.** This group wanted to end slavery by sending freed slaves to an independent colony in Africa. Few African Americans decided to go to Africa, a place most had never known. During the mid-1800s, a growing number of reformers spoke out against slavery. These reformers were white and black, men and women. They were known as **abolitionists.** (See diagram.)

Some abolitionists helped people escape from slavery on the **Underground Railroad.** Both white and black "conductors" guided runaway slaves to secret "stations" where they could hide. One of the most famous conductors was Harriet Tubman. After escaping slavery herself, Tubman went back to the South 19 times. She guided more than 300 slaves to freedom.

Many Americans reacted angrily to the abolitionists. Some northerners owned businesses that depended on southern cotton. They saw attacks on slavery as a threat to their livelihood. Some northern workers feared that freed slaves would take their jobs away by working for less money. Sometimes, mobs attacked abolitionists and broke up antislavery meetings.

Slave owners defended slavery. They argued that slaves were treated well and were better off than northern workers. Many southerners believed that northerners wanted to destroy their way of life.

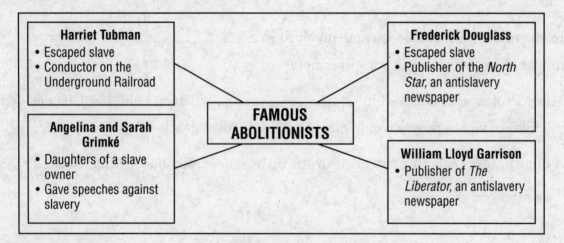

Harriet Tubman
- Escaped slave
- Conductor on the Underground Railroad

Angelina and Sarah Grimké
- Daughters of a slave owner
- Gave speeches against slavery

FAMOUS ABOLITIONISTS

Frederick Douglass
- Escaped slave
- Publisher of the *North Star,* an antislavery newspaper

William Lloyd Garrison
- Publisher of *The Liberator,* an antislavery newspaper

REVIEW

Answer the following questions on a separate sheet of paper.

1. Why did some northern business owners oppose abolitionists?

2. **Diagram Skills** What were two ways that abolitionists fought slavery?

CHAPTER

15 Section 2 Guided Reading and Review
Opposing Slavery

A. As You Read

Directions: Write in the missing cause or effect as you read Section 2 in your textbook.

1. Cause: In the 1800s, many Americans worked to end slavery.	1. Effect: _____ _____
2. Cause: _____ _____	2. Effect: A few thousand African Americans moved to Liberia.
3. Cause: Abolitionists formed the Underground Railroad.	3. Effect: _____ _____
4. Cause: _____ _____	4. Effect: Slave owners offered a $40,000 reward for the capture of Harriet Tubman.
5. Cause: _____ _____	5. Effect: Some northern manufacturers and workers opposed abolition.

B. Reviewing Key People

Directions: Briefly explain each person's contribution to the abolitionist movement.

6. Samuel Cornish _____

7. Maria Stewart _____

8. Frederick Douglass _____

9. William Lloyd Garrison _____

10. the Grimké sisters _____

11. Harriet Tubman _____

CHAPTER 15 Section 3 Guide to the Essentials
A Call for Women's Rights

VOCABULARY

Seneca Falls Convention the first women's rights meeting, held in Seneca Falls, New York

women's rights movement an organized campaign for equal rights for women

SUMMARY

Women had few political or legal rights in the early 1800s. They could not vote or hold office. When a woman married, her husband became owner of all her property. If a woman worked, her wages belonged to her husband. A husband could hit his wife, as long as he did not seriously hurt her. In the mid-1800s, some women and men began to work for women's rights.

In 1848, 200 women and 40 men met to discuss problems faced by women. This meeting was called the **Seneca Falls Convention.** The people at the meeting wrote a declaration that demanded equality for women. They also demanded the right to vote for women.

The situation of women slowly improved in some ways. (See chart.) Legal rights were given to women in some states. In New York, for example, married women were allowed to keep their own property and wages. Educational opportunities for women also increased. Reformers like Emma Williard opened a high school for women in Troy, New York. Mary Lyon opened a female seminary in Massachusetts. And during the late 1830s, a few men's colleges began to admit women. However, leaders of the **women's rights movement,** including Susan B. Anthony and the former enslaved African American Sojourner Truth, knew that their work was just beginning. The struggle for equal rights for women would last for many years.

- Women lack the rights to vote, to own property, and to keep their wages.

- Women who support antislavery causes find that their actions are limited. They must sit behind curtains at the World Antislavery Convention in London in 1840.

CAUSES

EARLY WOMEN'S RIGHTS MOVEMENT

EFFECTS

- Women's rights leaders demand equal rights for women, including education, careers, and the right to vote.

- Leaders use a variety of tactics, such as giving speeches.

- By mid-1800s, more schools are open to women, women gain legal rights in some states, and some women enter "male" careers.

REVIEW

Answer the following questions on a separate sheet of paper.

1. What rights did women lack in the early 1800s?
2. **Chart Skills** What were two effects of the women's rights movement?

CHAPTER

15 Section 3 Guided Reading and Review

A Call for Women's Rights

★

A. As You Read

Directions: Answer the following questions as you read Section 3 in your textbook.

1. What rights did women lack in the mid-1800s?

   _____

   _____

2. Why was Sojourner Truth an effective leader in the fight for women's rights?

   _____

   _____

3. What was the purpose of the Seneca Falls Convention?

   _____

   _____

4. What educational opportunities did women have in the mid-1800s?

   _____

   _____

B. Reviewing Key People

Directions: Briefly explain the contributions of each person to the campaign for women's rights.

5. the Grimké sisters _____

6. Sojourner Truth _____

7. Lucretia Mott _____

8. Elizabeth Cady Stanton _____

9. Susan B. Anthony _____

10. Amelia Bloomer _____

11. Elizabeth Blackwell _____

CHAPTER

15 Section 4 Guide to the Essentials

American Art and Literature

VOCABULARY

Hudson River School a group of artists who painted the landscape of the Hudson River region

individualism a way of thinking that stresses the importance of each individual person

transcendentalist a person who believes that the most important truths in life go beyond human reason

civil disobedience the idea that people have a right to disobey unjust laws if their consciences demand it

SUMMARY

Until the early 1800s, American writers and painters looked to Europe for inspiration. In the 1820s, however, American artists began to explore American themes in their work. (See diagram.)

American painters in the 1800s began to develop their own styles. The first group was the **Hudson River School.** These artists painted landscapes of the Hudson River region of New York. Other American painters painted scenes of country people and frontier life. Still others attempted to show the culture of Native Americans.

Two writers, Washington Irving and James Fenimore Cooper, wrote about the American past. A later writer, Henry

Wadsworth Longfellow, wrote poems about historical events. The poet Walt Whitman celebrated democracy and the diversity of the United States.

Two major American writers were Ralph Waldo Emerson and Henry David Thoreau. Both believed in **individualism,** and they were also **transcendentalists.** Emerson stressed that people had an "inner light" they could use to guide their lives. Thoreau urged people to live as simply as possible. He set an example by living alone in a cabin in the woods for a year. He also practiced **civil disobedience.** He went to jail because he did not believe in paying taxes to support a war that promoted slavery.

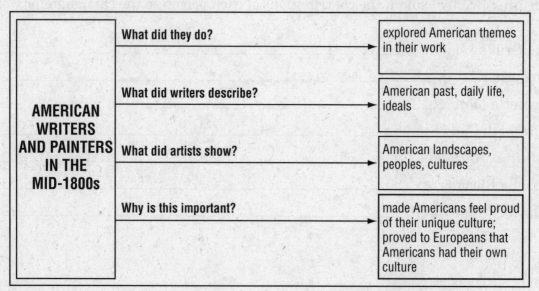

AMERICAN WRITERS AND PAINTERS IN THE MID-1800s	What did they do?	explored American themes in their work
	What did writers describe?	American past, daily life, ideals
	What did artists show?	American landscapes, peoples, cultures
	Why is this important?	made Americans feel proud of their unique culture; proved to Europeans that Americans had their own culture

REVIEW

Answer the following questions on a separate sheet of paper.

1. How did American writers change in the 1820s?

2. **Diagram Skills** How did the literature and art created in the mid-1800s affect the way people felt about being American?

CHAPTER 15

Section 4 Guided Reading and Review
American Art and Literature

A. As You Read

Directions: As you read Section 4 in your textbook, complete the chart below by writing in the names of important American artists and writers in each category. Briefly identify each person. One example is given.

painting	1.
	2.
	3.
poetry	4. Henry Wadsworth Longfellow, "Paul Revere's Ride" and "Hiawatha"
	5.
	6.
	7.
novels and stories	8.
	9.
	10.
	11.
	12.
	13.
	14.
philosophy	15.
	16.

B. Reviewing Key Terms

Directions: Define the following terms.

17. transcendentalists _____

18. civil disobedience _____

CHAPTER

15 TEST
Identifying Main Ideas
Write the letter of the correct choice in the answer space.

___ 1. The political roots of reform can be traced to
    A George Washington's term as President.
    B the Declaration of Independence.
    C the first colonies in North America.
    D the War of 1812.

___ 2. Reformers in the temperance movement worked against
    A slavery.
    B poor prison conditions.
    C mistreatment of the mentally ill.
    D the abuse of alcohol.

___ 3. By the 1850s, public elementary schools existed in
    A most northern states.
    B most southern states.
    C almost all states.
    D one or two states.

___ 4. The Underground Railroad helped to free slaves by
    A providing them with train tickets.
    B encouraging slave revolts.
    C teaching slaves to read and write.
    D providing secret hiding places and routes to the North.

___ 5. How did Harriet Tubman work against slavery?
    A by helping slaves to escape
    B by giving speeches in the North
    C by organizing meetings against slavery
    D by publishing a book attacking slavery

___ 6. Some northern workers opposed abolition because they thought
    A freed slaves might take their jobs.
    B southern states might stop buying northern goods.
    C more factories would open in the South.
    D it harmed trade with other countries.

___ 7. Which statement was NOT true for women in the early 1800s?
    A A woman's wages belonged to her husband.
    B Women were able to keep their own property when they married.
    C Women were unable to vote.
    D Women were unable to hold elected offices.

___ 8. How did conditions for women improve by the mid-1800s?
    A Women won full equality at work.
    B Women won new educational opportunities.
    C Women were able to hold office.
    D Women won the right to vote.

___ 9. In the 1820s, American artists and writers began to
    A use American themes in their work.
    B return to European ideas for inspiration.
    C show their art and publish only in other countries.
    D copy Asian art forms.

___ 10. Artists of the Hudson River School painted
    A portraits.
    B country people.
    C battle scenes.
    D landscapes.

Slavery Divides the Nation
(1820–1861)

Vocabulary Development

Using what you have learned in Chapter 16, write a sentence using each of the following pairs of vocabulary terms below to show that you understand the relationship or difference between the two terms.

Vocabulary
civil war
fugitive
Kansas-Nebraska
   Act
martyr
Missouri
   Compromise
popular sovereignty
secede
Wilmot Proviso

Kansas-Nebraska Act/Missouri Compromise

_____

_____

_____

_____

fugitive/martyr

_____

_____

_____

_____

popular sovereignty/Wilmot Proviso

_____

_____

_____

_____

secede/civil war

_____

_____

_____

_____

CHAPTER 16 Section 1 Guide to the Essentials

Slavery in the Territories

VOCABULARY

popular sovereignty control by the people

Free-Soil party a new political party formed by antislavery members of both political parties

SUMMARY

In the early to mid-1800s, fierce debates about slavery arose in the United States. Missouri asked to join the Union as a slave state. If Missouri were to be accepted as a slave state, there would be more slave states than free states. In 1820, Senator Henry Clay helped Congress work out the ***Missouri Compromise.*** Missouri joined as a slave state, and Maine joined as a free state.

Then, in the 1840s, the issue of slavery arose again. One problem was whether to allow slavery in the lands won from Mexico. Supporters of slavery, mostly southerners, wanted to allow it in every new territory and state of the West.

Opponents of slavery, mostly northerners, wanted to make it illegal in the West.

Again, northerners were afraid of losing power to southerners. In 1846, the House passed the ***Wilmot Proviso.*** It banned slavery in western territories. The Senate, however, defeated the Wilmot Proviso, and a solution to slavery was not reached. Some members of Congress supported the idea of **popular sovereignty.** This meant that voters in a new territory would decide for themselves whether to allow slavery.

The debate over slavery led to a new political party, the **Free-Soil party.** Its main goal was to keep slavery out of the western territories. It ran Martin Van Buren, a former President, as a candidate for President in 1848. Van Buren lost, but he showed that slavery had become a national issue.

MISSOURI COMPROMISE OF 1820

- Missouri joins the Union as a slave state.

- Maine joins the Union as a free state.

- Congress draws an imaginary line across the southern border of Missouri. Except for Missouri, all territories above the line are to be free of slavery. Slavery is permitted south of the line.

REVIEW

Answer the following questions on a separate sheet of paper.

1. What was the main goal of the Free Soil party?
2. **Chart Skills** Name two parts of the Missouri Compromise of 1820.

CHAPTER

16 Section 1 Guided Reading and Review
Slavery in the Territories

A. As You Read

As you read Section 1 in your textbook, fill in the missing causes and effects.

Causes	Effects
Missouri applied for statehood as a slave state.	1.
2.	Slavery was legal in the Louisiana Purchase south of the Missouri border.
Many northerners opposed the spread of slavery into the West.	3.
4.	People opposed to the spread of slavery founded the Free-Soil party.

B. Reviewing Key Terms

Explain the relevance of each term to the debate over slavery.

5. Missouri Compromise _____

_____

_____

6. Wilmot Proviso _____

_____

_____

7. popular sovereignty _____

_____

_____

8. Free-Soil party _____

_____

_____

CHAPTER

16 Section 2 Guide to the Essentials

The Compromise of 1850

VOCABULARY

secede to withdraw from an organization, country or political party

civil war a war between people of the same country

fugitive runaway

SUMMARY

The issue of slavery became important again in 1850. At that time, California requested to join the Union as a free state. If California were accepted, the North would gain control of the Senate. Southerners threatened to **secede** from the Union. Henry Clay, known as "the Great Compromiser," tried to avoid **civil war** and save the Union again. His *Compromise of 1850* helped the two sides reach agreement—but only for a short time. (See chart.)

One key part of the Compromise of 1850 was the *Fugitive Slave Act.* This law required every American citizen to help catch **fugitive** slaves. This law pleased southerners but upset antislavery

northerners. Northerners who believed that slavery was wrong did not like being forced to help slave owners. As a result, tensions over slavery remained high.

In 1852, Harriet Beecher Stowe wrote a book called *Uncle Tom's Cabin.* Stowe told the story of Tom, a kind and religious slave who is treated cruelly. Many northerners read this powerful book. It persuaded more people that slavery was wrong and must be ended. Within a short time, the book sold millions of copies and was translated into many languages. But, despite its popularity, most southerners objected to *Uncle Tom's Cabin.* They said it did not give an accurate picture of slave life.

THE COMPROMISE OF 1850
• California joins the Union as a free state.
• New Mexico and Utah use popular sovereignty to decide the question of slavery.
• Slave trading is banned in the nation's capital, Washington, D.C.
• The Fugitive Slave Law is passed.
• The border between Texas and New Mexico is set.

REVIEW

Answer the following questions on a separate sheet of paper.

1. Why did slavery become an issue in 1850?
2. **Chart Skills** Name two parts of the Compromise of 1850.

CHAPTER

16 Section 2 Guided Reading and Review
The Compromise of 1850

A. As You Read

As you read Section 2 in your textbook, answer the following questions:

1. Why were southerners against California's admission to the Union as a free state?

   _____

   _____

2. Why did congressmen believe that Henry Clay could resolve the debate? _____

   _____

3. What was Calhoun's position on slavery in the West? _____

   _____

4. Why was Daniel Webster willing to agree to a fugitive slave law? _____

   _____

5. What were the five provisions of the Compromise of 1850? _____

   _____

   _____

   _____

   _____

   _____

6. What was the northern reaction to the passage of the Fugitive Slave Act? _____

   _____

7. What effect did *Uncle Tom's Cabin* have on the nation? _____

   _____

B. Reviewing Key Terms

Briefly explain each person's contribution to the controversy over slavery.

8. Henry Clay _____

9. John C. Calhoun _____

10. Daniel Webster _____

11. Stephen Douglas _____

12. Harriet Beecher Stowe _____

CHAPTER

16 Section 3 Guide to the Essentials

The Crisis Deepens

VOCABULARY

guerrilla warfare the use of hit-and-run tactics

lawsuit a legal case brought to settle a dispute between persons or groups

SUMMARY

In 1854, the issue of slavery in the western territories arose again. Two new states—Kansas and Nebraska—were created by the ***Kansas-Nebraska Act.*** In each state, the issue of slavery would be decided by popular sovereignty. Both proslavery and antislavery settlers moved to Kansas. Proslavery bands from the state of Missouri flooded Kansas. Known as "Border Ruffians," members of the bands used violence and voted illegally. As a result, the proslavery group won control of the legislature. It soon passed laws in support of slavery. The antislavery settlers refused to accept these laws. People on each side engaged in **guerrilla warfare.** More than 200 people were killed in what became known as "Bleeding Kansas."

Violence even spilled onto the floor of the Senate. During one session, an abolitionist senator from Massachusetts, Charles Sumner, denounced the proslavery legislature of Kansas and criticized one of its supporters, Andrew Butler, an elderly southern senator. A few days later, Butler's nephew stormed into the Senate chamber and viciously beat Sumner with a cane. It took Sumner three years to recover from the beating.

During this time, people hoped that the Supreme Court could settle the issue of slavery. In 1857, however, the Court ruled on a **lawsuit** that divided the nation even further. Dred Scott, a slave whose owner had died, asked the courts for his freedom. He claimed he should be free because he had lived for a time in a free state and free territory. The Supreme Court decided against Scott. It went on to say that Congress did not have the power to outlaw slavery in any territory. The Court's ruling on ***Dred Scott*** v. ***Sandford***—that slaves were considered property, not people, and that Congress could not outlaw slavery anywhere in the United States—pleased slave owners but outraged opponents of slavery. (See chart.)

THE DRED SCOTT DECISION	
WHO	Dred Scott, a slave, asked for freedom because he had lived temporarily in a free state.
WHEN	1857
RESULT	Supreme Court ruled that a slave was property, not a citizen, and could not file requests in court. It also ruled that Congress could not outlaw slavery in any of the territories.

REVIEW

Answer the following questions on a separate sheet of paper.

1. Why was Kansas known as "Bleeding Kansas"?
2. **Chart Skills** Why did the Supreme Court decide that Dred Scott could not file a request in court?

CHAPTER

16 Section 3 Guided Reading and Review
The Crisis Deepens

A. As You Read

As you read Section 3 in your textbook, mark each statement true or false. Correct each false statement.

_____ 1. Henry Clay suggested that the people of Kansas and Nebraska decide for themselves whether their territories would allow slavery.

_____

_____ 2. Southerners argued that the Kansas-Nebraska Act would overturn the Missouri Compromise.

_____

_____ 3. Most people who moved to Kansas did so in search of cheap land.

_____

_____ 4. In 1855, Kansas ended up with two governments.

_____

_____ 5. A southern senator was severely beaten on the Senate floor for speaking out in favor of the Kansas legislature.

_____

_____ 6. The Supreme Court ruled that the Missouri Compromise was unconstitutional.

_____

B. Reviewing Key Terms

Write a sentence describing each person's role in the escalating battle over slavery.

7. Stephen Douglas _____

_____

8. John Brown _____

_____

9. Charles Sumner _____

_____

10. Dred Scott _____

_____

11. Frederick Douglass _____

_____

CHAPTER

16 Section 4 Guide to the Essentials

The Republican Party Emerges

VOCABULARY

Republican party the new political party formed by Free-Soilers, northern Democrats, and antislavery Whigs

arsenal a place for storing weapons

treason an act against one's country

martyr one who gives up one's life for one's beliefs

SUMMARY

In 1854, the **Republican party** came into being. The party was formed because the Whig party and the Democratic party would not take a strong stand against slavery. Antislavery members of the Whigs and the Democrats, along with the Free-Soilers, formed the Republican party.

In 1858, Abraham Lincoln ran for the Senate in Illinois as a Republican. He and his opponent, Senator Stephen Douglas, held a series of famous debates. (See chart.) The main issue in these debates was slavery. Lincoln believed that slavery was a "moral, social, and political wrong." Lincoln lost the election but became nationally known during the campaign.

John Brown, an abolitionist who had fought in Kansas, wanted to start an armed revolt against slavery. In 1859, Brown led a raid on an **arsenal** in Harpers Ferry, Virginia. He hoped to get guns from the arsenal. Brown planned to give the guns to enslaved African Americans and lead them in a revolt. Brown was caught and sentenced to death for **treason.** Southerners thought he deserved his sentence. Northerners were impressed by the dignity he showed at his trial. On the day of his death, church bells rang in the North. In the South, people were outraged that a man who tried to lead a slave revolt could be considered a **martyr** and a hero in the North.

LINCOLN-DOUGLAS DEBATES	
Abraham Lincoln	**Stephen Douglas**
believed slavery to be morally wrong	disliked slavery
opposed slavery in the western territories	would allow popular sovereignty to decide slavery issue in the western territories
would not interfere with slavery in the South	would not interfere with slavery in the South

REVIEW

Answer the following questions on a separate sheet of paper.

1. Who formed the Republican party? Why?
2. **Chart Skills** Compare the views of Douglas and Lincoln about slavery.

CHAPTER

16 Section 4 Guided Reading and Review
The Republican Party Emerges

A. As You Read

As you read Section 4 in your textbook, complete each sentence.

1. The main goal of the new Republican party was _____

2. The Republican candidate's popularity in the national election of 1856 made southerners _____

3. The Senate campaign between Lincoln and Douglas received national attention because _____

4. Before running for the Senate, Lincoln _____

5. At Harpers Ferry, John Brown _____

B. Reviewing Key Terms

Match each person with his description.

_____ 6. John C. Frémont

_____ 7. James Buchanan

_____ 8. Abraham Lincoln

_____ 9. Stephen Douglas

_____ 10. John Brown

a. first Republican candidate for President

b. Democrat who became President in 1856

c. Illinois senator who believed slavery question should be settled by popular sovereignty

d. Republican who ran for Illinois senate; gained national attention for his speeches against slavery

e. led what was planned to be a national slave uprising; tried for treason and executed

Section 5 Guide to the Essentials
A Nation Divides

SUMMARY

Abraham Lincoln ran for President as a Republican in 1860. He was able to win because the Democratic party was split over slavery. Northern Democrats chose Stephen Douglas to run for President. Southern Democrats picked John Breckinridge from Kentucky. Lincoln also won because there were now many more voters in the North than in the South. He received very few southern votes.

In the South, there was a great unhappiness about Lincoln's election. Many southerners thought that they no longer had a voice in the national government. They thought that their only choice was to leave the Union. South Carolina was the first to secede in 1860. Six states followed. They formed the Confederate States of America, or the Confederacy. Jefferson Davis was named president of the Confederacy.

President Lincoln did not believe that the southern states had the right to secede. However, he wanted to avoid war. While he was deciding what to do, Confederate forces began to seize federal forts in the South. Then Confederate forces fired on Union troops in Fort Sumter in South Carolina. The firing on the fort on April 11, 1861, marked the beginning of the Civil War. (See chart.) This war would last four long years.

EVENTS LEADING TO THE CIVIL WAR, 1860–1861

Abraham Lincoln is elected President.

↓

South Carolina secedes.

↓

Alabama, Florida, Georgia, Louisiana, Mississippi, and Texas secede.

↓

Confederate States of America is created.

↓

Confederate forces seize federal forts in the South.

↓

Confederates fire on Fort Sumter.

REVIEW
Answer the following questions on a separate sheet of paper.

1. What did Lincoln's election mean to the South?
2. **Chart Skills** Which event occurred first: the secession of South Carolina or the formation of the Confederate States of America?

CHAPTER

16 Section 5 Guided Reading and Review
A Nation Divides

A. As You Read

As you read Section 5 in your textbook, list supporting ideas for each main idea below:

Main Idea A: The national election of 1860 reflected sectional divisions.

1. _____

2. _____

3. _____

Main Idea B: The South reacted strongly to the election results.

4. _____

5. _____

6. _____

7. _____

B. Reviewing Key Terms

Briefly identify the importance of each place to the 1860 elections and/or the start of the Civil War.

8. Chicago, Illinois _____

9. South Carolina _____

10. Fort Sumter _____

CHAPTER
16 TEST

Identifying Main Ideas

Write the letter of the correct choice in the answer space.

___ 1. The idea of control by the people is called
A right of secession.
B popular sovereignty.
C compromise.
D sectionalism.

___ 2. Keeping slavery out of the western territories was the main goal of the
A Free Soil party.
B Whig party.
C Democrat party.
D United Democrat party.

___ 3. California was admitted to the Union as a free state in the
A Wilmot Proviso.
B Fugitive Slave Law.
C Compromise of 1850.
D Lincoln and Douglas debates.

___ 4. *Uncle Tom's Cabin* was an important book because it
A caused people to support slavery.
B told a true story about slavery.
C supported southern slave masters.
D persuaded many people that slavery was wrong.

___ 5. An effect of the Dred Scott decision was to
A divide the nation further over slavery.
B help the North and the South reach a compromise.
C weaken the Supreme Court's power.
D increase the Supreme Court's power.

___ 6. The Republican party was formed because
A the Senate passed a law.
B the Whigs and the Democrats would not take a strong stand about the slavery issue.
C southerners believed that they had no voice in the national government.
D Abraham Lincoln proposed it.

___ 7. Which of the following BEST states Lincoln's view of slavery in 1858?
A Slavery is not a political issue.
B Slavery should be abolished everywhere immediately.
C Slavery is acceptable in the western territories.
D Slavery is wrong.

___ 8. John Brown led a raid on Harpers Ferry to get
A boats for escaping slaves.
B help from trained military forces.
C guns for a slave revolt.
D southern support for antislavery ideas.

___ 9. Abraham Lincoln won the 1860 election for President because
A the Democratic party was split.
B he won the debates with Stephen Douglas.
C Jefferson Davis supported him.
D he won many southern votes.

___ 10. All of the following were causes of the Civil War EXCEPT
A the firing on Fort Sumter.
B Abraham Lincoln's election.
C the secession of South Carolina.
D John Breckinridge's death.

CHAPTER

17 The Civil War
(1861–1865)

Vocabulary Development

In this chapter, you will read about the battles and issues of the Civil War in the United States. The term *civil war* refers to a war between groups of people in the same country.

The word *civil* is used in other ways. Used alone, *civil* refers to citizens (civil duties). It is also used with other terms such as *civil defense, civil disobedience, civil rights*, and *civil service*.

Civil is also used to describe people or situations that are not part of the military. A civilian is a person who is not serving in the military. The word *military* refers to the armed forces, or those who train to fight in wars.

Directions: *The following concept map will help you to explore the word* military. *Some entries have been added to help you get started.*

- First, you will define the word. (Definition)
- What do you think about when you hear the word *military*? What are its characteristics? (Essential Characteristics)
- What groups or people are part of the military? (Examples)
- What groups of people are not part of the military? (Nonexamples)

Definition	Essential Characteristics
1. the armed forces	1. trained for war
Examples	**Nonexamples**
1.	1.
2.	2.
	3.

CHAPTER 17

Section 1 Guide to the Essentials

The Conflict Takes Shape

SUMMARY

As the Civil War began, each side believed its cause was right. The South believed it had the right to leave the Union and to preserve its traditions. One of its traditions was slavery. The North believed that it was right to save the Union, but not all northerners believed that slavery had to be abolished.

Both sides in the Civil War had strengths and weaknesses. The main strength of the Confederacy was that the southerners were defending their homeland. They had a strong reason to fight. Also, many southerners had skills, such as riding horses and using guns, that made them good soldiers. Before the war, many of the best officers in the United States Army were southerners. The main weakness of the Confederacy was its lack of resources. (See chart.)

The most important strength of the Union came from its abundant resources. The North had four times as many free citizens as the South. It had more people to fight and more people to grow food. The North also had more factories, which produced supplies for the Union army. The Union had many more ships than the Confederacy. However, the North had a major weakness. To bring the South back into the Union, the North would have to invade unfamiliar land and conquer a huge area.

The leaders of the two sides had strengths and weaknesses as well. President Jefferson Davis of the Confederacy had served as a soldier and as Secretary of War. He was widely respected for his honesty and courage. In making decisions, however, he did not always pay attention to the advice of others.

At first, some northerners doubted President Abraham Lincoln's ability to lead. He had little experience in national politics or in military affairs. Lincoln turned out to be a patient but strong leader and a fine war planner. His sense of humor helped him get along with others.

RESOURCES OF NORTH AND SOUTH, 1861		
Resources	**North**	**South**
Farmland	105,835 acres	56,832 acres
Railroad Track	21,847 miles	8,947 miles
Factories	119,500	20,600
Workers in Industry	1,198,000	111,000
Population	22,340,000	9,103,000 (of which 3,954,000 were slaves)

REVIEW

Answer the following questions on a separate sheet of paper.

1. What were one strength and one weakness of Jefferson Davis? of Abraham Lincoln?

2. **Chart Skills** How many factories did each side have in 1861?

CHAPTER 17

Section 1 Guided Reading and Review

The Conflict Takes Shape

A. As You Read

As you read Section 1 in your textbook, use the graphic organizer to compare and contrast the two sides fighting in the Civil War.

	United States of America	Confederate States of America
1. President		
2. Number of states		
3. Reasons for fighting		
4. Position on states' rights		
5. Population		
6. Economy		
7. Army		
8. Military leaders		

B. Reviewing Key Terms

Briefly define each term.

9. border state _____

10. martial law _____

CHAPTER
17

Section 2 Guide to the Essentials
No Easy Victory

SUMMARY

The North and the South had different plans for the war. (See chart.) Southerners planned to fight a defensive war. They would wait for northern armies to attack and then drive them back north. The Confederates believed that they could fight off the Union until northerners tired of fighting. When the war became unpopular, the North would be forced to accept the Confederacy.

The North had a three-part plan. First, it would use ships to blockade southern ports and prevent supplies from entering the South. Second, the Union hoped to quickly capture Richmond, Virginia, the Confederate capital. Third, the Union planned to seize control of the Mississippi River. This would cut the Confederacy into two parts and prevent the movement of southern troops and supplies along the river.

The North soon was successful in two parts of its war plan. The Union navy was able to blockade southern ports. Trade to the South dropped by more than 90 percent. The navy also moved to gain control of the Mississippi River. Union gunboats

captured New Orleans, and more ships seized Memphis, Tennessee. The Union now controlled both ends of the Mississippi. At the same time, Union General Ulysses S. Grant led his army to victory during the **Battle of Shiloh** on the Tennessee River. The North was slowly gaining control of the western part of the Confederacy.

In the east, however, Union armies did not win any major battles in the first years of the war. The **Battle of Bull Run** was the first of the war. Neither side could claim a victory. The battle did show, however, that the war would be long and difficult. The naval battle between the Confederate ship *Virginia* and the Union ship *Monitor* also ended in a draw. The Union was not able to capture Richmond as it had hoped. The Confederates won the **Battle of Fredericksburg**—one of the Union army's worst defeats in Virginia—and the **Battle of Chancellorsville,** but at great cost. The South's best general, Stonewall Jackson, was killed at Chancellorsville.

WHAT WERE THE PLANS OF EACH SIDE?	
NORTH	**SOUTH**
• blockade southern ports • take Richmond, Virginia, the Confederate capital • seize control of the Mississippi River to cut the Confederacy in two	• fight a defensive war until northerners tire of fighting • depend on European money and supplies

REVIEW

Answer the following questions on a separate sheet of paper.

1. Which parts of its war plan did the North achieve early in the war?

2. **Chart Skills** What part did the European nations play in the plans of the South?

CHAPTER

17 Section 2 Guided Reading and Review
No Easy Victory

A. As You Read
As you read Section 2 in your textbook, answer the following questions.

1. What was the Union strategy for winning the war? _____
_____

2. Why did the Confederacy expect help from Europe? _____
_____

3. Where and how did General Stonewall Jackson get his nickname? _____
_____

4. What did both sides learn from the Battle of Bull Run? _____
_____

5. What kind of commander was General McClellan? _____
_____

6. What was the purpose of the Union blockade of southern ports? _____
_____

7. What was the United States Navy's contribution to the war? _____
_____

B. Reviewing Key Terms
Briefly describe each battle, including the location and the winner.

8. Bull Run _____
_____

9. Antietam _____
_____

10. Fredericksburg _____
_____

11. Chancellorsville _____
_____

12. Shiloh _____
_____

CHAPTER

17 Section 3 Guide to the Essentials

A Promise of Freedom

VOCABULARY

emancipate set free

SUMMARY

On January 1, 1863, President Lincoln issued the ***Emancipation Proclamation***. His goal was to **emancipate** all slaves in the Confederate states. (See chart.)

Lincoln believed that the Union could be saved by broadening the goals of the war. The goals were now to restore the Union and free slaves. However, the Emancipation Proclamation did not free all slaves. In the Union, and in Confederate lands controlled by the Union, slaves were not freed. Lincoln wanted to introduce freedom for slaves gradually. He was not sure that northerners would support freedom for all slaves.

Because the rebelling states were not under Union control, no slaves actually gained freedom on January 1, 1863. However, the Emancipation Proclamation had important effects. First, Union troops were

now fighting to end slavery as well as to save the Union. Also, the Emancipation Proclamation won the Union sympathy from European countries. It became less likely that these countries would help the South. And it made both free and enslaved African Americans enthusiastic supporters of the North.

African Americans contributed a great deal to the Union war effort. At first, black troops faced discrimination. However, by the end of the war, large numbers of African Americans—about 200,000—had fought for the Union. The most famous African American unit, the **54th *Massachusetts Regiment,*** fought bravely at Fort Wagner, near Charleston, South Carolina. Behind Confederate lines, slaves did what they could to weaken the southern war effort.

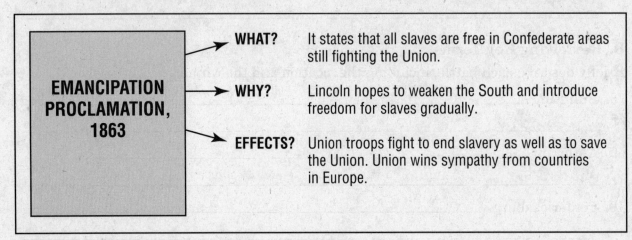

EMANCIPATION PROCLAMATION, 1863		
	WHAT?	It states that all slaves are free in Confederate areas still fighting the Union.
	WHY?	Lincoln hopes to weaken the South and introduce freedom for slaves gradually.
	EFFECTS?	Union troops fight to end slavery as well as to save the Union. Union wins sympathy from countries in Europe.

REVIEW

Answer the following questions on a separate sheet of paper.

1. About how many African Americans fought for the Union during the Civil War?

2. **Chart Skills** What were the effects of the Emancipation Proclamation?

CHAPTER
17 Section 3 Guided Reading and Review
A Promise of Freedom

★

A. As You Read

As you read Section 3 in your textbook, complete the following sentences:

1. Lincoln approached the issue of emancipation cautiously because _____
_____
_____

2. The Emancipation Proclamation stated that _____
_____
_____

3. European reaction to the Emancipation Proclamation was _____
_____
_____

4. African Americans fought in the Union army because _____
_____
_____

5. The 54th Massachusetts Regiment is famous because _____
_____
_____

6. Slaves in the Confederacy responded to the Emancipation Proclamation by _____
_____
_____

B. Reviewing Key Terms

Briefly explain the relevance of each term to the Civil War.

7. Emancipation Proclamation _____
_____

8. 54th Massachusetts Regiment _____
_____

9. Fort Wagner _____
_____

CHAPTER

17 Section 4 Guide to the Essentials
Hardships of War

VOCABULARY

draft selection for required service in the military

inflation rise in prices

income tax tax on earnings

SUMMARY

Life for soldiers during the Civil War was difficult. They slept on the ground in rain and snow. New weapons made fighting even more deadly. In most battles, one fourth or more of the soldiers were killed or wounded. Because of poor medical care, many soldiers died of infections and diseases. If captured, they faced terrible conditions in prison camps.

Both sides faced difficult problems at home. In the North, many people, called *Copperheads,* opposed the war. Fewer men volunteered to fight, so Congress passed a **draft** law. This law led to violent riots in several cities.

The North and the South also faced economic problems. Both regions experienced **inflation.** In order to pay for the war, both sides began an **income tax.** Profiteers charged high prices for needed supplies.

However, the economic problems were much more difficult in the South than in the North. The war stopped the cotton trade, the most important part of the southern economy. The northern blockade also created severe shortages of food in the South.

In both the North and the South, women played a key role. (See chart.) Many women served as nurses, improving medical care. Some women were soldiers and spies. At home, women raised money and collected supplies, including food. As men left for the battlefields, women even took jobs in industry and on farms.

WOMEN IN THE CIVIL WAR	
Loreta Janeta Velazquez	fought for South at Bull Run and Shiloh
Rose Greenhow	spied for South in Washington, D.C.
Dorothea Dix	served as chief of nurses for Union
Clara Barton	served as nurse and founded Red Cross
Sojourner Truth	worked in Union hospitals and camps for freed slaves
Sally Tompkins	opened a hospital in Richmond, Virginia

REVIEW

Answer the following questions on a separate sheet of paper.

1. Describe the life of a soldier during the Civil War.

2. **Chart Skills** Which of the women listed on the chart worked with the sick and wounded?

CHAPTER

17

Section 4 Guided Reading and Review
Hardships of War

A. As You Read

As you read Section 4 in your textbook, fill in supporting details for each main idea listed below:

Main Idea A: Army life was like a nightmare.

1. _____

2. _____

Main Idea B: Both sides faced difficulties on the home front.

3. _____

4. _____

Main Idea C: The war affected the economy on both sides.

5. _____

6. _____

Main Idea D: Women on both sides played an active role in the war.

7. _____

B. Reviewing Key Terms

Match each term with its definition.

_____ 8. draft

_____ 9. Copperhead

_____ 10. inflation

_____ 11. profiteer

a. northerner who opposed using force to keep the South in the Union

b. military service requirement

c. rise in prices and decrease in the value of money

d. manufacturer who charged excessive prices for goods that the government needed for war

CHAPTER

17

Section 5 Guide to the Essentials
The War Ends

VOCABULARY

total war war in which troops destroy food and equipment useful to an enemy

SUMMARY

In July 1863, the North won two key battles. Union forces took the town of Vicksburg on the Mississippi River. The Union soon controlled the entire river. Another major northern victory was the **Battle of Gettysburg** in Pennsylvania. Pickett's Charge was the Confederates' last attempt to invade the North. If the Confederates had defeated the Union in Pennsylvania, they could have marched on Washington, D.C. However, the Confederates would never invade the North again.

At a ceremony after the battle, President Lincoln gave the **Gettysburg Address.** In this speech, Lincoln reminded people that the United States was founded on the belief that "all men are created equal." The Union was fighting, he said, so that "government of the people, by the people, and for the people, shall not perish from the Earth." This short but famous speech has been honored as an important statement of American ideals.

The North finally defeated the South through a strategy of **total war.** General Ulysses S. Grant, the commander of Union forces in 1864, wanted to destroy the South's ability to fight. He sent General William Tecumseh Sherman to attack Atlanta and march from there to the sea. Union troops burned farms, houses, and cities along the way. In 1865, General Lee surrendered the main southern army at **Appomatox Court House.** After four long and terrible years, the Civil War was over. (See chart.)

Lincoln nearly lost reelection in 1864 because of the war. Sherman's success, however, helped him keep the Presidency. He knew that the next four years would be difficult. He hoped to rebuild the Union. The war had taken a terrible toll on the nation, yet it was an important turning point. The national government became more powerful than state governments. Slavery ended, and millions of African Americans became free citizens. In the end, the war unified the nation.

CAUSES

- South fears loss of power in the national government

- Issue of slavery in the western territories divides North and South

THE CIVIL WAR

EFFECTS

- Lincoln issues Emancipation Proclamation

- Total war destroys the South

- Hundreds of thousands of Americans killed

REVIEW

Answer the following questions on a separate sheet of paper.

1. What was the importance of the Battle of Gettysburg?

2. **Chart Skills** What were the effects of the Civil War?

Name_____ Class_____ Date_____

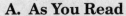

CHAPTER
17
Section 5 Guided Reading and Review
The War Ends

A. As You Read

As you read Section 5 in your textbook, mark each statement true or false. Correct each false statement.

_____ 1. Lincoln appointed Grant commander of the army because Grant was efficient and an effective leader.

_____

_____ 2. A great victory at Vicksburg turned the tide of war in the Confederacy's favor.

_____

_____ 3. Union control of the Mississippi cut the Confederacy in two.

_____

_____ 4. The Battle of Gettysburg was a decisive victory for Robert E. Lee.

_____

_____ 5. The South would continue to fight for a year after the Battle of Gettysburg.

_____

_____ 6. Only five thousand men died at the Battle of Gettysburg.

_____

_____ 7. Grant believed that total war against the southerners was the only way to win the war.

_____

_____ 8. Lee was forced to sign harsh and inhuman terms of surrender to the Union.

_____

B. Reviewing Key Terms

Fill in each blank with the correct term.

9. Lincoln's brief speech in honor of the war dead is known as the _____.

10. _____ was the last attack at Gettysburg, in which the Confederate soldiers were to cross open ground, climb a steep hill, and open fire on the enemy.

11. As part of the policy of _____ against the South, railroads and crops were destroyed and cities were burned to the ground.

12. Lee surrendered to Grant at _____.

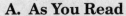

Identifying Main Ideas

Write the letter of the correct choice in the answer space.

___ 1. A disadvantage for the North in the Civil War was that it
A had fewer people.
B had more factories.
C would have to invade the South.
D had more rail lines.

___ 2. When the Civil War began, many northerners
A doubted Lincoln's ability to lead.
B had great respect for Lincoln.
C feared that Lincoln might join the Confederacy.
D were confident because Lincoln had military experience.

___ 3. As war began, the Confederates believed that
A they did not need a war plan.
B the North would not attack them.
C they could conquer the North.
D northerners would grow tired of the war.

___ 4. What was the effect of the northern blockade?
A Southern trade dropped slightly.
B Southern trade dropped sharply.
C The blockade had no effect.
D Southern trade stopped and then began again.

___ 5. Which was NOT an effect of the Emancipation Proclamation?
A It encouraged European countries to sympathize with the North.
B It meant the Union was fighting to end slavery.
C It encouraged free and enslaved African Americans to support the North.
D It freed all slaves.

___ 6. During the Civil War, African American troops
A fought on the Union side in large numbers.
B were not allowed into battle.
C were very few in number.
D did not face discrimination.

___ 7. The life of soldiers during the Civil War was
A dangerous and difficult.
B boring and uneventful.
C difficult but not deadly.
D comfortable yet deadly.

___ 8. What economic problem did both the North and the South face?
A lack of goods
B inflation
C destruction of factories
D economic ruin

___ 9. What was the importance of the Battle of Vicksburg to the Union?
A The Union would soon control the entire Mississippi River.
B The Union now controlled both ends of the Mississippi River.
C It prevented a Confederate attack on Washington, D.C.
D The Union could go on to capture the southern end of the river.

___ 10. In total war,
A fighting is limited to soldiers.
B food and equipment are destroyed.
C enemy resources are not affected.
D destruction occurs only during battles.

CHAPTER

18 Reconstruction and the Changing South (1863–1896)

Vocabulary Development

Write the correct vocabulary word on the line next to each definition below.

1. _____ a northerner in the South after the Civil War

2. _____ the government pardon of a group of people

3. _____ a farmer who does not own the land but works for a portion of the crops he or she farms

4. _____ to bring formal charges against someone, especially a public official

5. _____ a southerner helping the Republican administration of the South after the Civil War

6. _____ the separation of races, classes, or ethnic groups

Directions: *Using at least four of the listed vocabulary words, write a paragraph about the chapter on the lines below. Be sure to use complete sentences and correct spelling in your writing.*

_____

_____

_____

_____

_____

_____

_____

_____

_____

_____

_____

CHAPTER

18 Section 1 Guide to the Essentials

Early Steps to Reunion

VOCABULARY

freedmen men and women who were once slaves

amnesty a government pardon

SUMMARY

After the Civil War ended, the South lay in ruins. Most of the battles had been fought in the South. Many homes, farms, and cities had been destroyed. Nearly four million **freedmen** needed food, clothing, and jobs.

As the war was ending, President Lincoln planned for *Reconstruction,* the rebuilding of the South. He wanted to reunite the Union quickly. In his Ten Percent Plan, a southern state could form a new state government after 10 percent of its voters swore loyalty to the United States. After the state abolished slavery, it could rejoin the Union. The plan also granted **amnesty** to former Confederate soldiers. However, many members of Congress wanted a stricter form of Reconstruction.

Congress created the *Freedman's Bureau,* which gave food, clothing, and other kinds of help to the freedmen. Congress also passed the *Thirteenth Amendment* in January 1865 ending slavery in the United States.

Lincoln and the Congress never had time to agree on a plan for Reconstruction. The President was shot and killed by John Wilkes Booth on April 14, 1865. Vice President Andrew Johnson became President.

Johnson also proposed a plan for Reconstruction. Republicans in Congress were outraged and opposed his plan. (See chart.)

RECONSTRUCTION PLAN OF ANDREW JOHNSON

THE PLAN
- In each southern state, a majority of voters must swear loyalty to the United States.
- Each state must approve the Thirteenth Amendment.
- After meeting the conditions, each state could rejoin the Union.

RESPONSE OF THE SOUTH
- Southern states met Johnson's demands.
- President approved their new state governments.
- Southern voters elected representatives to Congress.

RESPONSE OF CONGRESS
- Republicans were outraged that southern states had not let African Americans vote and that former Confederate leaders were elected to Congress.
- Republicans kept southern representatives from taking seats in Congress.

REVIEW

Answer the following questions on a separate sheet of paper.

1. What hardships did the freedmen face after the Civil War?

2. **Chart Skills** Why did Republicans prevent the new southern representatives from taking seats in Congress?

CHAPTER

18 Section 1 Guided Reading and Review

Early Steps to Reunion

A. As You Read

As you read Section 1 in your textbook, answer the following questions:

1. Why was it harder for southerners than for northerners to adjust to peacetime?

_____

_____

2. What were Lincoln's intentions toward the South after the war ended? _____

_____

_____

3. (a) What was the main goal of the Freedmen's Bureau? (b) What services did it provide?

_____

_____

4. What effect did Lincoln's assassination have on the United States? _____

_____

_____

5. What did Andrew Johnson do when he became President? _____

_____

_____

B. Reviewing Key Terms

Match each description at the left with a term or name at the right.

_____ 6. rebuilding of the South after the Civil War

_____ 7. required majority of white men in former Confederate states to swear loyalty to the Union

_____ 8. agency that aided former slaves

_____ 9. actor who shot President Lincoln and died soon after while hiding from police

_____ 10. abolished slavery throughout the United States

a. John Wilkes Booth

b. Reconstruction

c. Freedmen's Bureau

d. Thirteenth Amendment

e. Wade-Davis Bill

CHAPTER 18 Section 2 Guide to the Essentials

Radical Reconstruction

VOCABULARY

black codes laws that severely limited the rights of African Americans

impeach to bring formal charges against an elected official

SUMMARY

After the war, most southern states quickly ratified the ***Thirteenth Amendment,*** which ended slavery. However, they also passed **black codes,** which limited the rights of African Americans.

When President Johnson did nothing about the black codes, some members of Congress decided to take over Reconstruction themselves. This group was called ***Radical Republicans.*** They had two main goals. First, they wanted to break the power of the southern planters. Second, they wanted to make sure African Americans had the right to vote. To make sure that this happened, Congress passed the Civil Rights Act of 1866. It gave citizenship to African Americans.

Although not all Republicans were Radicals, the Republicans in Congress worked together against the southern Democrats to carry out Radical Reconstruction. They passed the ***Fourteenth Amendment*** and later the ***Fifteenth Amendment.*** (See chart.) These amendments protected the rights of African Americans and all citizens of the United States. Then Congress passed the ***Reconstruction Act.*** This act threw out southern state governments that refused to ratify the Fourteenth Amendment and also stated that African Americans must be allowed to vote. African American votes were important to Republicans. When allowed to vote, almost all African Americans voted for Republicans. Their votes kept Republicans in power.

However, Republicans feared that Johnson would not enforce their Reconstruction laws. In 1868, the House of Representatives voted to **impeach** Johnson. The charges against the President were not proved, however. The Senate vote against Johnson fell short of the two thirds needed to convict him. He was not removed from office. Soon after, Republican Ulysses S. Grant won the presidential election of 1868.

THREE AMENDMENTS

THIRTEENTH AMENDMENT, 1865
Slavery is illegal throughout the United States.

FOURTEENTH AMENDMENT, 1868
All people born in the United States are citizens. No state may take away rights of citizens.

FIFTEENTH AMENDMENT, 1870
The right to vote cannot be denied to citizens because of their race or color or because they were once enslaved.

REVIEW

Answer the following questions on a separate sheet of paper.

1. What were two goals of the Radical Republicans?

2. **Chart Skills** What right did the Fifteenth Amendment guarantee?

CHAPTER 18 Section 2 Guided Reading and Review
Radical Reconstruction

A. As You Read

As you read Section 2 in your textbook, complete each sentence.

1. Southern legislatures' response to the Thirteenth Amendment was _____
_____

2. Republicans were outraged at the black codes and President Johnson because
_____
_____

3. Radical Republicans' two chief goals were _____
_____
_____

4. The Fourteenth Amendment stated that _____
_____

5. The 1866 elections resulted in _____
_____

6. The Reconstruction Act required that _____
_____
_____

7. President Johnson was impeached because _____
_____

8. Republicans supported the Fifteenth Amendment because _____
_____
_____

B. Reviewing Key Terms

Briefly identify the following terms.

9. Radical Reconstruction _____
_____

10. black codes _____
_____

CHAPTER 18

Section 3 Guide to the Essentials

The South Under Reconstruction

VOCABULARY

sharecropper person who farms land owned by someone else and who is paid with a share of the crops

SUMMARY

During Reconstruction, new groups gained political power in the South. One such group was white southerners who had opposed the Confederacy and now supported the Republicans. They were viewed as traitors by some other southerners. A second group was northerners who moved south after the war. African Americans were a third group. They were now able to vote and take part in government. (See chart.)

White southerners who held power before the war resisted Reconstruction. They were known as Conservatives. They did everything they could to keep freedmen from owning land or voting. Many joined secret societies that used violence to terrorize African Americans. The most dangerous was the Ku Klux Klan. These actions kept Reconstruction from going ahead smoothly.

In the South, opportunities were still limited for many people. The freedmen had little money to buy land. Many freedmen and poor whites became **sharecroppers.** The sharecropping system kept many farmers poor. They were unable to earn much money or to buy land of their own.

RECONSTRUCTION: AFRICAN AMERICANS ENTER POLITICS

African Americans are able to vote in large numbers for the first time.

↓

Many are elected to local and state government offices.

↓

Sixteen are elected to Congress, including two senators from Mississippi.

↓

Many southern whites are opposed to African Americans' voting and taking office.

↓

The *Ku Klux Klan* and other secret groups use violence to prevent African Americans from voting.

↓

Many African Americans stop voting as a result of these threats.

REVIEW

Answer the following questions on a separate sheet of paper.

1. How did the sharecropping system keep many farmers poor?

2. **Chart Skills** Which group used violence to prevent African Americans from voting?

CHAPTER

18 Section 3 Guided Reading and Review

The South Under Reconstruction

A. As You Read

As you read Section 3 in your textbook, fill in the missing causes and effects.

Causes	Effects
1.	Many northerners came South after the war.
African Americans in the South went to the polls in large numbers.	2.
3.	Some southerners formed a terrorist group called the Ku Klux Klan.
Reconstruction governments spent a lot of money on railroads, school systems, and telegraph lines.	4.
5.	Most freedmen worked the land and remained poor.

B. Reviewing Key Terms

Match each term with its definition.

_____ 6. scalawag

_____ 7. carpetbagger

_____ 8. sharecropper

a. farmer who rented land and was given seeds, fertilizer, and tools in return for a share of the crop at harvest time

b. southern Democrat's derogatory nickname for southern Republican

c. northerner who went to the South after the war

CHAPTER

18 Section 4 Guide to the Essentials

The End of Reconstruction

VOCABULARY

segregation separating people of different races in public places

Jim Crow laws laws, such as segregation laws, that trapped southern African Americans in a hopeless situation

SUMMARY

In the 1870s, Radical Republicans were losing power in Congress. Many northerners were tired of Reconstruction. They thought that it was time to forget the Civil War. They wanted to let southerners run their own governments—even if that meant African Americans might lose their rights. Republicans were also hurt when people found out about corruption in President Grant's government. Many northerners lost faith in Republican leaders. By the late 1870s, Reconstruction had ended.

After Reconstruction, southern leaders worked to expand the southern economy. The South built industries to process agricultural goods. For example, investors built textile mills to turn cotton into cloth. The South also developed its natural resources.

Steel, oil, and lumber became important industries. By 1900, the South had developed a more balanced economy. Still, it failed to keep up with even more rapid growth in the North and in the West.

When Reconstruction ended, African Americans lost their rights. Southern whites stopped African Americans from voting. (See diagram.) After 1877, **segregation** became the law of the South. African Americans brought lawsuits to challenge segregation. In 1896, the Supreme Court upheld segregation in *Plessy v. Ferguson.* The Court ruled that **Jim Crow laws** that separated the races in public places such as schools and restaurants were legal if places for blacks and whites were equal. In reality, separate places were rarely equal.

Poll Tax—
charged African Americans money to vote because most were poor and could not afford to pay

Literacy Test—
set up tests to make African Americans fail so that they could not vote

HOW SOUTHERN WHITES KEPT AFRICAN AMERICANS FROM VOTING

Violence—
threatened African Americans with death if they voted

Grandfather Clause—
allowed whites to vote without taking tests because their grandfathers had voted

REVIEW

Answer the following questions on a separate sheet of paper.

1. What did the Supreme Court decide in *Plessy* v. *Ferguson*?
2. **Diagram Skills** What was the purpose of a poll tax?

CHAPTER

18 Section 4 Guided Reading and Review

The End of Reconstruction

A. As You Read

As you read Section 4 in your textbook, fill in supporting details for each of the main ideas listed below.

Main Idea A: Reconstruction came to an end in the 1870s.

1. _____

2. _____

3. _____

Main Idea B: After Reconstruction ended, African Americans in the South began losing their rights.

4. _____

5. _____

Main Idea C: Industries flourished in the New South.

6. _____

7. _____

B. Reviewing Key Terms

Briefly explain the relevance of each of the following terms to the end of the Reconstruction era.

8. poll tax _____

_____

9. literacy test _____

_____

10. grandfather clause _____

_____

11. segregation _____

_____

12. *Plessy* v. *Ferguson* _____

_____

CHAPTER

18 TEST
Identifying Main Ideas
Write the letter of the correct choice in the answer space.

___ 1. Which of the following was NOT a hardship faced by the South after the Civil War?

A Many farms had been destroyed.

B Southern cities were in ruins.

C Freedmen needed jobs.

D The South lacked natural resources.

___ 2. Reconstruction refers to the period in which

A the South was rebuilt.

B the Civil War was fought.

C African Americans were enslaved.

D Republicans lost power.

___ 3. The Reconstruction plan of President Johnson was

A the same as the plan proposed by Lincoln.

B supported by Republicans.

C opposed by Republicans.

D opposed by all southerners.

___ 4. One goal of the Radical Republicans was to

A provide support for the black codes.

B break the power of southern planters.

C offer support for President Johnson.

D prevent passage of the Fifteenth Amendment.

___ 5. The Fourteenth Amendment to the Constitution

A freed the slaves.

B gave African Americans the right to vote.

C granted citizenship to those born in the United States.

D gave land to the freedmen.

___ 6. Congress impeached President Johnson because members feared he would

A refuse to enforce Reconstruction laws.

B win the election of 1868.

C attack the black codes.

D throw out the new southern governments.

___ 7. All of the following groups gained power in the South after the Civil War EXCEPT

A settlers from the West.

B white southerners who supported Republicans.

C northerners who had moved south.

D African Americans.

___ 8. Under the sharecropping system, many farmers

A saved enough money to buy land.

B stayed very poor.

C shared land with state governments.

D lost their jobs.

___ 9. Reconstruction ended because

A it did not improve the economy of the South.

B Radical Republicans gained power.

C northerners lost interest in it.

D freedmen got the right to vote.

___ 10. In *Plessy* v. *Ferguson,* the Supreme Court

A imprisoned Ku Klux Klan leaders.

B gave African Americans the vote.

C outlawed lynching.

D upheld segregation.

CHAPTER

19 The New West
(1865–1914)

Vocabulary Development

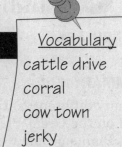

Vocabulary
cattle drive
corral
cow town
jerky

Write a short, original dialogue that might take place between two cowhands. Good dialogue not only sounds like real speech but also uses a lot of particular details. For instance, look at this mini-dialogue between two imaginary miners from the mid-1800s. Also, pay attention to the use of quotation marks, since you will be using them in your writing.

Miner 1: "Tom, I'm telling you, we need to leave Colorado and head west to Nevada to start mining that Comstock Lode."

Miner 2: "Yeah, Mike. I'm all for getting our picks on some of that silver and gold!"

Directions: *Write an imagined dialogue between two cowhands. This conversation should use all of the vocabulary words above. The words need to be used in a way that shows you understand the meanings. The dialogue should contain several specific details in order to make it realistic.*

_____

_____

_____

_____

_____

_____

_____

_____

_____

_____

_____

_____

_____

_____

Name_____ Class_____ Date_____

CHAPTER
19 Section 1 Guide to the Essentials
Indian Peoples of the Great Plains

VOCABULARY

tepee tent made by stretching buffalo skins on tall poles

SUMMARY

Many different Native American nations lived on the Great Plains. At one time, most Plains people were farmers. Then, during the 1600s, their way of life began to change. First, Pueblo Indians in the South learned to ride and care for the horses brought to the Americas by the Spanish. Later, they traded horses with Indians from the Plains. On horseback, the Plains Indians could travel farther and faster. They could follow buffalo herds and hunt buffalo more successfully. Hunting replaced farming as their most important way of getting food.

The Plains Indians depended on the buffalo for more than food. They lived in **tepees** made by stretching buffalo skins on poles. They wove buffalo fur into cloth. They carved buffalo horns and bones into tools. The Plains people followed the buffalo herds, moving their tepees from place to place. (See chart.)

In summer, many Native American groups met on the Plains. They hunted together, played games, and ran races. Leaders met to discuss problems that affected the people. They also held a religious ceremony, the Sun Dance. Thousands of people gathered to ask the Great Spirit for help in the coming year.

Among the Plains people, men and women had different roles. Men were responsible for hunting and fighting in wars. Women were responsible for the home. They made clothing, baskets, and tepees. In some Native American groups, women hunted and helped govern.

A WAY OF LIFE DEVELOPS

Plains Indians learn to ride horses.

Horses allow them to travel farther and faster, so they hunt buffalo more successfully.

Buffalo hunting replaces farming as the main way to get food.

Plains Indians follow buffalo herds. They use buffalo for food, clothing, shelter, and tools.

REVIEW

Answer the following questions on a separate sheet of paper.

1. What were three ways that the Plains Indians used the buffalo?

2. **Chart Skills** How did the introduction of horses change the Plains people's way of life?

Section 1 Guided Reading and Review

Indian Peoples of the Great Plains

A. As You Read

As you read Section 1 in your textbook, complete the graphic organizer by filling in supporting details for each main idea.

Main Idea A: Horses and buffalo played a central role in the culture of the Plains Indians.

1. _____

2. _____

3. _____

4. _____

5. _____

Main Idea B: Men's and women's activities and duties differed.

6. _____

7. _____

8. _____

9. _____

10. _____

11. _____

B. Reviewing Key Places

Match each term with its definition.

_____ 12. tepee

_____ 13. travois

_____ 14. corral

_____ 15. jerky

a. sled pulled by a dog or horse

b. dried buffalo meat

c. enclosure for livestock

d. tent made by stretching buffalo skins on tall poles

CHAPTER
19
Section 2 Guide to the Essentials
Mining and Railroading

⋆

VOCABULARY

transcontinental railroad railroad that stretches across a continent from coast to coast

SUMMARY

In the middle 1800s, mining brought great change to the West. Gold and silver were discovered, and thousands of miners traveled west. Towns grew up near the mines. Although many turned into "ghost" towns when all the gold and silver was mined, others survived and grew.

Life was hard for miners. Few people ever got rich mining gold and silver, which were difficult to find. Immigrant miners from countries such as Mexico and China were treated unfairly. Mining also caused problems. Miners polluted streams and cut down forests.

People in mining towns needed supplies. Trains could move people and supplies quickly and cheaply. Therefore, railroads were needed to link mining towns with cities. With the help of the federal government, railroad companies built railroads across the western United States.

Railroad building was dangerous. Wages were low. Railroad companies hired Chinese, Mexican, and Irish immigrants. Workers had to cross deserts and cut through mountains. Many workers died.

The first **transcontinental railroad** was completed in 1869. The country was then united by railroad. Towns and cities grew up near the train lines. Railroads helped the West develop. (See diagram.)

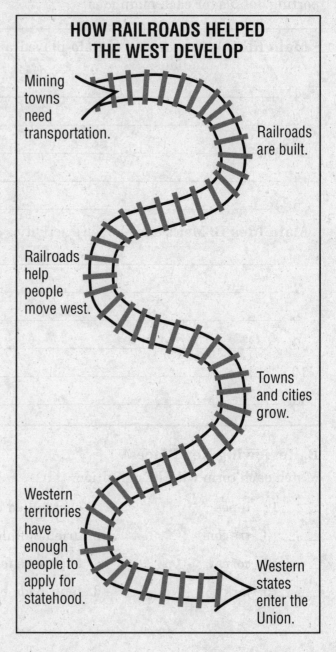

HOW RAILROADS HELPED THE WEST DEVELOP

Mining towns need transportation.

Railroads are built.

Railroads help people move west.

Towns and cities grow.

Western territories have enough people to apply for statehood.

Western states enter the Union.

REVIEW
Answer the following questions on a separate sheet of paper.

1. In what ways did mining change the West?

2. **Diagram Skills** What effect did the railroads have on the population of the West?

CHAPTER

19 Section 2 Guided Reading and Review
Mining and Railroading

A. As You Read

As you read Section 2 in your textbook, list one cause and one effect of each of the following events:

1. Miners began to leave boomtowns.

Cause: _____

Effect: _____

2. Few miners ever got rich.

Cause: _____

Effect: _____

3. Lawlessness and disorder often were characteristics of boomtowns.

Cause: _____

Effect: _____

4. Construction of a transcontinental railroad was completed in 1869.

Cause: _____

Effect: _____

B. Reviewing Key Terms
Briefly define each term.

5. lode _____

6. vigilante _____

7. transcontinental railroad _____

8. subsidy _____

CHAPTER 19

Section 3 Guide to the Essentials
The Cattle Kingdom

VOCABULARY

cattle drive long trips on which cattle were driven to markets near railroads

cow town town that grew up around railroad lines, where cattle were held before being shipped east

vaquero skilled rider who herded cattle in the Southwest, Mexico, and California

SUMMARY

After the Civil War, the demand for beef increased. People in growing eastern cities wanted more meat. Miners and railroad workers in the West also added to the demand. Wild herds of cattle, known as longhorns, roamed freely across the grassy plains of Texas. Ranchers there began to round up the cattle. They then drove the animals north to railroad lines in Kansas and Missouri. These trips were known as **cattle drives.** The towns in which the cattle were brought were known as **cow towns.** Cow towns attracted settlers, as well as cowhands. Many cow towns became thriving communities.

Ranchers employed cowhands to tend the cattle and drive the herds. Many cowhands were Mexican Americans and African Americans. Many of the skills that cowhands used—riding, roping, and branding—were learned from Spanish and Mexican **vaqueros.** For the cowhands, life on the trail was difficult. The work was hot, dirty, and tiring. Cowhands faced dangers such as bad weather, stampedes, and cattle thieves.

In the 1870s, ranching spread north. Cattle grazed from Kansas to present-day Montana. Ranchers had built a Cattle Kingdom in the West.

However, this Cattle Kingdom soon came to an end. By the 1880s, many farmers had moved to the Plains. Farmers put up fences that prevented the cattle from roaming freely. Then, in the late 1880s several cold winters killed many cattle. This bad weather also helped end the Cattle Kingdom.

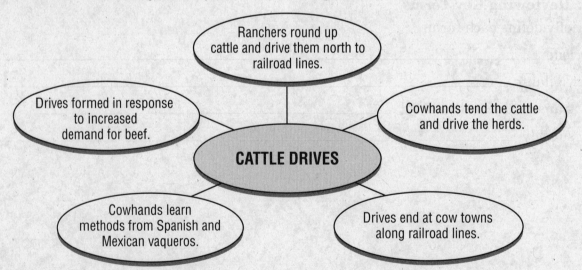

Ranchers round up cattle and drive them north to railroad lines.

Drives formed in response to increased demand for beef.

Cowhands tend the cattle and drive the herds.

CATTLE DRIVES

Cowhands learn methods from Spanish and Mexican vaqueros.

Drives end at cow towns along railroad lines.

REVIEW

Answer the following questions on a separate sheet of paper.

1. Why did ranchers in Texas start cattle drives?

2. **Chart Skills** Who taught cowhands methods of tending and driving cattle?

CHAPTER

19 Section 3 Guided Reading and Review
The Cattle Kingdom

A. As You Read

As you read Section 3 in your textbook, describe each of the following in two or three sentences:

1. cowhand _____

_____

_____

_____

2. cattle drive _____

_____

_____

_____

3. cow town _____

_____

_____

_____

B. Reviewing Key Terms

Fill in the blanks with the correct terms.

4. A _____ was a long journey of cattle from the Southwest to railroad lines in Kansas and Missouri.

5. A _____ was a skilled Mexican rider who herded cattle on Southwestern ranches.

6. A _____ is used to lasso cattle.

7. _____ protected a rider's legs from thorny plants.

8. A gunshot or clap of thunder could start a _____, in which cattle set off at a run.

9. A _____ was a town in which cattle were held until they could be shipped east.

CHAPTER

19 Section 4 Guide to the Essentials

Indian Peoples in Retreat

SUMMARY

After the Civil War, many Americans moved west. Settlers began to take Native American land. White hunters began killing thousands of buffalo. Thousands had already died because of drought, disease, and the destruction of their habitat.

Native Americans tried to preserve their ways of life. They signed agreements with the United States, giving up some land in return for food and supplies and respect for their rights to their land forever. However, many of these agreements were broken.

Native Americans resisted losing their lands. Many turned to war. Leaders such as the Lakota chief Sitting Bull won some battles. However, in the end, the United States was too strong. The Apache warrior Geronimo surrendered in 1886.

In 1889, many Plains people turned to a ceremony called the Ghost Dance. They believed that performing this dance would bring about a happier world. However, settlers feared the dance. When an army of troops killed 300 Lakota at Wounded Knee, the Ghost Dance religion ended.

By the late 1800s, the United States had forced many Native Americans onto reservations. Reservations are limited areas set aside for Native Americans. Government officials replaced traditional leaders and made decisions about Indians' lives. Many officials believed Indians should give up their old ways. Government policies changed the Native Americans ways of life. (See chart.)

Some people—both Native American and white—spoke out against the government's treatment of Native Americans. Call for reform led to the passage of the 1887 Dawes Act. The act encouraged more Native Americans to become farmers and divided some tribal land into small family plots. However, the Dawes Act was unsuccessful. Most Native Americans held fast to their traditional ways, preferring open land for riding and hunting instead of fenced-in farms.

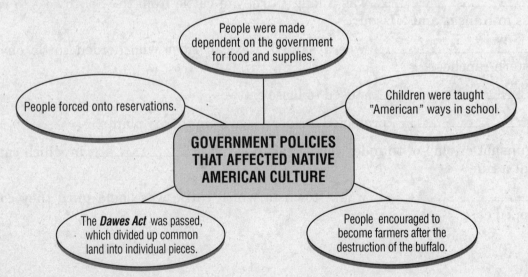

People were made dependent on the government for food and supplies.

People forced onto reservations.

Children were taught "American" ways in school.

GOVERNMENT POLICIES THAT AFFECTED NATIVE AMERICAN CULTURE

The *Dawes Act* was passed, which divided up common land into individual pieces.

People encouraged to become farmers after the destruction of the buffalo.

REVIEW

Answer the following questions on a separate sheet of paper.

1. Why did Native Americans and settlers come into conflict?

2. **Chart Skills** List one government policy that affected Native American culture.

CHAPTER

19 Section 4 Guided Reading and Review

Indian Peoples in Retreat

A. As You Read

As you read Section 4 in your textbook, answer the following questions:

1. What were the terms of the Fort Laramie Treaty? _____
_____

2. What happened at the Chivington Massacre? _____
_____

3. What happened to the buffalo of the Great Plains? _____
_____

4. What was the cause of the Sioux War of 1876? _____
_____

5. What happened at the Battle of Little Bighorn? _____
_____

6. What effect did the Ghost Dance have on non-Native Americans? _____
_____

7. What happened at Wounded Knee Creek? _____
_____

8. What was the intention of the Dawes Act? _____
_____

B. Reviewing Key Terms

Briefly identify each person listed below.

9. Sitting Bull _____

10. John Chivington _____

11. George Armstrong Custer _____

12. Chief Joseph _____

13. Geronimo _____

14. Susette La Flesche _____

15. Helen Hunt Jackson _____

CHAPTER

19 Section 5 Guide to the Essentials
Farming

★

VOCABULARY

sodbuster Plains farmer who used steel plows to cut through tough sod

sod house a house built of soil held together by grass roots

SUMMARY

Different groups of farmers settled in the West. (See chart.) Many began farming because of the ***Homestead Act.*** Congress passed the act in 1862 to encourage people to move west. It promised 160 free acres of land to anyone who farmed it for five years.

Life was difficult for farmers on the Plains. They became known as **sodbusters.** In order to farm, they had to cut through sod, a layer of thick, hard soil held together by grass roots. Trees were scarce, so many farmers built leaky **sod houses** from the soil. In the summer, there was little rain. The winters were windy and cold. Sometimes huge swarms of grasshoppers came out and ate everything in their path.

In the late 1880s, the United States government forced several Native American nations to sell their land in Oklahoma. The government then announced that settlers and farmers could stake their claims to free homesteads on that land. On April 22, 1889,

land seekers lined up at the Oklahoma border for the start of the Oklahoma Land Rush. When a shot rang out from the starting gun at noon, 100,000 people—on foot, on horseback, and in wagons—streamed into Oklahoma. They all hoped to stake a claim on a fertile piece of land.

Despite the harsh conditions, farmers began to harvest huge crops of wheat and corn. However, since the supply of these crops was increasing, prices began to fall. By the late 1800s, farmers were facing a crisis. Soon, many farmers could not repay money they had borrowed to buy equipment and land. Farmers began to organize to improve their lives. In 1891, they helped form the Populist party. It supported candidates who wanted to improve conditions for farmers and other workers. Many Populist ideas, such as the eight-hour workday, eventually became accepted in American life.

ORIGINS OF WESTERN FARMERS	
Homesteaders	Easterners and immigrants who came west to get free land under the Homestead Act
Exodusters	African Americans who left the South (they took their name from Exodus, the book of the Bible describing how the Jews escaped slavery in Egypt)
Mexicanos	Spanish-speaking people who already lived in the lands that the United States won in the Mexican War

REVIEW

Answer the following questions on a separate sheet of paper.

1. Why was life difficult for farmers on the Plains?

2. **Chart Skills** How did the Exodusters get their name?

CHAPTER

19 Section 5 Guided Reading and Review
Farming

A. As You Read

As you read Section 5 in your textbook, complete the following sentences:

1. To encourage people to settle the West, the government passed the

   _____.

2. African American homesteaders called themselves the _____ after a book of the Bible that described the Jewish flight from slavery in Egypt.

3. The first farmers to settle Oklahoma were called _____ because they grabbed their land before the official date.

4. Dangers caused by the dry climate of the Plains included _____

   _____

5. Women's duties on the Plains farms included _____

   _____

   _____

6. Farmers formed the National Grange and the Farmer's Alliance because _____

   _____

7. The Populist party supported these ideas: _____

   _____

B. Reviewing Key Terms

Briefly explain the relevance of each term to the settlement of the West.

8. sod house _____

   _____

9. sodbuster _____

   _____

10. cooperative _____

   _____

11. wholesale _____

   _____

CHAPTER

19 TEST

Identifying Main Ideas

Write the letter of the correct choice in the answer space.

___ 1. Which did NOT happen after the Plains Indians tamed wild horses?

A They could travel farther and faster.

B They could hunt more buffalo.

C The buffalo became their main source of food.

D Their way of life stayed the same.

___ 2. Among the Plains Indians, men

A were responsible for hunting.

B oversaw village life.

C made tepees.

D spent most of their time farming.

___ 3. The transcontinental railroad

A led north.

B led south.

C crossed the United States.

D was completed in the 1900s.

___ 4. Which was NOT a result of the building of the railroads?

A Many workers died.

B Cities grew up along railroad lines.

C Supplies could be moved quickly and cheaply.

D The population of western territories fell.

___ 5. Cowhands on cattle drives used skills

A brought over by Irish immigrants.

B learned from Mexican vaqueros.

C that destroyed the buffalo herds.

D that made the work more difficult.

___ 6. What action of Plains farmers helped end the Cattle Kingdom?

A They hunted buffalo.

B They put up fences.

C They gave up farming.

D They quickly passed into areas farther west.

___ 7. What did Native Americans hope to gain in return for agreeing to give up some land?

A respect for rights to the rest of the land

B the return of the buffalo herds

C rights to mine gold and silver

D the passage of the Dawes Act

___ 8. Some Native Americans turned to the Ghost Dance as a way to

A earn money.

B frighten settlers.

C create a new, happier world.

D share their cultures with white Americans.

___ 9. The Homestead Act

A set a price for land.

B promised land only to African Americans.

C helped farmers settle the East.

D promised land to people who would farm it for five years.

___ 10. What new problem did farmers face in the late 1800s?

A They had to cut through tough sod.

B Crop prices began to fall.

C Winters turned cold and windy.

D Grasshoppers attacked their lands.

CHAPTER

20 Industrial Growth
(1865–1914)

Vocabulary Development

<u>Vocabulary</u>
corporation
dividend
free enterprise
  system
mass production
moving assembly
  line
stock

You can often figure out the meaning of an unfamiliar word by looking at the words that surround it. These words are called the context.

Imagine that you are a journalist in 1927 who is writing an article on the growth of the U.S. economy. Use all of the vocabulary terms listed on the right to describe the factors that have helped bring about the success of business in the Roaring Twenties. Remember to define all these words using context clues. You may choose to open with the sentence provided, or you may write your own opening sentence.

The U.S. economy is still growing, continuing the boom times of the past several years.

_____

_____

_____

_____

_____

_____

_____

_____

_____

_____

_____

_____

_____

_____

_____

_____

CHAPTER

20 Section 1 Guide to the Essentials

Railroads Spur Industry

VOCABULARY

gauge the width of a railroad track

consolidate combine

competition a rivalry between companies to win business or customers

rebate a discount for a product or service

SUMMARY

After the Civil War, railroad companies built lines all over the United States. Most railroads covered only 50 miles or so. Few railroads used the same width of track. When passengers rode to the end of the line, they had to get out and switch railroads. Switching was inconvenient and costly for shippers of goods. Finally, in the 1880s, all railroad companies decided to use the same **gauge** track to create a network of connected railroad lines.

As railroads grew, railroad companies got bigger. Some consolidated to become even larger. A few tough-minded business people, such as Cornelius Vanderbilt, led the drive for **consolidation** and gained control of most of the railroad industry.

As the railroad industry grew, the **competition** became greater. Railroad companies rushed to get their share of profits. Some companies cut fares to get customers. Other companies offered

rebates to their biggest customers. These discounts forced many small railroad companies out of business. The discounts also hurt small shippers, who had to pay full price. Some railroad companies realized that competition was hurting their business. Some joined together and formed a pool. They divided up business in an area, reduced competition, and kept prices high.

The growth in railroad building helped the economy. (See chart.) New jobs were created. Workers turned iron into steel for tracks. Workers cut down forests to provide wood for railroad ties. Miners dug coal for the engines. Railroad companies employed thousands of workers. Large railroad companies also created new ways of managing business. Other large companies copied these techniques. In addition, railroads opened many parts of the country to settlement, especially in the West.

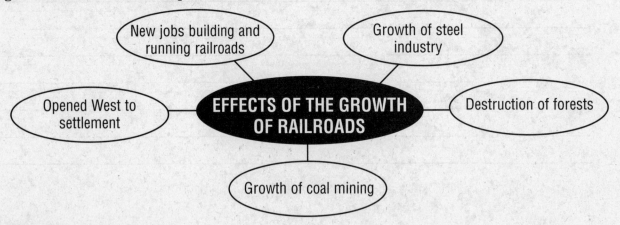

REVIEW

Answer the following questions on a separate sheet of paper.

1. Why did railroad companies decide to use the same type of tracks?

2. **Chart Skills** What effect did the growth of the railroad have on workers?

20 Section 1 Guided Reading and Review

Railroads Spur Industry

A. As You Read

As you read Section 1 in your textbook, explain the importance of each of the following developments in the national railroad on American society and on the economy.

1. In 1886, Southern railroads adopted the Northern gauge. _____
_____

2. George Westinghouse invented the air brake. _____
_____

3. Companies began buying up small rail lines. _____
_____

4. Many industries boomed because of the railroad. _____
_____

B. Reviewing Key Terms

Use each term correctly in an accurate statement about the growth of the railroad.

5. gauge _____
_____

6. network _____
_____

7. consolidate _____
_____

8. rebate _____
_____

9. pool _____

CHAPTER

20 Section 2 Guide to the Essentials
The Rise of Big Business

VOCABULARY

corporation a business owned by investors

stock shares in a corporation

investor a person who commits money to earn a financial return

monopoly a company that controls all or nearly all the businesses of an industry

SUMMARY

After the Civil War, the steel industry began to grow. Inventors discovered a way to make steel cheaply. The growth of railroads meant more demand for steel. Steel rails were stronger than iron and resisted rust. Steel was used for building skyscrapers. Steel mills employed many workers.

As industry expanded, Americans developed new ways of doing business. Growing businesses needed money to buy raw materials and to build factories. Many businesses became **corporations.** To raise money, a corporation sells **stock** to **investors.** The corporation uses this money and money borrowed from banks to keep expanding. Bankers like J. P. Morgan invested, or put money into, corporations even during economic hard times.

As corporations got larger, many small businesses failed. By the late 1800s, many corporations had become **monopolies.** For example, Standard Oil controlled 95 percent of all of the oil refining in the United States. Its owner, John D. Rockefeller, had bought out almost all the competition.

Many people were opposed to monopolies. They argued that monopolies reduced competition. Without competition, companies had no reason to keep prices low or to make better products. Monopolies also made it difficult for new companies to begin. Workers thought that large corporations treated them badly. (See chart.)

Defenders of monopolies said that large corporations brought lower prices and a better quality of life. Some business leaders argued that competition ruined businesses and put people out of work.

CAUSES

- **Railroad growth helps other businesses grow**

- **Businesses become corporations**

- **Nation has rich supply of natural resources**

THE RISE OF INDUSTRY IN THE UNITED STATES

EFFECTS

- **Steel and oil become giant industries**

- **Monopolies control important industries**

- **Factory workers face harsh conditions**

REVIEW

Answer the following questions on a separate sheet of paper.

1. Why did the steel industry become so important after the Civil War?

2. **Chart Skills** What were two causes of the rise of industry in the United States?

Name_____ Class_____ Date_____

Section 2 Guided Reading and Review
The Rise of Big Business

A. As You Read
As you read Section 2 in your textbook, fill in the missing causes and effects.

Causes	Effects
The Bessemer process allowed stronger steel to be produced more cheaply.	1.
2.	Carnegie had a great advantage over other steel producers.
J. P. Morgan invested in troubled corporations.	3.
Rockefeller knew that oil was not profitable until it was refined.	4.
5.	Corporations usually found ways to avoid regulations.

B. Reviewing Key Terms
Match each person with his description.

_____ 6. Henry Bessemer

_____ 7. Andrew Carnegie

_____ 8. J. P. Morgan

_____ 9. John D. Rockefeller

a. discovered a new way to convert iron into steel

b. Scottish immigrant to the United States who made a fortune in steel mills

c. built up his oil refineries into the Standard Oil Company of Ohio

d. banker who eventually gained control of U.S. Steel

CHAPTER

20 Section 3 Guide to the Essentials
Inventions Change the Nation

VOCABULARY

assembly line a system of production in which workers add parts to a product as a moving belt carries it by them

mass production making large quantities of a product cheaply and quickly

SUMMARY

In the late 1800s, Americans created many inventions. (See chart.) These inventions helped industry grow.

Some inventions improved communication. The telegraph had been in use since the 1840s. In 1866, Cyrus Field laid an underground telegraph cable across the Atlantic Ocean. Now fast communication was possible between the United States and Europe. In 1876, Alexander Graham Bell tested his "talking machine"—a telephone. By 1885, Bell had sold more than 300,000 phones, mostly to businesses.

In Menlo Park, New Jersey, Thomas Edison and his co-workers created an "invention factory." Teams of experts made Edison's ideas into practical inventions.

Edison was responsible for inventing the light bulb, the electric power plant, and hundreds of other devices.

Henry Ford introduced the **assembly line** in his automobile factory. The assembly line allowed **mass production** of cars. As prices dropped, more people could afford to buy cars. Cars soon became part of everyday American life.

By 1917, more than 4.5 million cars were rolling along the nation's roads. Life in the United States changed very quickly. Because of the automobile—and eventually, the airplane—men and women could travel much farther and conduct business more quickly than ever before.

A TIME OF INVENTION		
Elijah McCoy	1872	engine-oiling machine
Stephen Dudley Field	1874	electric streetcar
Alexander Graham Bell	1876	telephone
Thomas Alva Edison	1877	phonograph
Anna Baldwin	1878	milking machine
Jan Matzeliger	1883	shoemaking machine
Charles and J. Frank Duryea	1893	gasoline-powered car
John Thurman	1899	motor-driven vacuum cleaner
Leo H. Baekeland	1909	plastic

REVIEW

Answer the following questions on a separate sheet of paper.

1. How did Henry Ford change the automobile industry?

2. **Chart Skills** Who invented the electric streetcar?

CHAPTER

20 Section 3 Guided Reading and Review
Inventions Change the Nation

A. As You Read

As you read Section 3 in your textbook, correct each of the following false statements:

1. The telephone was an instant success. _____

_____

2. Movies became possible with the invention of the light bulb. _____

_____

3. Assembly lines made it possible for people to eat fresh meat. _____

_____

4. Henry Ford charged less for his cars because he didn't care about making a profit.

_____

_____

5. The first airplane could fly 40 miles per hour and was used for wartime

reconnaissance. _____

_____

B. Reviewing Key Terms

Identify the invention or inventions for which each of the following people is known.

6. Elisha Otis _____

7. Thomas Edison _____

8. Alexander Graham Bell _____

9. Lewis E. Waterman _____

10. King C. Gillette _____

11. George Pullman _____

CHAPTER

20 Section 4 Guide to the Essentials
The Rise of Organized Labor

VOCABULARY

sweatshop a workplace in which people labor long hours in poor conditions for low pay

union a confederation of workers

collective bargaining the right of unions to negotiate with management for workers as a group

strike work stoppage by a group of workers because of a grievance

SUMMARY

As industry in the United States grew, the lives of workers changed. Factories were larger. Bosses did not always know workers. Workers spent long days tending dangerous machines in large, crowded rooms. In **sweatshops,** they learned few skills and worked for low wages fixed by their bosses. Owners were often more interested in profits than in worker safety. Many workers were hurt or killed.

Workers got together to improve working conditions. They formed **unions.** One early union was the Knights of Labor. Its goals included an end to child labor and equal pay for men and women. However, by the late 1880s, membership dropped and the Knights of Labor failed.

Another important union was the American Federation of Labor (AFL). (See chart.) Workers in a trade joined a union, and then that union joined the AFL. The AFL worked for higher wages, shorter hours, improved working conditions, and **collective bargaining.** It became the most powerful union in the nation.

In some industries women outnumbered men. Some formed unions. One, the International Ladies Garment Workers Union (ILGWU), worked to improve conditions for women workers. In 1911, nearly 150 young women were killed in the Triangle Fire in New York. New laws to improve work conditions were soon passed.

However, labor unions made very slow progress after 1870. When the economy was bad, workers lost their jobs or took pay cuts. To get higher pay, workers sometimes went on **strike.** However, strikes were often unsuccessful. The federal government usually supported the factory owners during a strike. Also, many Americans did not like unions. They believed that people who worked hard would be rewarded. Others feared unions were controlled by foreigners.

THE AMERICAN FEDERATION OF LABOR (AFL)

Founded
1886

Founder
Samuel Gompers,
cigarmaker

Membership
skilled laborers in specialized trade unions

Strategy
supported use of strikes; collected money from its member unions to help workers in a striking union feed their families

REVIEW

Answer the following questions on a separate sheet of paper.

1. Describe the working conditions for factory workers in the late 1800s.

2. **Chart Skills** Who founded the American Federation of Labor (AFL)?

CHAPTER

20 Section 4 Guided Reading and Review

The Rise of Organized Labor

A. As You Read

As you read Section 4 in your textbook, answer the following questions:

1. How did the relationship between worker and boss change after the Civil War?

_____

_____

2. What were the results of the 1885 strike at the Missouri Pacific Railroad?

_____

_____

3. What happened in Haymarket Square when workers clashed with strikebreakers?

_____

_____

4. What were the goals of the American Federation of Labor?

_____

_____

5. What is Mother Jones best known for?

_____

6. Why is the Triangle Shirtwaist Company fire significant in the labor movement?

_____

_____

7. Why were unions not popular in the United States in the late 1800s?

_____

_____

B. Reviewing Key Terms

Complete each sentence below by writing the correct term in the blank.

8. A _____ is a workplace in which people labor long hours in poor conditions for low pay.

9. A _____ replaces a worker who has gone on strike.

10. _____ is the right of unions to negotiate with management on behalf of a group of workers.

11. The initials _____ stand for the famous union of garment workers that was founded in 1900.

Name_____ Class_____ Date_____

TEST

Identifying Main Ideas

Write the letter of the correct choice in the answer space.

___ 1. Cornelius Vanderbilt's drive to consolidate the railroad industry allowed him to
   A build the Great Northern Railway.
   B gain control of most of the railroad industry.
   C invent the first railroad tie.
   D create new time zones.

___ 2. By offering discounts to their biggest customers, railroads
   A forced many small railroad companies out of business.
   B reduced costs to all customers.
   C improved the quality of service.
   D pleased small farmers.

___ 3. All of the following industries were helped by the growth of railroads EXCEPT the
   A lumber industry.
   B steel industry.
   C canal-building industry.
   D coal industry.

___ 4. Steel was important after the Civil War because
   A corporations controlled the production of iron.
   B it could be transported by train.
   C iron was no longer available.
   D it was used to make steel rails for railroads.

___ 5. Critics of monopolies argued that large corporations
   A reduced competition.
   B made prices of goods too low.
   C encouraged competition.
   D allowed workers too much free time.

___ 6. Which of the following inventions improved communication?
   A plastic
   B vacuum cleaner
   C engine-oiling machine
   D telephone

___ 7. How did the assembly line affect the automobile industry?
   A Mass production of cars was no longer possible.
   B Factories became safer for workers.
   C The quality of cars improved and prices rose.
   D More people could afford cars.

___ 8. In the late 1800s, factories became places
   A that were safe and clean.
   B where bosses knew workers.
   C with dangerous conditions.
   D where hours were short.

___ 9. All of the following were goals of early labor unions EXCEPT
   A ending child labor.
   B increasing wages.
   C making workdays shorter.
   D putting factories out of business.

___ 10. During the labor strikes of the late 1800s, the federal government usually
   A supported factory owners.
   B remained uninvolved in the struggles.
   C supported factory workers.
   D urged state governments to support workers.

CHAPTER

21 A New Urban Culture
(1865–1914)

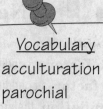

Vocabulary Development

When you come across a word you do not know, you can often figure out its meaning from the word's context—the words alongside it in the sentence or paragraph. For example, consider the word *anarchist,* which is one of the vocabulary words from Chapter 20. You may not be immediately familiar with the definition of this word. Don't panic! Look at the word in the context of this sentence:

The political protesters seemed determined to start a riot during the President's speech, so many onlookers believed them to be anarchists.

The context tells you that anarchists are political protesters, and that these protesters are not peaceful but are determined to start a riot. You know that a riot is an uncontrolled public demonstration that can be violent and destructive. Based on this knowledge, you can figure that an anarchist is someone who wants political disorder.

Directions: *Look at the sentences below. Then write your own definition of each underlined word based on the context clues contained in each sentence. After doing this, check your definition against the definition provided in the dictionary.*

1. For any foreign athlete coming to play a sport in the United States, the process of acculturation can be long and difficult.

   _____

2. The boy's parents moved their son out of a public high school and into a parochial school because they felt the influence of religion would help him.

   _____

3. The Holocaust that occurred in Europe during World War II is considered the largest pogrom in the history of humanity.

   _____

4. Passengers who paid the least to travel aboard the *Titanic* were put in steerage.

   _____

5. One result of urbanization is that farmland is lost, causing a decline in agricultural output.

   _____

Vocabulary
acculturation
parochial
pogrom
steerage
urbanization

CHAPTER

21

Section 1 Guide to the Essentials

New Immigrants in a Promised Land

VOCABULARY

push factor a condition that drives people from their homes

pull factor a condition that attracts immigrants to a new area

assimilation the process of becoming part of another culture

SUMMARY

Between 1866 and 1915, more than 25 million immigrants came to the United States. Most were from southern and eastern Europe and Asia. Both **push factors** and **pull factors** led people to immigrate. (See chart.)

Adjusting to life in the United States was difficult for these new immigrants. They had to find jobs and places to live. Most immigrants stayed in the cities where they had landed. They often lived in poor, crowded neighborhoods with others of their own ethnic group. There, they could speak their own language and celebrate their special holidays. Fitting into American culture was difficult at first. These immigrants spoke a variety of languages that were new

to America. They also practiced different religions. Eventually, the new immigrants began the process of **assimilation.** They began to learn English and adopt American customs while keeping their own special traditions.

Some Americans felt overwhelmed by the huge numbers of new immigrants. Some believed that these new immigrants would never fit in. Many were worried that the immigrants might take their jobs. Congress passed laws that limited immigration. One law, the ***Chinese Exclusion Act of 1882,*** nearly stopped immigration from China. Another law did not allow immigrants to enter the country if they could not read their own language.

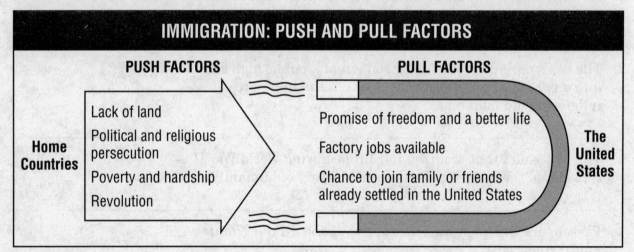

IMMIGRATION: PUSH AND PULL FACTORS

PUSH FACTORS

Home Countries

Lack of land

Political and religious persecution

Poverty and hardship

Revolution

PULL FACTORS

Promise of freedom and a better life

Factory jobs available

Chance to join family or friends already settled in the United States

The United States

REVIEW

Answer the following questions on a separate sheet of paper.

1. What was a reason anti-immigrant feelings grew in the late 1800s and early 1900s?

2. **Chart Skills** Identify one push factor and one pull factor that brought immigrants to the United States.

CHAPTER

21 Section 1 Guided Reading and Review

New Immigrants in a Promised Land

A. As You Read

Directions: As you read Section 1 in your textbook, fill in the following chart with details about immigration in the late 1800s.

	Immigration
1. place of origin	
2. reasons for resettling	
3. journey to the United States	
4. life in the United States	
5. American response	

B. Reviewing Key Terms

Directions: Briefly identify each of the following terms.

6. pogrom _____

7. steerage _____

8. Statue of Liberty _____

9. acculturation _____

10. nativist _____

CHAPTER

21 Section 2 Guide to the Essentials
An Age of Cities

VOCABULARY

tenement a building divided into small apartments with poor living conditions

settlement house a community center that offers services to the poor

Social Gospel the duty of rich Christians to help society's poor

SUMMARY

During the late 1800s, the population of the United States exploded. (See graph.) Jobs drew people to the cities. As industries grew, factories needed more workers. Immigrants came to fill this need. Also, people from farming areas moved into cities. Some were African Americans leaving poverty in the South.

The face of most cities changed during this time. Many of the people who lived in the centers of the cities were poor. They faced unhealthy and even dangerous living conditions. Most lived in buildings called **tenements.** The middle class lived in neat homes on tree-lined streets. The wealthy lived in mansions just outside the cities.

As the cities and their problems grew, reformers worked to improve conditions for the poor. They convinced city governments to make sure that buildings were constructed more safely. Cities hired workers to clean the streets. New laws kept factories out of neighborhoods where people lived. Water tunnels were built to bring clean water into cities. Some reformers, such as Jane Addams, worked directly with poor people. Addams set up a **settlement house** in a poor area of Chicago. Religious groups preached the **Social Gospel** and urged the rich to provide services to the poor.

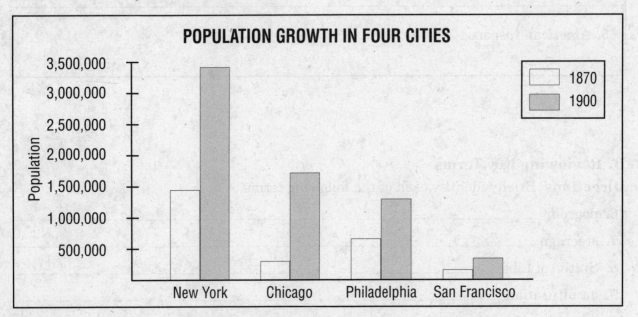

POPULATION GROWTH IN FOUR CITIES

Legend: 1870, 1900

REVIEW

Answer the following questions on a separate sheet of paper.

1. What groups of people added to the populations of cities in the late 1800s?

2. **Graph Skills** Which cities shown had more than 1 million people in 1870? in 1900?

CHAPTER

21 Section 2 Guided Reading and Review
An Age of Cities

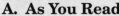

A. As You Read

Directions: As you read Section 2 in your textbook, mark each statement true or false. Correct each false statement.

_____ 1. By 1890, the majority of Americans lived in cities.

_____

_____ 2. Many African Americans migrated to northern cities to escape prejudice and find work.

_____

_____ 3. Many slum apartments had no windows, heating, or indoor bathrooms.

_____

_____ 4. The rich, the middle classes, and the urban poor all lived in the same neighborhoods.

_____

_____ 5. Unpleasant aspects of city life included garbage, pollution, and pickpockets.

_____

_____ 6. Religious organizations founded settlement houses to help the poor.

_____

_____ 7. Jane Addams is best known for helping to establish professional police and fire departments in Chicago.

_____

B. Reviewing Key Terms

Directions: Complete each sentence.

8. _____ meant that cities were becoming more and more crowded.

9. Only the poorest people in a city would live in a _____, with its lack of air, heat, and sanitation.

10. By the 1880s, _____ set standards for construction and safety of city housing.

11. The _____ spread the teachings of Christianity but also offered food and shelter to the poor.

12. The _____ helped preserve Jewish culture and provided community services.

CHAPTER

21 Section 3 Guide to the Essentials
Life in the Changing Cities

★

VOCABULARY

skyscraper a tall building with many levels, supported by a lightweight steel frame

department store a store that sells a variety of products in different sections

vaudeville a variety show that included comedians, song-and-dance routines, and acrobats

ragtime a lively, rhythmic form of music that was popular in the early 1900s

SUMMARY

The population growth of the late 1800s brought great change to the cities of the United States. (See chart.) **Skyscrapers,** new kinds of transportation, and parks were all part of a new look for cities.

A building boom changed the face of American cities. Because cities ran out of space in their downtown areas, builders decided to build tall skyscrapers. The development of electric street cars relieved traffic on city streets. Public parks were built and gave city dwellers a place to enjoy nature. Shoppers could stroll the streets and look at the displays of goods in **department store** windows.

As more people worked in factories, Americans began to think of work and play as separate activities. People felt a greater need to rest and relax. Americans found escape from their factories, stores, and offices in leisure activities. People played and watched sports, such as football, basketball, and especially baseball. People went to **vaudeville** shows. The invention of the phonograph allowed them to listen to new kinds of music. **Ragtime** was a popular form of dance music.

A NEW LOOK FOR CITIES	
CAUSE	**EFFECT**
Downtown land is scarce; new building technologies include lightweight steel frames and elevators.	→ Builders construct skyscrapers.
Growth of population leads to traffic jams.	→ Cities build streetcars and subways.
With cities growing up and out, land is quickly used up.	→ Cities set aside land for parks and gardens.

REVIEW

Answer the following questions on a separate sheet of paper.

1. Why did people begin to think of work and play as separate activities?

2. **Chart Skills** What new technologies led to the building of skyscrapers?

CHAPTER

21 Section 3 Guided Reading and Review
Life in the Changing Cities

A. As You Read

Directions: As you read Section 3 in your textbook, complete the graphic organizer by filling in supporting details for each main idea.

Main Idea A: A building boom made remarkable changes to city life.

1. _____

2. _____

3. _____

Main Idea B: New diversions made life in cities much more entertaining and fun.

4. _____

5. _____

6. _____

B. Reviewing Key Terms

Directions: Briefly define each term.

7. skyscraper _____

8. suburb _____

9. department store _____

10. vaudeville _____

11. ragtime _____

CHAPTER

21 Section 4 Guide to the Essentials

Public Education and American Culture

VOCABULARY

yellow journalism a sensational reporting style that focused on scandal, gossip, and crime

SUMMARY

In the years after the Civil War, growing industries needed educated people to work in their stores and factories. States responded by improving their public schools. (See chart.) New education laws required children to attend school. Schools began special programs to educate students for jobs in business and industry. More colleges and universities opened.

As more Americans learned to read, reading habits changed in the late 1800s. Americans read more newspapers, magazines, and books. Many newspapers began to publish with the immigrant audience in mind. They introduced bold headlines, illustrations, and comics. To grab reader attention, they reported on crimes, gossip, and scandals. Critics called this kind of

reporting **yellow journalism.** Newspapers also published sections meant to attract women readers. New technologies, such as the mechanical typesetter, made books cheaper. Low-priced magazines and adventure novels gained many readers.

A new group of American writers appeared in the late 1800s. They were known as realists because they attempted to show life as it really was. Stephen Crane wrote about the Civil War and city slums. In the *Adventures of Huckleberry Finn,* Mark Twain captured local color—the special features of a region and the way its people spoke. Some American painters were also realists. They, too, showed the reality of modern life in their work.

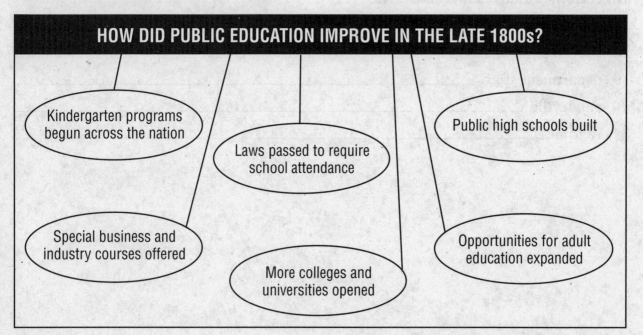

HOW DID PUBLIC EDUCATION IMPROVE IN THE LATE 1800s?

- Kindergarten programs begun across the nation
- Laws passed to require school attendance
- Public high schools built
- Special business and industry courses offered
- More colleges and universities opened
- Opportunities for adult education expanded

REVIEW

Answer the following questions on a separate sheet of paper.

1. What was one reason that American reading habits changed in the late 1800s?

2. **Chart Skills** Identify two ways in which education improved in the late 1800s.

CHAPTER

21

Section 4 Guided Reading and Review

Public Education and American Culture ★

A. As You Read

Directions: As you read Section 4 in your textbook, fill in the missing causes and effects.

Causes	Effects
An industrial society needed educated workers.	1.
2.	The number of newspapers grew dramatically.
Girls as well as boys were sent to school and taught to read.	3.
4.	Realists wanted to show the costs of urbanization and industrial growth.
5.	Mark Twain's stories and novels were widely popular.

B. Reviewing Key Terms

Directions: Match each person with his or her description.

_____ 6. Joseph Pulitzer

_____ 7. William Randolph Hearst

_____ 8. Horatio Alger

_____ 9. Stephen Crane

_____ 10. Kate Chopin

_____ 11. Mark Twain

_____ 12. Winslow Homer

_____ 13. Thomas Eakins

_____ 14. Mary Cassatt

a. author of more than 100 rags-to-riches stories for children

b. moved to France and painted everyday scenes of mothers and children

c. writer of satirical stories and novels about serious issues

d. painter of medical and sporting scenes

e. publisher of the New York *World*

f. writer of stories about life in New Orleans

g. publisher of the New York *Journal*

h. painter of realistic scenes of New England coast

i. realist writer of *The Red Badge of Courage*

CHAPTER
21 TEST

Identifying Main Ideas

Write the letter of the correct choice in the answer space.

____ 1. Which of the following was NOT a pull factor drawing immigrants to the United States in the late 1800s?

  A jobs

  B lack of land

  C freedom

  D family

____ 2. What does it mean to assimilate?

  A to continue to keep customs one is born with

  B to become part of another culture

  C to celebrate special holidays

  D to take new jobs in a new land

____ 3. Which of the following best describes tenements in the late 1800s?

  A crowded but clean

  B small houses with open spaces

  C dirty, crowded, and unhealthy

  D skyscrapers with elevators, heat, and water

____ 4. In the late 1800s, reformers attempted to

  A force immigrants out of the city.

  B build more tenements.

  C hide conditions in poor neighborhoods.

  D improve conditions for the poor in the cities.

____ 5. A settlement house was a place where

  A services were offered to the poor.

  B immigrants first settled.

  C reformers met to plan new housing.

  D the middle class spent leisure time.

____ 6. Which of the following did NOT contribute to the building of skyscrapers?

  A the development of lightweight steel frames

  B the use of public transportation

  C the invention of the elevator

  D the lack of land in cities

____ 7. Public parks were built to

  A relieve traffic on city streets.

  B give city dwellers a place to enjoy nature.

  C allow shoppers to look into department store windows.

  D end crowding in downtown areas.

____ 8. Baseball was popular because of

  A reformers' belief in the importance of fresh air.

  B the growth of ethnic neighborhoods.

  C newspapers' attempts to appeal to women.

  D the demand for new leisure activities.

____ 9. What new reading habits developed in the late 1800s?

  A Most people began to read plays.

  B Fewer people read newspapers.

  C More people began reading magazines and adventure novels.

  D People rejected yellow journalism in favor of real news.

____ 10. What did writers who were realists try to do?

  A describe life in foreign lands

  B help people forget their troubles

  C write about characters who were larger than life

  D show life as it really was

CHAPTER

22 The Progressive Era
(1876–1920)

Vocabulary Development

These vocabulary words are all related to the Progressive Movement. This movement came about in response to the urbanization and industrialization that occurred after the Civil War.

<u>Vocabulary</u>
muckraker
political boss
suffragist
trustbuster

Directions: *Use the vocabulary words to complete the concept maps below. Each column of the graphic organizer below presents a concept map for each vocabulary word. Fill in the blank spaces in each column.*

Term	Muckraker	Political Boss	Suffragist	1.
Definition	A writer who stirs public opinion against corruption	A corrupt political leader who uses public office for selfish profit	2.	A person who breaks apart business monopolies
Use in Sentence	A muckraker exposed a scandal that involved a member of the city council.	3.	Suffragists marched to the capital, demanding the right to vote.	4.
Historical Figure	5.	William M. "Boss" Tweed	Carrie Chapman Catt	6.

Directions: *Using the four listed vocabulary words, write a paragraph about the chapter on the lines below. Be sure to use complete sentences and correct spelling in your writing.*

_____

_____

_____

_____

_____

_____

_____

CHAPTER

22 Section 1 Guide to the Essentials

Reform in the Gilded Age

VOCABULARY

regulate control

trust groups of corporations run together as one large company

SUMMARY

In the 1870s and 1880s, Americans were concerned about corruption in government. Many feared "special interests"—bankers, industrialists, and other wealthy leaders—had gained control of politicians.

One source of corruption was the spoils system. (See Chapter 12.) This practice had grown since the early 1800s. Now many officeholders lacked the skills to do their jobs correctly. Some stole from the government. In 1881, President James Garfield was killed by a disappointed office seeker. Garfield's murder sparked new efforts to end the spoils system.

Reformers called for action. (See chart.) Congress created the *Civil Service Commission.* The commission conducted

tests so that only qualified people got federal jobs. By 1900, it controlled about 40 percent of all federal jobs.

The government also tried to **regulate** big business. It set up the *Interstate Commerce Commission,* or ICC. The ICC made sure that railroads did not engage in unfair practices, such as reducing competition or keeping prices high.

In 1890, Congress passed a law to regulate **trusts.** The *Sherman Antitrust Act* made it illegal for businesses to limit competition. Although the government efforts were weak at first, attempts to control big business slowly gained strength.

NEW LAWS BRING REFORM	
LAW	**REFORM**
Pendleton Act (1883)	created Civil Service Commission to make sure that only qualified people got federal jobs
Interstate Commerce Act (1887)	created Interstate Commerce Commission to oversee the railroad companies
Sherman Antitrust Act (1890)	made it illegal for companies to restrict competition

REVIEW

Answer the following questions on a separate sheet of paper.

1. Why did reformers want to end the spoils system?
2. **Chart Skills** What was one goal of the Civil Service Commission?

CHAPTER

22 Section 1 Guided Reading and Review

Reform in the Gilded Age

A. As You Read

Directions: As you read Section 1 in your textbook, answer the following questions:

1. What two concerns shaped politics in the Gilded Age? _____

_____

2. What did President Hayes do about corruption at the New York customhouse?

_____

_____

3. What did the Pendleton Act create? _____

_____

4. What did the Interstate Commerce Act of 1887 do? _____

_____

5. What were the results of the passage of the Sherman Antitrust Act? _____

_____

B. Reviewing Key Terms

Directions: Explain the relevance of each term to reform in the Gilded Age.

6. patronage _____

_____

7. merit _____

_____

8. civil service _____

_____

9. interstate commerce _____

_____

CHAPTER

22 Section 2 Guide to the Essentials
The Progressives

VOCABULARY

primary election in which voters choose their party's candidates

initiative way for voters to put a bill before the legislature

referendum way for voters to vote a bill directly into law

recall way for voters to remove an elected official from office

SUMMARY

During the late 1800s, corruption had become common in many American cities. Many politicians demanded money from businesses in exchange for city jobs. Reformers tried to replace corrupt officials with honest leaders. These reformers were called Progressives. They believed that the problems of society could be solved. The late 1800s and early 1900s were called the Progressive Era.

The Progressives were helped by the press. Some reporters began to describe the horrible conditions in poor areas of the cities. Others exposed the unfair practices of big businesses. These journalists became known as muckrakers. They helped turn public opinion in favor of reform.

Progressives wanted the government to act for the good of the people. They especially promoted education and democratic values. Many Progressives wanted voters to have more power. A number of states passed measures to achieve this goal. Most states began to hold **primaries.** In the past, party leaders picked candidates. Other changes included the **initiative, referendum,** and **recall.** (See chart.)

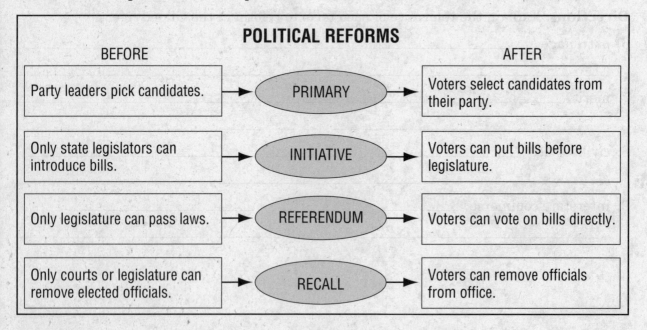

POLITICAL REFORMS

BEFORE		AFTER
Party leaders pick candidates.	PRIMARY	Voters select candidates from their party.
Only state legislators can introduce bills.	INITIATIVE	Voters can put bills before legislature.
Only legislature can pass laws.	REFERENDUM	Voters can vote on bills directly.
Only courts or legislature can remove elected officials.	RECALL	Voters can remove officials from office.

REVIEW

Answer the following questions on a separate sheet of paper.

1. What role did the press play in the reform movement?

2. **Chart Skills** How was the choosing of candidates changed by primaries?

CHAPTER

22 Section 2 Guided Reading and Review
The Progressives

A. As You Read

Directions: As you read Section 2 in your textbook, correct each false statement.

1. Political bosses fought corruption at all levels of government. _____

_____

2. Muckraking journalists ignored the need for reform. _____

_____

3. The Progressives were a unified political party. _____

_____

4. Robert La Follette's actions helped increase railroad rates. _____

_____

5. The Supreme Court decreed that after 1912, senators would be elected by the people
instead of by legislatures. _____

_____

B. Reviewing Key Terms

Directions: Match each person with his or her description.

Column I

_____ 6. Thomas Nast

_____ 7. William Tweed

_____ 8. Jacob Riis

_____ 9. Ida Tarbell

_____ 10. Upton Sinclair

_____ 11. John Dewey

_____ 12. Robert La Follette

Column II

a. journalist and photographer who exposed slum conditions in New York

b. author of *The Jungle,* which exposed the meatpacking industry

c. Wisconsin governor who introduced reforms

d. corrupt political boss of New York City

e. journalist who exposed the Standard Oil Company

f. newspaper cartoonist who satirized corrupt politicians

g. Progressive educator

CHAPTER

22 Section 3 Guide to the Essentials

Progressives in the White House

VOCABULARY

conservation protection of natural resources

national park land set aside and run by the federal government for people to visit

SUMMARY

When President William McKinley was assassinated in 1901, Vice President Theodore Roosevelt took office. Roosevelt thought that trusts could be good or bad. He wanted the government to stop bad trusts. Bad trusts abused workers or cheated the public. In 1902, he had the government bring a lawsuit against Northern Securities. The lawsuit charged that the company was trying to limit trade. Such actions were illegal according to the Sherman Antitrust Act. The Supreme Court agreed with Roosevelt. It ordered the trust to be broken up. The President then took similar actions against other trusts.

President Roosevelt supported a number of other reforms. (See chart.) Unlike earlier Presidents, he sided with labor unions in their disputes with big businesses. When he ran for President in 1904, Roosevelt promised Americans a *Square Deal.* By this, he meant that all Americans should have the same opportunities to succeed. He sent government inspectors into meatpacking houses. He attacked drug companies that made false claims. Roosevelt also believed in **conservation,** the protection of natural resources. While Roosevelt was President, the government set aside 170,000 acres of land to create **national parks.**

Roosevelt's successor, William Howard Taft, had the support of Progressives until he agreed to raise tariffs. Progressives also accused him of blocking conservation efforts. In the election of 1912, Roosevelt ran against Taft and Woodrow Wilson. Because Roosevelt and Taft split the Republican vote, Wilson won.

Wilson's main goal was to increase competition in the economy. He persuaded Congress to create the *Federal Trade Commission,* or FTC. The FTC had the power to investigate businesses and order them to stop using practices that destroyed their competition. Wilson also supported laws that regulated banks.

WHAT REFORMS DID THEODORE ROOSEVELT SUPPORT?

• Government should control or break up bad trusts.	• Government should regulate the railroads, setting rates and preventing abuses.	• Government should act to make food and medicines healthful.	• Government should promote conservation.

REVIEW

Answer the following questions on a separate sheet of paper.

1. How did Woodrow Wilson try to increase competition in the economy?

2. **Chart Skills** Identify two reform efforts supported by Theodore Roosevelt.

CHAPTER

22 Section 3 Guided Reading and Review

Progressives in the White House

A. As You Read

Directions: As you read Section 3 in your textbook, compare and contrast the three Progressive Presidents by filling in details about each.

1. Theodore Roosevelt	
2. William Howard Taft	
3. Woodrow Wilson	

B. Reviewing Key Terms

Directions: Briefly identify each reform, specifying which President established each. Mark an R for Roosevelt, a T for Taft, or a W for Wilson.

_____ 4. Square Deal _____

_____ 5. Pure Food and Drug Act _____

_____ 6. New Freedom _____

_____ 7. Federal Reserve Act _____

_____ 8. Federal Trade Commission _____

CHAPTER

22 Section 4 Guide to the Essentials

Women Win Reforms

VOCABULARY

suffragist person who worked for women's right to vote

SUMMARY

In the late 1800s and early 1900s, women continued their efforts to win the right to vote. They organized marches, met with elected officials, picketed, and even went to jail. **Suffragists,** or people who campaigned for women's right to vote, were active all around the country. Their work resulted in the passage of the *Nineteenth Amendment* in 1919. This amendment guaranteed women the right to vote in national elections.

Besides the vote, women won new opportunities in a number of other areas. (See chart.) More colleges were accepting women as students. Professions such as medicine and law were beginning to open up to women. By 1900, 1,000 woman lawyers and 7,000 woman doctors were in practice. Women were entering the sciences, too.

Women also took part in the reform movement. Women were leaders in the temperance movement, fighting against alcohol abuse. Many wives and mothers believed that alcohol abuse was a threat to their families. In 1917, Congress passed the *Eighteenth Amendment,* which made the sale of alcoholic drinks illegal.

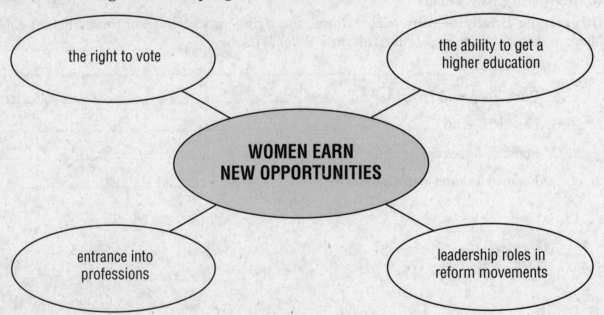

the right to vote

the ability to get a higher education

WOMEN EARN NEW OPPORTUNITIES

entrance into professions

leadership roles in reform movements

REVIEW

Answer the following questions on a separate sheet of paper.

1. For what cause did suffragists work?

2. **Chart Skills** Identify two areas in which women earned new opportunities in the early 1900s.

CHAPTER

22 Section 4 Guided Reading and Review
Women Win Reforms

★

A. As You Read
Directions: As you read Section 4 in your textbook, complete each sentence.

1. The Seneca Falls Convention was the beginning of _____
   _____

2. Western states granted women the right to vote because _____
   _____

3. Carrie Chapman Catt helped the cause of suffrage by _____
   _____

4. While picketing outside the White House, Alice Paul, Rose Winslow, and others
   _____
   _____

5. Women's clubs contributed to the fight for rights by _____
   _____

6. Women supported the temperance drive because _____
   _____

B. Reviewing Key Terms
Directions: Match each term or person with the correct description.

Column I

_____ 7. Carrie Chapman Catt

_____ 8. suffragist

_____ 9. Alice Paul

_____ 10. Nineteenth Amendment

_____ 11. Carrie Nation

_____ 12. Eighteenth Amendment

Column II

a. banned the sale of alcoholic drinks

b. gave women the right to vote

c. one who fought for women's right to vote

d. radical temperance advocate

e. often arrested for her marches and protests in favor of suffrage for women

f. organized a plan to fight for women's suffrage one state at a time

CHAPTER

22 Section 5 Guided Reading and Review

Other Americans Seek Justice

VOCABULARY

barrio a Spanish-speaking neighborhood in a city or town, often found in California or the Southwest

SUMMARY

In general, white Progressives had little concern for nonwhites. African Americans and other minorities had to fight for justice themselves.

In the late 1800s and early 1900s, life for African Americans remained difficult. In the South, segregation was a way of life. In both North and South, African Americans faced discrimination. They found it difficult to find well-paying jobs or to rent homes in white neighborhoods. When whites lost their jobs, some took out their anger on African Americans. In the 1890s, angry mobs murdered more than 1,000 African Americans.

African American leaders had different ideas about how to fight discrimination. (See diagram.) Booker T. Washington urged African Americans to learn trades and earn money. Equality, he believed, would come later. In the meantime, he accepted segregation. Other leaders, such as W.E.B. Du Bois,

disagreed. Du Bois believed African Americans should insist immediately on their rights. Du Bois and others founded the **NAACP,** or the National Association for the Advancement of Colored People, in 1909.

Other groups faced challenges in the early 1900s. Thousands of Mexicans had moved north to the American Southwest. They lived in neighborhoods called **barrios.** They found jobs harvesting crops and building roads. The West Coast became home to many immigrants from Asian countries. Many Japanese immigrants were farmers, but they were not allowed to own land in California. Immigrants from Mexico, Japan, and other countries met discrimination and sometimes violence in the United States. Native Americans were, once again, cheated out of their reservation land. Speculators would often trick them into selling their land at very low prices.

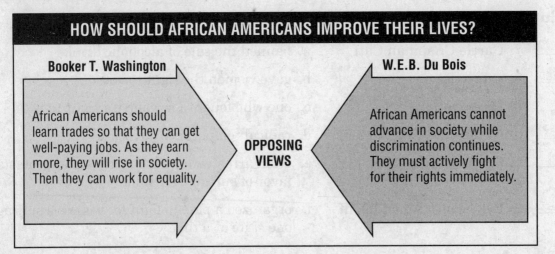

HOW SHOULD AFRICAN AMERICANS IMPROVE THEIR LIVES?

Booker T. Washington

African Americans should learn trades so that they can get well-paying jobs. As they earn more, they will rise in society. Then they can work for equality.

OPPOSING VIEWS

W.E.B. Du Bois

African Americans cannot advance in society while discrimination continues. They must actively fight for their rights immediately.

REVIEW

Answer the following questions on a separate sheet of paper.

1. What problems did African Americans face during the late 1800s and early 1900s?

2. **Diagram Skills** Explain how the viewpoints of Booker T. Washington and W.E.B. Du Bois differed.

CHAPTER

22 Section 5 Guided Reading and Review

Other Americans Seek Justice

A. As You Read

Directions: As you read Section 5 in your textbook, fill in the outline with details describing the experience of each ethnic group during the Progressive era.

Main Idea A: African Americans

1. _____

2. _____

3. _____

Main Idea B: Mexican Americans

4. _____

5. _____

6. _____

Main Idea C: Asian Americans

7. _____

8. _____

Main Idea D: Native Americans

9. _____

10. _____

B. Reviewing Key Terms

Directions: Briefly define or identify each term.

11. lynch _____

_____

12. NAACP _____

_____

13. barrio _____

_____

14. Gentleman's Agreement _____

_____

Reading and Vocabulary Study Guide   **235**

CHAPTER 22 TEST

Identifying Main Ideas

Write the letter of the correct choice in the answer space.

____ 1. Which of the following was NOT a feature of American politics in the 1870s and 1880s?

A too much government control of big business

B the spoils system

C fears about "special interests" controlling government

D concern over political corruption

____ 2. In the spoils system, politicians gave jobs

A to both supporters and opponents.

B through the civil service.

C to experts.

D to supporters.

____ 3. During the late 1800s, the muckrakers

A ignored unfair practices of big business.

B supported political bosses.

C helped expose corruption.

D demanded money from city leaders.

____ 4. The recall allowed voters to

A pass a bill into law.

B put a bill before the legislature.

C remove an elected official.

D choose their party's candidates.

____ 5. Which idea was supported by Theodore Roosevelt?

A Big corporations have no place in American life.

B Trusts engaging in illegal practices should be controlled or broken up.

C The government can do nothing about trusts.

D All trusts should be broken up.

____ 6. Efforts to regulate trusts were a reaction to

A corporations that cheated the public or tried to limit competition.

B the lack of national parkland.

C lower fees on imported goods.

D too much competition in the economy.

____ 7. The Nineteenth Amendment

A allowed women to become doctors.

B allowed women to go to college.

C forbade suffragists to protest.

D gave women the right to vote.

____ 8. Many leaders of the temperance movement were women because

A wives and mothers feared the effect of alcohol on their families.

B women wanted to drink in public bars just as men did.

C men urged them to lead.

D men were not affected by drinking alcohol.

____ 9. Booker T. Washington believed that African Americans should

A learn trades and wait for equal rights.

B attack white mobs.

C fight for equal rights under the law.

D march to end discrimination.

____ 10. Both Mexican and Japanese immigrants

A were able to farm the best land.

B settled mainly in the Southeast.

C were welcomed to the United States.

D faced discrimination.

CHAPTER

23 Becoming a World Power
(1865–1916)

Vocabulary Development

Vocabulary
expansionism
imperialism
isolationism
racism

All of the vocabulary terms on the right end in the suffix *-ism*, which means "system." Each word expresses a philosophy that became a system or institution. Each of these systems has held a place in our national history.

For each of the situations from U.S. history below, decide which of the *-ism* words on the right applies, and label it accordingly.

1. In 1941, a number of politicians argued that the United States should stay out of World War II.

_____

_____

2. After the Spanish-American War, the United States took control of Cuba, Puerto Rico, Guam, and the Philippines.

_____

_____

3. The Union Pacific and the Central Pacific met near Ogden, Utah, in May 1869, and the first transcontinental railroad was completed.

_____

_____

4. The Supreme Court in the *Plessy* v. *Ferguson* case of 1896 decided that "separate but equal" facilities for whites and African-Americans on railroad cars were constitutional.

_____

_____

Directions: *Using the four listed vocabulary words, write a paragraph about the chapter on the lines below. Be sure to use complete sentences and correct spelling in your writing.*

_____

_____

_____

_____

_____

CHAPTER 23 Section 1 Guide to the Essentials

A Pacific Empire

VOCABULARY

imperialism policy by which one country controls the economy and politics of another country

annex to take control of a territory or country

SUMMARY

By the late 1800s, the United States was becoming one of the most powerful countries in the world. Treaties with Japan and Russia benefited the United States. Japan was closed to foreign trade when American warships landed there in 1853. Impressed by American strength, the Japanese agreed to trade with the United States. In 1867, the United States bought the huge and valuable territory of Alaska from Russia.

In the late 1800s, some Americans argued that the United States should adopt a policy of **imperialism.** Supporters of imperialism argued that the United States needed new markets for foreign trade. They also argued that Americans should bring Western culture to the other peoples of the world. In addition, they pointed out that the United States no longer had a western frontier. They said that the country's growing population needed new lands to settle.

As a result of these arguments, the government took action. The United States **annexed** Hawaii and gained territory in Samoa in the 1890s. In China, the United States competed with other imperialist nations to gain trade. In 1899, the United States persuaded other nations—Britain, France, Germany, Russia, and Japan—to follow an *Open Door Policy* in China. This policy meant that these nations would not stop the United States from trading in China. American foreign trade continued to grow. (See graph.)

NEW LAWS BRING REFORM	
LAW	**REFORM**
Pendleton Act (1883)	created Civil Service Commission to make sure that only qualified people got federal jobs
Interstate Commerce Act (1887)	created Interstate Commerce Commission to oversee the railroad companies
Sherman Antitrust Act (1890)	made it illegal for companies to restrict competition

REVIEW

Answer the following questions on a separate sheet of paper.

1. Identify three examples of growing American power in the middle and late 1800s.

2. **Graph Skills** In which five-year period did American foreign trade grow the most?

CHAPTER

23 Section 1 Guided Reading and Review
A Pacific Empire

A. As You Read

Directions: As you read Section 1 in your textbook, use the chart to compare and contrast the relationships between the United States and the nations listed.

1. Japan	
2. Russia	
3. Samoa	
4. Hawaii	
5. China	

B. Reviewing Key Terms

Directions: Use each term correctly in an accurate statement about the policy and actions of the United States in the Pacific.

6. isolationism _____

_____

7. expansionism _____

_____

8. annex _____

_____

9. imperialism _____

_____

10. sphere of influence _____

_____

23 Section 2 Guide to the Essentials
War With Spain

SUMMARY

In 1898, the United States and Spain fought the **Spanish-American War.** The war had several causes. Cuba, one of the last Spanish colonies in the Western Hemisphere, rebelled against Spain. Many Americans wanted to support Cuban independence. Some American newspaper publishers also wanted war, thinking that it would help sell newspapers. They printed stories about cruel Spanish treatment of Cubans that were not always true. Finally, the United States battleship *Maine* sunk after an explosion in a Cuban harbor. The cause of the explosion remains a mystery, but many Americans suspected that it was caused by Spain. Congress declared war on Spain in April 1898.

The war lasted only four months. American ships quickly defeated the Spanish navy in the Philippines, a major Spanish colony. In Cuba, Theodore Roosevelt led American troops to victory at the **Battle of San Juan Hill.** American ships also destroyed the Spanish fleet in the waters off Cuba. In August, Spain and the United States agreed to end the fighting.

The war had important results. (See chart.) Cuba was now independent of Spain, but it did not have full independence. United States troops remained in Cuba.

WHAT WERE THE RESULTS OF THE SPANISH-AMERICAN WAR?
Spain gives the Caribbean island of Puerto Rico and the Pacific island of Guam to the United States.
Spain sells the Philippines to the United States.
The United States defeats Filipino rebels and takes control of the Philippines in 1901.
Spain grants independence to Cuba.
American troops remain on Cuba, limiting its independence.
The United States declares the right to intervene in Cuban government.

REVIEW
Answer the following questions on a separate sheet of paper.

1. What role did newspapers play in starting the Spanish-American War?
2. **Chart Skills** Identify two results of the Spanish-American War.

CHAPTER

23 Section 2 Guided Reading and Review
War With Spain

A. As You Read

Directions: As you read Section 2 in your textbook, answer the following questions:

1. Why did President McKinley declare war on Spain? _____
_____

2. What was the cause of the Cuban rebellion of 1895? _____
_____

3. What was the reaction of the United States to the rebellion in Cuba? _____
_____

4. How did the newspapers of the day affect the situation? _____
_____

5. Why did the Americans fight in the Philippines? _____
_____

6. What was the outcome of the Spanish-American War? _____
_____

B. Reviewing Key Terms

Directions: Identify each person's role in the Spanish-American War.

7. William McKinley _____

8. José Martí _____

9. Joseph Pulitzer _____

10. William Randolph Hearst _____

11. Theodore Roosevelt _____

12. George Dewey _____

13. John J. Pershing _____

CHAPTER

23 Section 3 Guided Reading and Review

The United States in Latin America

VOCABULARY

isthmus narrow strip of land connecting two larger bodies of land

SUMMARY

In the early 1900s, the United States increased its involvement in the affairs of Latin America. One example was the building of the Panama Canal. President Theodore Roosevelt wanted to build a canal across the **Isthmus of Panama.** This canal would allow ships to cross from the Atlantic to the Pacific oceans much more quickly. Until this time, ships had to sail around South America in order to get from New York to San Francisco. Colombia rejected Roosevelt's plan. However, some people in Panama wanted to secede from Colombia. Roosevelt supported their rebellion. In 1903, the new independent government of Panama agreed to sell land to the United States. Canal builders completed the canal in 1914.

Ever since the Monroe Doctrine, the United States had shown a strong interest in the countries of Latin America. Now, President Roosevelt declared that the United States had the right to use military force to keep order and to protect its interests in Latin America. This statement was called the *Roosevelt Corollary.*

After Roosevelt, other Presidents followed a similar "Big Stick" policy to control events in Latin American countries. In 1916, for example, President Woodrow Wilson sent troops into Mexico to support the Mexican government in a civil war. The use of force angered many Latin Americans. Their leaders criticized the United States for interfering in the affairs of other countries. (See chart.)

CAUSES

- Businesses seek raw materials and new markets.

- Americans want quicker route between the Atlantic and Pacific Oceans.

- United States has longstanding interest in Latin America.

INCREASED INVOLVEMENT IN LATIN AMERICAN AFFAIRS

EFFECTS

- United States gains island of Puerto Rico and limited control over Cuba.

- United States builds the Panama Canal.

- United States sends troops to Latin America to protect its interests.

REVIEW

Answer the following questions on a separate sheet of paper.

1. What was the Roosevelt Corollary?

2. **Chart Skills** List two causes of increased United States involvement in Latin America.

CHAPTER
23 Section 3 Guided Reading and Review

The United States in Latin America

A. As You Read

Directions: As you read Section 3 in your textbook, complete the following sentences:

1. President Roosevelt wanted to build a canal across Panama because _____

_____

2. The greatest obstacle to the workers digging the canal was _____

_____

3. Merchants and manufacturers benefited from the building of the Panama Canal because

_____

_____

4. Roosevelt extended the Monroe Doctrine to state that _____

_____

5. The United States wanted to keep Europe out of Latin America because _____

_____

6. The United States invested in Latin America because _____

_____

7. Relations between the United States and Mexico grew strained because _____

_____

B. Reviewing Key Terms

Directions: Match each term with its definition.

Column I	Column II
_____ 8. isthmus	a. policy of building strong economic ties between nations
_____ 9. corollary	b. addition
_____ 10. dollar diplomacy	c. strip of land connecting two larger bodies of land

CHAPTER

23 TEST

Identifying Main Ideas

Write the letter of the correct choice in the answer space.

___ 1. After 1853, Japan agreed to
  A trade with the United States.
  B refuse to trade with imperialist nations.
  C help shipwrecked sailors.
  D stop all foreign trade.

___ 2. Which of the following was NOT an argument in favor of imperialism?
  A the end of the western frontier
  B a belief in spreading Western culture
  C a need for new markets
  D the decreasing population in the United States

___ 3. The Open Door Policy
  A ended trade with China.
  B caused the United States to take over part of China.
  C kept other nations from blocking American trade with China.
  D made China a colony.

___ 4. From 1865 to 1915, American foreign trade generally
  A increased.
  B decreased.
  C went up and down.
  D stayed the same.

___ 5. Which of the following was NOT a cause of the Spanish-American War?
  A the sinking of the battleship *Maine*
  B newspaper stories about Spanish treatment of Cubans
  C American support for Cuban independence
  D American desire to conquer Spain

___ 6. The Spanish-American War
  A dragged on for many years.
  B was over in four months.
  C spread to the mainland United States.
  D did not involve fighting on the seas.

___ 7. At the end of the war, the United States
  A acquired overseas territories.
  B helped Filipino rebels gain independence.
  C refused to take over Spanish colonies.
  D gave full independence to Cuba.

___ 8. In the early 1900s, the United States
  A avoided involvement in Latin American affairs.
  B increased involvement in Latin American affairs.
  C abandoned the Monroe Doctrine.
  D rejected the Roosevelt Corollary.

___ 9. The building of the Panama Canal
  A showed that the United States had no interest in Latin America.
  B allowed ships to pass quickly between the Atlantic and Pacific Oceans.
  C was supported by the government of Colombia.
  D was never completed.

___ 10. President Wilson angered many Latin Americans by
  A remaining neutral during the Mexican civil war.
  B refusing to get involved in foreign affairs.
  C sending troops into Mexico.
  D forbidding the use of military force in Latin America.

CHAPTER

24 World War I
(1914–1919)

Vocabulary Development

Sometimes, you will recognize a root word, but the attached suffix, or word ending, will confuse you. Like root words, many suffixes have Latin and Greek origins. The following list includes several of the most common suffixes, their meanings, and an example.

Vocabulary
bureaucracy
isolationists
militarism
nationalism
reparations
self-
determination
Socialist

-able (capable of):	enjoy*able*
-an (belonging to):	Americ*an*
-cracy (government):	auto*cracy*
-en (consisting of):	wood*en*
-er (performer of action):	kick*er*
-est (most):	farth*est*
-graph (written material):	auto*graph*
-hood (condition):	father*hood*
-ic(s) (pertaining to):	hydraul*ics*
-ion (process; act):	telecommunicat*ion*
-ish (like; of):	child*ish*
-ism (system):	commun*ism*
-ist (doer; agent):	dent*ist*
-less (without):	hope*less*
-logy (study of):	zoo*logy*
-ment (process; act):	encircle*ment*
-ness (quality; state):	light*ness*

Directions: *Identify the suffixes in each word. Then, using your knowledge of the root word and the suffix, write out the complete word's meaning.*

1. bureaucracy _____

2. isolationists _____

3. militarism _____

4. nationalism _____

5. reparations _____

6. self-determination _____

7. Socialist _____

CHAPTER

24 Section 1 Guide to the Essentials
War in Europe

VOCABULARY

nationalism loyalty and devotion to a nation

militarism policy of building up armed forces to prepare for war

SUMMARY

In the early 1900s, tensions were high in Europe. Extreme feelings of **nationalism** had created mistrust among European nations. Competition among imperialist nations for colonies added to the tension. **Militarism** also caused tension. Nations raced against each other to build larger armies and navies. The alliance system was another danger. Allies agreed to support one another in the case of attack. Thus, a dispute between two countries could expand to include the allies of each country.

World War I began in 1914 when Franz Ferdinand, a prince of Austria-Hungary, was killed in Bosnia. A Serbian nationalist, angry that Bosnia remained under Austro-Hungarian rule, shot the prince. Austria-Hungary responded by declaring war on Serbia. Russia decided to protect Serbia, its ally. Germany, an ally of Austria-Hungary,

also entered the war. Before long, the alliance system had drawn all the powerful countries of Europe into the struggle. War raged between the Central Powers and the Allied Powers. (See chart.) Soon, the armies of every European nation dug and lived in trenches. For three years, troops fought bloody battles over a few yards of land that lay between their trenches.

When war broke out, the United States remained neutral. Still, the war affected the United States. Orders for war goods from Europe strengthened the American economy. German submariners, however, attacked neutral ships, including American ships, that traded with Germany's enemies. When the United States threatened to join the Allies, Germany agreed to stop attacking neutral ships without warning.

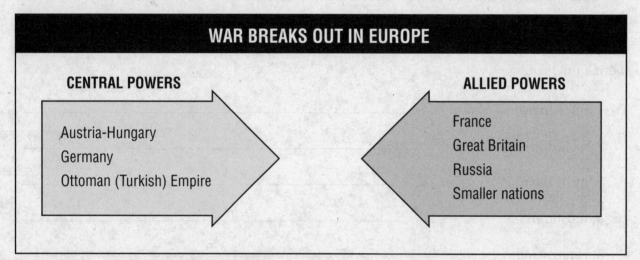

WAR BREAKS OUT IN EUROPE

CENTRAL POWERS

Austria-Hungary
Germany
Ottoman (Turkish) Empire

ALLIED POWERS

France
Great Britain
Russia
Smaller nations

REVIEW

Answer the following questions on a separate sheet of paper.

1. How did alliances increase tension in Europe?

2. **Chart Skills** Which alliance included Russia and France?

CHAPTER

24 Section 1 Guided Reading and Review
War in Europe

A. As You Read

Directions: As you read Section 1 in your textbook, list one cause and one effect of each of the following events:

1. European nationalists demanded freedom and self-government.

   Cause: _____

   Effect: _____

2. The Archduke of Austria-Hungary and his wife were assassinated in Sarajevo in

   1914.

   Cause: _____

   Effect: _____

3. Germany declared war on Russia and France.

   Cause: _____

   Effect: _____

4. Neither side gained much territory during four years of trench warfare.

   Cause: _____

   Effect: _____

5. The United States remained neutral for most of the war.

   Cause: _____

   Effect: _____

B. Reviewing Key Terms

Directions: Briefly define each term.

6. nationalism _____

7. militarism _____

8. terrorist _____

9. kaiser _____

10. stalemate _____

11. propaganda _____

CHAPTER

24 Section 2 Guide to the Essentials

From Neutrality to War

VOCABULARY

draft a law requiring people of a certain age to serve in the military

bureaucracy system of managing government through departments run by appointed officials

SUMMARY

As World War I continued, Americans debated entering the war. Although most Americans wanted to support the Allied Powers, some did not want to declare war on Germany. (See chart.) President Wilson even tried to bring both sides to peace talks.

By 1917, many reasons pushed the United States toward war. Germany started attacking neutral ships again. It also sent a secret note, the Zimmermann telegram, to Mexico, asking it to attack the United States. News of this telegram outraged many Americans. In Russia, a revolution had overthrown the czar, a powerful ruler. All three Allied Powers were now democracies. President Wilson told Congress that the war would make the world "safe for democracy." In April 1917, Congress declared war.

The United States organized for the war effort. To build an army, the government started a **draft.** It also set up large **bureaucracies.** One department was responsible for boosting food production.

As wartime industries grew, the need for workers increased. Women joined the work force. Many African Americans left the South to find jobs in northern cities and factories. Many met with discrimination and violence. In the Southwest, almost 100,000 Mexican workers contributed to the war effort.

Some Americans opposed the war. The government moved to silence these critics. Congress passed a law making it a crime to criticize the government or interfere with the war effort.

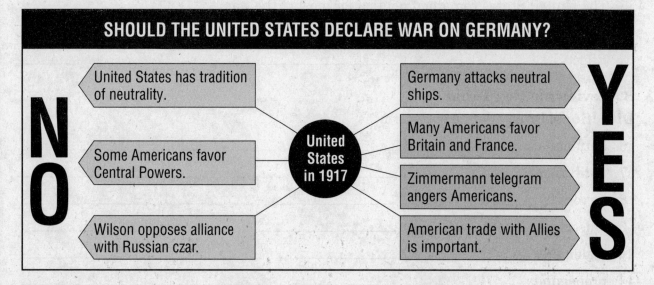

SHOULD THE UNITED STATES DECLARE WAR ON GERMANY?

NO
- United States has tradition of neutrality.
- Some Americans favor Central Powers.
- Wilson opposes alliance with Russian czar.

United States in 1917

YES
- Germany attacks neutral ships.
- Many Americans favor Britain and France.
- Zimmermann telegram angers Americans.
- American trade with Allies is important.

REVIEW

Answer the following questions on a separate sheet of paper.

1. How did the government respond to critics of the war?

2. **Chart Skills** Identify one argument for and one against the United States declaring war on Germany.

CHAPTER

24 Section 2 Guided Reading and Review

From Neutrality to War

A. As You Read

Directions: As you read Section 2 in your textbook, fill in supporting details for each main idea below:

> **Main Idea A:** President Wilson tried to bring about peace.
>
> 1. _____
>
> 2. _____
>
> **Main Idea B:** The United States began preparations to enter the war.
>
> 3. _____
>
> 4. _____
>
> 5. _____
>
> 6. _____
>
> **Main Idea C:** Americans on the home front responded to the war effort.
>
> 7. _____
>
> 8. _____
>
> 9. _____

B. Reviewing Key Terms

Directions: Match each term with its definition.

Column I	Column II
_____ 10. warmonger	a. law requiring people of a certain age to serve in the military
_____ 11. czar	b. emperor of Russia
_____ 12. draft	c. unable to read or write
_____ 13. illiterate	d. person who tries to stir up war
_____ 14. bureaucracy	e. a system of managing government through departments run by appointed officials
_____ 15. pacifist	f. one who refuses to fight because of a belief that violence is wrong

CHAPTER

24 Section 3 Guide to the Essentials

Americans in Battle

VOCABULARY

armistice agreement to stop fighting

SUMMARY

By 1917, the Allies faced hard times. Their armies had suffered millions of casualties. The troops in the field were exhausted and ill. In late 1917, a group who believed in communism seized power in Russia. This new government opposed the war. By early 1918, Russia signed a separate peace treaty with Germany. The treaty hurt the Allies because Germany could now concentrate on fighting the other Allies.

American soldiers, however, helped change the course of the war. By June 1918, the American Expeditionary Force was arriving in Europe in huge numbers. American soldiers were fresh and ready for battle. They helped fight a series of battles that slowly pushed Germany out of the territory it had captured. The *Battle of the Argonne Forest* in the autumn of 1918 lasted for 47 days. More than a million Americans took part in the battle. Finally, the Allies smashed through the German defense.

Germany could fight no longer and agreed to an **armistice** in November 1918. The costs of the war were huge. (See graph.) Much of northern France lay in ruins. Between 8 and 9 million people died in battle. The United States lost over 50,000 troops in combat.

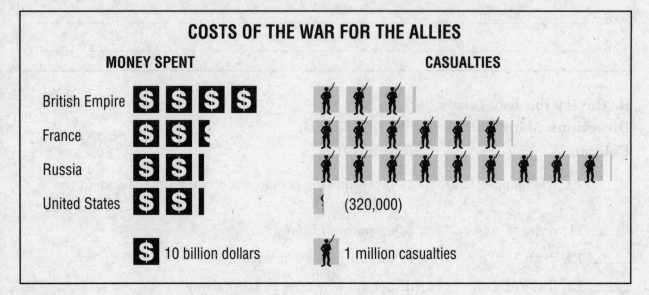

COSTS OF THE WAR FOR THE ALLIES

MONEY SPENT   CASUALTIES

British Empire

France

Russia

United States   (320,000)

$ 10 billion dollars   1 million casualties

REVIEW

Answer the following questions on a separate sheet of paper.

1. What difficulties did the Allies face in 1917?

2. **Graph Skills** Which countries suffered the most and the fewest casualties in the war?

CHAPTER

24 Section 3 Guided Reading and Review

Americans in Battle

A. As You Read

Directions: As you read Section 3 in your textbook, answer the following questions:

1. Why did Russia withdraw from the war? _____

_____

_____

2. What was the result of the Treaty of Brest-Litovsk? _____

_____

_____

3. What was the battle at Amiens like? _____

_____

_____

4. What did the United States Marines do at Belleau Wood? _____

_____

_____

5. What happened at the Battle of the Argonne Forest? _____

_____

_____

6. How did the war end? _____

_____

_____

7. What were the costs of the war? _____

_____

_____

B. Reviewing Key Terms

Directions: Briefly explain the importance of each place to the Great War.

8. Amiens _____

9. Belleau Wood _____

10. the Argonne Forest _____

CHAPTER

24 Section 4 Guide to the Essentials
The Failed Peace

VOCABULARY

self-determination right of national groups to their own territory and forms of government

reparations compensation in money or materials made by a defeated nation

isolationist person who wanted the United States to stay out of foreign affairs

SUMMARY

In 1918, President Woodrow Wilson proposed a plan to bring peace to Europe. Wilson's fourteen-point peace plan contained a number of important ideas. (See chart.) One idea was the principle of **self-determination.** The most important part of the plan was Wilson's idea of an association of nations. The association, called the *League of Nations,* would work to bring about world peace and cooperation.

Wilson's goals were different from those of the other Allied leaders. Wilson wanted a "peace without victory" in which the defeated countries would not be punished. He hoped to build good relations between countries in order to prevent further wars. The other Allies, however, wanted mainly to punish Germany. They insisted that Germany pay cash payments for the losses the Allies had suffered during the war. By June 1919, the Allied Powers had reached an agreement called the *Treaty of Versailles.* The treaty included many of Wilson's ideas, such as the League of Nations. However, it also included many measures that were harsh on Germany. For example, Germany had to pay huge **reparations.** It also lost its colonies, which were put under the control of other nations.

In the United States, the treaty had to be approved by the Senate. A number of powerful senators were **isolationists** who opposed the treaty. They believed that membership in the League of Nations might involve the United States in future European wars. Wilson failed to win support for the treaty. In November 1919, the Senate rejected the Treaty of Versailles.

WILSON'S PEACE PLAN

- End to secret agreements among nations

- Freedom of the seas

- Free trade

- Limits on arms

- Self-determination

- League of Nations

REVIEW

Answer the following questions on a separate sheet of paper.

1. Why did the Senate reject the Treaty of Versailles?

2. **Chart Skills** List three important ideas in Wilson's plan for peace.

CHAPTER

24 Section 4 Guided Reading and Review
The Failed Peace

A. As You Read

Directions: As you read Section 4 in your textbook, complete each sentence.

1. Wilson's goals after the war were _____

_____

_____

2. The purpose of the League of Nations was _____

_____

_____

3. The Treaty of Versailles stated that Germany must _____

_____

_____

4. Americans reacted to the Versailles Treaty in the following way: ____

_____

_____

5. The League of Nations failed because _____

_____

_____

B. Reviewing Key Terms

Directions: Briefly define each term below.

6. Fourteen Points _____

7. League of Nations _____

8. Peace of Paris _____

9. Big Four _____

10. Treaty of Versailles _____

CHAPTER 24 TEST

Identifying Main Ideas

Write the letter of the correct choice in the answer space.

___ 1. Which was NOT a cause of tension in Europe in the early 1900s?
A alliances
B competition for colonies
C nationalism
D United States interference

___ 2. When war broke out in Europe in 1914, the United States
A remained neutral.
B favored the Central Powers.
C entered the war on the side of the Allies.
D declared war on Russia.

___ 3. What effect did World War I have on the American economy?
A It caused a decline in foreign trade.
B It had no effect.
C The economy grew stronger.
D The economy slowed.

___ 4. Which was a reason that the United States entered World War I?
A sympathy for Germany among some Americans
B American neutrality
C desire to help the Russian czar
D German threats to neutral shipping

___ 5. The draft required
A men to serve in the military.
B Americans to support the war.
C businesses to produce war goods.
D officials to run government departments.

___ 6. The United States government responded to American critics of its involvement in World War I by
A protecting freedom of speech.
B making criticism of the war illegal.
C ignoring them.
D allowing criticism of the government, but not of the war.

___ 7. Which of the following best describes the situation of the Allies in 1917?
A close to winning the war
B not worried about Russia
C suffering great losses
D ready with fresh soldiers

___ 8. The decision of Russia to leave the war meant that
A more American troops could travel to Europe.
B the Allies could stop fighting.
C Germany could concentrate on fighting the other Allies.
D the United States could also leave.

___ 9. Which of the following was NOT a part of Wilson's peace plan?
A limits on arms
B free trade
C self-determination
D payment for Allied losses

___ 10. Isolationists in the Senate opposed the Treaty of Versailles because
A President Wilson had not negotiated it.
B they believed it would draw the United States into European wars.
C it called for freedom of the seas.
D it did not call for the League of Nations.

CHAPTER 25
The Roaring Twenties
(1919–1929)

Vocabulary Development

Vocabulary
fad
flappers
jazz

Think about words that you use every day that are particular to the time in which you live. For instance, you might discuss "burning" music onto CDs without even realizing that CD technology was brand new in the 1980s. Moreover, the slang term *burning* is even newer. The 1920s had its new words as well.

During the Roaring Twenties, Americans pursued a variety of **fads**, or short-lived crazes. Some of these fads included sitting atop flagpoles, marathon dances, swallowing goldfish, and dancing the Charleston. Women acquired more responsibilities and freedoms in the 1920s. Some women who rejected traditional rules of dress and conduct were known as **flappers**. For example, fashion-conscious flappers had their hair cut short and wore rolled-down stockings and straight, long-waisted dresses. A new style of music, **jazz**, became very popular during this period. Jazz was written and played primarily by African American composers and performers. Jazz had a style and rhythm that was totally different from any music that came before it. Most important, jazz was mostly improvised during performance rather than written ahead of time.

Directions: *Using your knowledge from reading Chapter 25 and this worksheet, write a short character sketch of an imaginary person living in the 1920s. Be sure to include the vocabulary terms in your description. Including other details from the chapter will help bring your character to life.*

_____

_____

_____

_____

_____

_____

_____

_____

_____

_____

CHAPTER

25

Section 1 Guide to the Essentials

Politics and Prosperity ★

VOCABULARY

recession period when business slows down temporarily

stock share of ownership in a business

communism an economic system in which wealth and property are owned by the community as a whole

disarmament a reduction of the armed forces and weapons of a country

SUMMARY

After World War I, soldiers coming home from the war began to look for jobs. At the same time, however, factories stopped turning out war materials. Fewer jobs were available. As a result, the American economy suffered a **recession,** or economic downturn. In the 1920 election, Warren G. Harding was elected President. Voters hoped that he would improve the economy. However, Harding was faced with a series of political scandals. Some of the people he appointed to office used their government jobs to enrich themselves. When Harding died of a heart attack in 1923, Vice President Calvin Coolidge became President.

Coolidge believed that the prosperity of all Americans depended on the prosperity of American businesses. Under his pro-business policies, the American economy had a period of rapid growth. (See diagram.) More people bought **stocks** than ever before. However, a few experts warned that stock market growth could not last forever.

During this period, the United States played a limited role in foreign affairs. The United States intervened to protect its economic interests in Latin America. It refused to recognize the Soviet Union, where the government was based on **communism.** The United States also joined other nations in supporting **disarmament.**

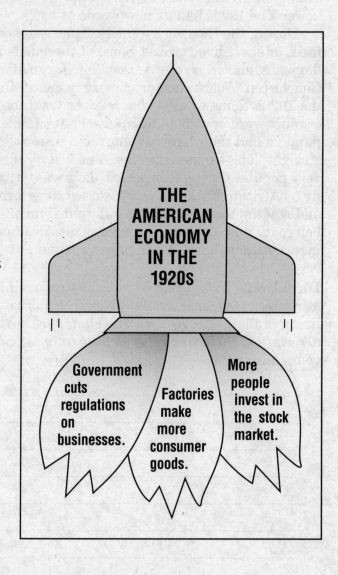

THE AMERICAN ECONOMY IN THE 1920s

Government cuts regulations on businesses.

Factories make more consumer goods.

More people invest in the stock market.

REVIEW

Answer the following questions on a separate sheet of paper.

1. What role did the United States play in foreign affairs in the 1920s?

2. **Diagram Skills** What government action helped the economy grow in the 1920s?

CHAPTER

25 Section 1 Guided Reading and Review
Politics and Prosperity

★

A. As You Read

Directions: As you read Section 1 in your textbook, answer the following questions:

1. Why did the Democrats lose the White House in 1920? _____

_____

2. Why were the 1920 Cabinet members called the "Ohio Gang"? _____

_____

3. What was the Teapot Dome scandal? _____

_____

4. What were the domestic presidential policies in the 1920s? _____

_____

5. What were the sources of the economic boom of the 1920s? _____

_____

6. How were relations between the United States and Latin America characterized during this period? _____

_____

7. What type of government was in place in the Soviet Union? _____

_____

8. What happened at the Washington Conference of 1921? _____

_____

B. Reviewing Key Terms

Directions: Identify each person listed.

9. Warren G. Harding _____

10. Andrew Mellon _____

11. Herbert Hoover _____

12. Albert Fall _____

13. Calvin Coolidge _____

14. Dwight Morrow _____

15. V. I. Lenin _____

16. Jane Addams _____

CHAPTER

25

Section 2 Guide to the Essentials

New Ways of Life

VOCABULARY

repeal to revoke or abandon a law

SUMMARY

American society went through dramatic changes in the 1920s. New ideas, new products, and new forms of entertainment changed the American way of life.

One such change began in January 1920, when the Eighteenth Amendment to the Constitution became law. This amendment made it illegal to make or sell alcohol anywhere in the United States. Because it prohibited people from drinking alcohol, the amendment began the period known as **Prohibition.** Prohibition had long been a goal of reformers, who hoped it would improve American life. In the end, however, it did not work. Many Americans found ways to get alcohol. Prohibition led to an increase in organized crime. Criminals provided alcohol to the illegal clubs where it was served. Prohibition was **repealed** in 1933.

The Nineteenth Amendment, passed in 1920, brought more changes to American life. It gave women the right to vote. The lives of women were changing in other ways, too. During World War I, thousands of women had begun working outside the home. While many lost their jobs when the troops came home, some remained in the work force. In the home, new appliances such as refrigerators and vacuum cleaners made housework easier.

Other changes occurred in the 1920s. The automobile came into much wider use, allowing people to move more easily from place to place. A new mass culture that crossed state lines began to develop. New types of entertainment, such as radio and movies, became very popular. (See diagram.)

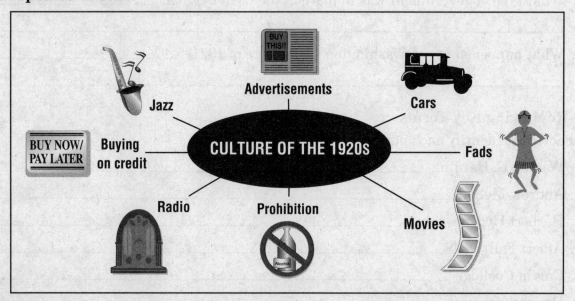

REVIEW

Answer the following questions on a separate sheet of paper.

1. How did the lives of women change during the 1920s?

2. **Diagram Skills** List four factors that contributed to a change in American culture in the 1920s.

CHAPTER
25 Section 2 Guided Reading and Review
New Ways of Life

A. As You Read

Directions: As you read Section 2 in your textbook, complete the chart by describing the social changes in each category.

1. Prohibition	
2. Women's Rights	
3. Transportation	

B. Reviewing Key Terms

Directions: Use each term correctly in a sentence about the Roaring Twenties.

4. Prohibition _____

_____

5. bootleggers _____

_____

6. repeal _____

_____

7. League of Women Voters _____

_____

8. Equal Rights Amendment _____

_____

9. suburb _____

_____

CHAPTER 25

Section 3 Guide to the Essentials
The Roaring Twenties

VOCABULARY

fad activity or style that is popular for a short time

jazz strong, rhythmic music in which players or singers often make up parts as they go along

SUMMARY

In the United States, the 1920s became known as the Roaring Twenties. New dances, music, and games swept the country. Americans seemed to "roar" with fun and laughter. A number of **fads,** such as dance contests, flagpole sitting, and styles of dress, came and went.

The 1920s were also called the Jazz Age. **Jazz** was a popular new music created by African American musicians, such as Louis Armstrong. It first developed in New Orleans and then spread around the country. Today, jazz is considered one of the most significant cultural achievements of the United States.

A new generation of American writers gained worldwide fame in the 1920s. Many criticized Americans for caring too much about money and fun. Ernest Hemingway drew on his World War I experiences to write about the horrors of war. F. Scott Fitzgerald wrote about wealthy young people who attended countless parties but could not find happiness.

The neighborhood of Harlem in New York City became a center for the arts. There, large numbers of African American musicians, artists, and writers created a movement called the Harlem Renaissance. During the Harlem Renaissance, many great works of art were produced. (See chart.) African American writers and artists celebrated their heritage.

Radio, movies, and newspapers created heroes known across the country. Many athletes, such as Babe Ruth, star of the New York Yankees, became famous. The greatest hero of the decade was Charles Lindbergh. In 1927, he was the first person to fly nonstop across the Atlantic Ocean—alone.

WRITERS OF THE HARLEM RENAISSANCE		
WRITER	**AN IMPORTANT WORK**	**MESSAGE OF THAT WORK**
Langston Hughes	"My People," poem	Encouraged African Americans to be proud of their heritage.
Claude McKay	"If We Must Die," poem	Condemned violence against African Americans.
Zora Neale Hurston	*Mules and Men,* collection of folk tales, songs, and prayers	Celebrated African American folklore of the South.

REVIEW

Answer the following questions on a separate sheet of paper.

1. Who helped create jazz music?

2. **Chart Skills** What was Langston Hughes's message in "My People"?

CHAPTER

25 Section 3 Guided Reading and Review
The Roaring Twenties

A. As You Read

Directions: As you read Section 3 in your textbook, fill in the chart with examples of 1920s crazes, innovations, artists, and celebrities.

1. Dances	
2. Fashions	
3. Music	
4. Literature	
5. Celebrities	

B. Reviewing Key Terms

Directions: Match each person with his or her description.

Column I	Column II
_____ 6. Louis Armstrong	a. hit 60 home runs in one season; record stood for over 30 years
_____ 7. Bessie Smith	b. flew solo across the Atlantic Ocean
_____ 8. Ernest Hemingway	c. playwright; wrote realistic dramas
_____ 9. Sinclair Lewis	d. writer and collector of African American folktales
_____ 10. Eugene O'Neill	e. poet; wrote "The Negro Speaks of Rivers"
_____ 11. Langston Hughes	f. trumpeter who helped create jazz music
_____ 12. Zora Neale Hurston	g. jazz singer
_____ 13. Babe Ruth	h. author of *Babbitt* and *Main Street*
_____ 14. Charles Lindbergh	i. author of *The Sun Also Rises* and *A Farewell to Arms*

CHAPTER 25 Section 4 Guide to the Essentials
A Nation Divided

VOCABULARY

deport force a person to leave a country

quota system a policy that restricts the number of immigrants entering the United States

SUMMARY

Many Americans did not share in the prosperity of the 1920s. Railroad workers lost jobs as more people used cars. The power of labor unions decreased. Farmers suffered terribly. (See chart.)

Many Americans believed that too many people were immigrating to the United States. Some Americans believed that immigrants brought political ideas that posed a danger to the American way of life. In the South, a revived Ku Klux Klan terrorized African Americans, immigrants, Catholics, and Jews.

The government took harsh actions against communists. During the *Red Scare,* suspected communists were arrested. Many foreigners were **deported.** Congress passed new laws that limited immigration. Under the new **quota system,** only a certain number of people from each country could enter the United States.

In 1925, a legal case known as the Scopes Trial captured the nation's attention. Two of the best lawyers in the country argued for and against the teaching of evolution in schools. The side for evolution lost.

Three years later in 1928, voters had to choose between two presidential candidates: the Republican, Herbert Hoover, a prosperous businessman; and the Democrat, Alfred E. Smith, the son of Irish immigrants. Hoover won the presidency on the issues of prosperity and prohibition.

HARD TIMES FOR FARMERS

During World War I, Europeans buy American farm goods, driving prices up.

↓

American farmers borrow money to buy more land and equipment.

↓

After war, European farmers increase production.

↓

Farm prices in United States drop sharply.

↓

Income of American farmers drops sharply.

↓

American farmers cannot pay their debts.

REVIEW

Answer the following questions on a separate sheet of paper.

1. Why did the government pass laws to limit immigration?

2. **Chart Skills** What caused farm prices in the United States to drop sharply in the 1920s?

CHAPTER

25 Section 4 Guided Reading and Review
A Nation Divided

A. As You Read

Directions: As you read Section 4 in your textbook, fill in supporting details under each main idea below:

Main Idea A: Many Americans did not share in the boom of the 1920s.

1. _____

2. _____

3. _____

4. _____

Main Idea B: Communism's rise in the East made Americans fear a communist revolution in the West.

5. _____

6. _____

7. _____

B. Reviewing Key Terms

Directions: Briefly define each term.

8. company union _____

_____

9. sabotage _____

_____

10. anarchist _____

_____

11. deport _____

_____

12. nativism _____

_____

13. quota system _____

CHAPTER
25 TEST

Identifying Main Ideas

Write the letter of the correct choice in the answer space.

____ 1. Once in office, President Harding
   A continued the policies that had made the economy strong.
   B made the United States more active overseas.
   C pursued antibusiness policies.
   D faced political scandals.

____ 2. Under President Coolidge, the American stock market
   A was reformed so that stocks would not rise in value.
   B stayed the same in value.
   C declined in value.
   D grew in value.

____ 3. During the 1920s, the United States
   A intervened in Latin America.
   B immediately recognized the Soviet Union.
   C accepted the job of keeping world peace.
   D rejected disarmament.

____ 4. The Eighteenth Amendment
   A reversed the ban on alcohol.
   B gave women the right to vote.
   C made it illegal to make or sell alcohol.
   D led to a significant decrease in organized crime.

____ 5. What was one effect of the wider use of automobiles?
   A People could move more easily from place to place.
   B People remained interested only in local developments.
   C The development of a new national culture was weakened.
   D Housework became easier.

____ 6. The 1920s became known as the Roaring Twenties because
   A the noise of cars and trucks filled the air.
   B past ways of doing things regained their strength.
   C terrible social conflicts tore Americans apart.
   D new fads and ways to have fun swept across the country.

____ 7. The Harlem Renaissance was a movement of African American artists
   A working in the South.
   B calling for segregation.
   C urging other African Americans to leave the country.
   D celebrating their heritage.

____ 8. During the 1920s, farmers
   A suffered an economic downturn.
   B recovered from the hard times of World War I.
   C adopted European farming methods.
   D continued their economic success.

____ 9. The Red Scare caused
   A Congress to pass new laws limiting immigration.
   B the Ku Klux Klan to terrorize African Americans.
   C suspected communists to be arrested.
   D railroad workers to lose their jobs.

____ 10. The immigration quota system
   A provided jobs for new immigrants.
   B limited immigration.
   C increased immigration.
   D was rejected by Congress.

CHAPTER 26 The Great Depression (1929–1941)

Vocabulary Development

Franklin D. Roosevelt led the effort to create a variety of government programs and agencies designed to pull America out of the Great Depression. Roosevelt's overall plan for national economic recovery became known as the New Deal. So many programs and agencies were born during the New Deal that most became known by their abbreviations. An abbreviation is a shortened form of a phrase that is formed by combining the first letters in the key words of the phrase. For example, an an abbreviation of Franklin D. Roosevelt's name is FDR.

<u>Vocabulary</u>
Civilian Conservation
  Corps
National Labor
  Relations Act
National Recovery
  Administration
Social Security Act
Tennessee Valley
  Authority

Directions: *Draw a line from the New Deal agency or program and its matching abbreviation to its proper mission or function.*

Agency or Program and Abbreviation	Mission/Function
1. Civilian Conservation Corps (CCC)	A. Agency that supervised the codes of fair competition in various industries.
2. National Labor Relations Act (NLRA)	B. Law that created a board to investigate unfair labor practices.
3. National Recovery Administration (NRA)	C. Law that created a program that delivered benefits to retired workers who were 65 or older and to dependent survivors of deceased workers.
4. Social Security Act (SSA)	D. Agency that created employment for young men in the areas of reforestation, road construction, flood control, and soil conservation.
5. Tennessee Valley Authority (TVA)	E. Independent public corporation created to fully develop a geographic region.

Name_____ Class_____ Date_____

26 Section 1 Guide to the Essentials
The Great Crash

VOCABULARY

bankrupt unable to pay debts

public works projects built by the government for public use

SUMMARY

By the end of the 1920s, there were signs that the economy was failing. However, most Americans were not aware of any problems. Then, in 1929, there was a crash, or a severe fall in prices, in the stock market. It began when a few investors sold stocks because they thought that the prosperity of the 1920s might be over. More people began selling their stocks, and stock prices fell. Soon people panicked and tried to sell before prices fell even further. So many people lost their fortunes on October 29 that it was called *Black Tuesday.*

The stock market crash marked the beginning of a period of economic hard times known as the *Great Depression.* This period lasted until 1941. (See chart.) Factories cut back on production and laid off workers. Many businesses declared that they were **bankrupt.** The unemployment rate rose very high. Many Americans had no money to buy food or pay rent.

President Herbert Hoover responded cautiously. He did not believe that the government should help businesses directly. At first, he tried to restore confidence by predicting better times. When the hard times continued, Hoover took other steps. He set up **public works** programs. Still, the depression deepened. When the *Bonus Army* camped in a tent city along the

Potomac River, Hoover used the army to force veterans to leave. Many people were shocked by the use of force. By 1932, Americans wanted a new leader.

CAUSES

- Factories and farms produce more goods than people can buy.
- Banks make loans that borrowers cannot pay back.
- After the stock market crash, many businesses cannot find people who will invest in their growth.

THE GREAT DEPRESSION

EFFECTS

- Many banks fail.
- Many businesses and factories fail.
- Millions of Americans are out of work.
- Many are homeless and hungry.
- Families break up and people suffer.

REVIEW
Answer the following questions on a separate sheet of paper.

1. How did the reaction of President Hoover to the depression change over time?

2. **Chart Skills** What were two causes of the Great Depression?

CHAPTER 26

Section 1 Guided Reading and Review
The Great Crash

A. As You Read

Directions: As you read Section 1 in your textbook, list one cause and one effect for each of the following:

1. Farmers' incomes fell during the 1920s.

   Cause: _____

   Effect: _____

2. The stock market crashed on October 29, 1929.

   Cause: _____

   Effect: _____

3. The banking system was weakened.

   Cause: _____

   Effect: _____

4. Factories cut back on production.

   Cause: _____

   Effect: _____

5. Most Americans blamed President Hoover for the Great Depression.

   Cause: _____

   Effect: _____

B. Reviewing Key Terms

Directions: Complete each sentence by writing the correct term in the blank.

6. Many investors could not repay loans from stocks purchased _____.

7. October 29, 1929, the date of the stock market crash, is called _____.

8. People or businesses unable to pay their debts are described as _____.

9. Groups of shacks in which homeless people lived during the depression were called

   _____ because people blamed the President for the depression.

10. In 1932, the _____ marched to Washington to demand immediate

    payment of money not due to be paid until 1945.

CHAPTER 26 Section 2 Guide to the Essentials

FDR and the New Deal

VOCABULARY

fireside chat one of President Roosevelt's regular radio speeches

SUMMARY

In 1932, Franklin Delano Roosevelt, known as FDR, was elected President. During the campaign, FDR promised to help the unemployed, farmers, and the elderly. Many Americans believed that he would take action to improve the economy.

Once in office, Roosevelt first acted to help the banks. The depression had caused many banks to close. People lost the money they had deposited in those banks. Many depositors became afraid and took their savings out of other banks. FDR knew that the economy would not recover without strong banks. Urged by the President, Congress passed laws that strengthened the banks. Roosevelt gave a speech on the radio, called a **fireside chat,** to explain that the banks were now safe. Depositors

returned their money to the banks, and the American banking system grew stronger.

The bank bill was the first of many bills FDR sent to Congress during the first three months he was in office. Congress passed many of these in just a few months. This period was called the **Hundred Days.**

Roosevelt called his plan for economic recovery the **New Deal.** The New Deal had three main goals: relief for the unemployed, plans for recovery, and reforms to prevent another depression. (See chart.) The government began large public works programs to provide people with jobs. Other laws helped raise the prices of agricultural products. Government and industry agreed on new rules for doing business. Congress passed laws to regulate the stock market.

PROGRAMS OF THE NEW DEAL

RELIEF

- **Works Progress Administration (WPA)** Hires jobless people to build public buildings and parks.

- **Civilian Conservation Corps (CCC)** Employs young men to work on outdoor projects.

RECOVERY

- **National Industrial Recovery Act (NIRA)** Develops rules for doing business.

- **Tennessee Valley Authority (TVA)** Builds dams to provide electricity to seven southern states.

REFORM

- **Truth-in-Securities Act** Regulates the stock market.

- **Federal Deposit Insurance Corporation (FDIC)** Insured savings accounts in banks approved by the government.

REVIEW

Answer the following questions on a separate sheet of paper.

1. Which problem did Roosevelt concentrate on first?

2. **Chart Skills** What are two New Deal programs that tried to provide relief for the unemployed?

CHAPTER

26 Section 2 Guided Reading and Review
FDR and the New Deal

A. As You Read

Directions: As you read Section 2 in your textbook, complete the chart below by writing key steps the government took to achieve each main goal of the New Deal.

> **Goal A:** to provide relief for the unemployed
>
> 1. _____
>
> 2. _____
>
> **Goal B:** to plan the economic recovery
>
> 3. _____
>
> 4. _____
>
> 5. _____
>
> 6. _____
>
> 7. _____
>
> **Goal C:** to prevent another depression
>
> 8. _____
>
> 9. _____

B. Reviewing Key Terms

Directions: Briefly describe each New Deal program, and mark each A, B, or C to identify which of the above goals it helped achieve.

10. Civilian Conservation Corps _____

_____

11. Works Progress Administration _____

_____

12. National Industrial Recovery Act _____

_____

13. Public Works Administration _____

_____

14. Agricultural Adjustment Act _____

_____

CHAPTER
26 Section 3 Guide to the Essentials
Response to the New Deal

★

VOCABULARY

pension regular sum of money paid to people after they retire

SUMMARY

The first hundred days of the New Deal made Americans feel hopeful. Still, the depression continued. Criticism of FDR and his policies grew. Some people wanted the government to do more to help people. Others did not want the government to expand its power. They argued that the New Deal was interfering too much with business and with people's lives. New Deal critics thought that they could end the depression by increasing taxes or by insisting that people over age 60 retire.

The Supreme Court ruled that many New Deal laws were unconstitutional. Roosevelt wanted to appoint more judges who supported his programs. Many Americans feared that his plan to "pack" the Supreme Court would destroy the balance of powers. FDR withdrew his proposal.

Roosevelt continued to expand the New Deal. In 1935, Congress passed the *Social Security Act.* This act provided **pensions** for older people. It also set up a system through which unemployed people were given small payments until they found work, and states were given money to support dependent children and people with disabilities. In his second term, Roosevelt pushed for laws strengthening labor unions. Workers were given more power to negotiate with their employers.

The debate for and against the New Deal has continued to this day. (See chart.) Whether good or bad, the New Deal was a turning point in American history. For the first time, large numbers of people had direct contact with the federal government. New Deal programs such as Social Security have affected the lives of almost every American citizen.

THE NEW DEAL: WAS IT GOOD OR BAD?	
GOOD	**BAD**
• Government has a duty to help all citizens.	• Government should not interfere in business or in people's private lives.
• The New Deal helped the nation through the worst days of the Great Depression.	• New Deal spending led to increases in the **national debt.**
• At a time when people in other countries turned to dictators to solve the economic crisis, the New Deal saved the nation's democratic system.	• The New Deal did not end the Great Depression.

REVIEW

Answer the following questions on a separate sheet of paper.

1. What programs did the Social Security Act create?
2. **Chart Skills** Identify two arguments against the New Deal.

CHAPTER

26 Section 3 Guided Reading and Review
Response to the New Deal

A. As You Read

Directions: As you read Section 3 in your textbook, list three ways in which the New Deal changed the United States government. Then, fill in the chart with arguments for and against these changes.

1. _____

2. _____

3. _____

For	Against
4.	5.

B. Reviewing Key Terms

Directions: Briefly define each term.

6. pension _____

7. collective bargaining _____

8. sit-down strike _____

9. deficit spending _____

10. national debt _____

Section 4 Guide to the Essentials
The Nation in Hard Times ★

VOCABULARY

migrant worker person who moves in search of work

SUMMARY

During much of the depression, a severe drought hit the western Great Plains states. This area, which included parts of Texas, Oklahoma, and Arkansas, became known as the **Dust Bowl.** The soil became so dry that winds blew it away in blinding dust storms. Farming was nearly impossible. Many farmers left and traveled west to become **migrant workers** on the West Coast. There, new hardships awaited them. Those who were able to find work were paid very little. Many lived in tents and shacks without water or electricity.

Women, African Americans, and other minority groups faced hardships during the depression. (See chart.) Women and minorities were usually the first to lose jobs. Then, when jobs became available, white men were hired back first. However, under the New Deal, thousands of young African American men learned trades. Also, President Roosevelt encouraged new policies toward Native Americans.

Americans found ways to take their minds off the depression. Every night, millions of people tuned in to the radio. They also went to the movies to watch stories about happy families and people finding love and success. The radio and the movies helped people forget about their troubles at least for a little while. Some American artists used the depression as a backdrop for their art. Writer John Steinbeck's novel, *The Grapes of Wrath,* tells the story of a migrant family. Photographers like Dorothea Lange captured images of that time in their work.

HARDSHIPS FACED BY WOMEN AND MINORITIES

Women	→ face difficulty finding jobs; men usually hired before women.
African Americans	→ often first to lose jobs; face continued discrimination; a few leaders become advisers to President Roosevelt.
Mexican Americans	→ face discrimination; some forced to return to Mexico.
Asian Americans	→ face discrimination; competition over jobs leads to calls that they leave the country.
Native Americans	→ face terrible poverty; however, Congress passes new laws giving them more control over their own affairs.

REVIEW

Answer the following questions on a separate sheet of paper.

1. What were two ways people found to escape the hard times of the depression?

2. **Chart Skills** How were Asian Americans affected by the Great Depression?

CHAPTER

26 Section 4 Guided Reading and Review

The Nation in Hard Times

★

A. As You Read

Directions: As you read Section 4 in your textbook, answer the following questions:

1. What caused the dust storms that swept the Great Plains during the 1930s?

_____

_____

2. Why did farmers from the Great Plains pack up and migrate to California?

_____

_____

3. How did Eleanor Roosevelt change the job of First Lady? _____

_____

4. What special struggles did ethnic minorities face during the depression? _____

_____

_____

5. What did movies contribute to society during the depression? _____

_____

_____

B. Reviewing Key Terms

Directions: Briefly identify each artist's contribution to the depression.

6. John Steinbeck _____

_____

7. Thomas Hart Benton _____

_____

8. Dorothea Lange _____

_____

9. Orson Welles _____

_____

Identifying Main Ideas

Write the letter of the correct choice in the answer space.

___ 1. One reason for the stock market crash was that people

   A ignored the fall in stock prices.

   B refused to be involved in the stock market.

   C stopped selling stocks.

   D panicked and tried to sell their stocks before prices fell even further.

___ 2. President Hoover reacted to the Great Depression with

   A unconcern.

   B panic.

   C caution.

   D boldness.

___ 3. During the early years of the Great Depression, the unemployment rate

   A rose slightly.

   B fell.

   C remained stable.

   D rose very high.

___ 4. Roosevelt ended the banking crisis by

   A asking Congress to pass laws to strengthen the banks.

   B opening many new banks.

   C canceling his fireside chats.

   D bringing all banks under government control.

___ 5. Which of the following was NOT a goal of the New Deal?

   A plans to increase the national debt

   B reforms to prevent depressions

   C plans for recovery

   D relief for the unemployed

___ 6. The Social Security Act was designed to help

   A labor unions.

   B older people.

   C business owners.

   D bankers.

___ 7. During Roosevelt's time in office, labor unions were

   A outlawed.

   B ignored.

   C harmed.

   D strengthened.

___ 8. Some critics opposed the New Deal because they felt it

   A was a turning point in American history.

   B decreased the national debt too rapidly.

   C interfered too much with business and with people's lives.

   D decreased the power of the federal government.

___ 9. The Dust Bowl was an area in

   A the Great Plains.

   B the Northeast.

   C the Southwest.

   D the West Coast.

___ 10. Which groups were the first to lose jobs during the depression?

   A men and veterans

   B radio and movie entertainers

   C union members and skilled workers

   D women and minorities

CHAPTER

27 The World War II Era
(1935–1945)

Vocabulary Development

The Battle of Midway and the Battle of the Bulge were two important turning points in World War II. Review the information in your textbook, and complete the following concept diagrams to organize information about these two battles.

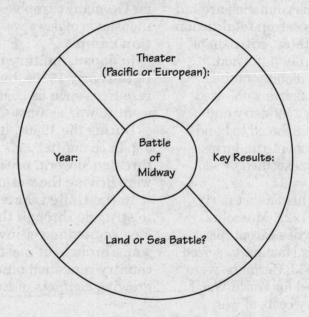

Theater
(Pacific or European):

Year:

Battle
of
Midway

Key Results:

Land or Sea Battle?

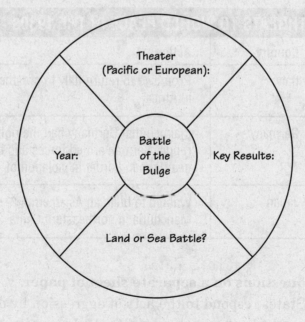

Theater
(Pacific or European):

Year:

Battle
of the
Bulge

Key Results:

Land or Sea Battle?

CHAPTER

27

Section 1 Guide to the Essentials
The Gathering Storm

VOCABULARY

concentration camp prison for civilians considered to be enemies of the state

aggression warlike act by one country against another without just cause

SUMMARY

During the 1920s and 1930s, dictators came to power in various countries around the world. The dictators set up totalitarian states. In totalitarian states, criticism of the government is severely punished.

Joseph Stalin was the dictator of the Soviet Union. Brutal measures were used to modernize the country's industry and agriculture. Peasants were forced to hand over their land to government-run farms. People who resisted were executed or sent to labor camps.

Benito Mussolini and his Fascist party seized power in Italy in 1922. Mussolini outlawed all political parties except his own. Adolf Hitler and his Nazi party seized power in Germany in 1933. Germans were bitter about being blamed for World War I and for bearing the heavy costs of war reparations. Hitler blamed Jews and others for Germany's troubles. As his power grew, thousands of Jews were sent to **concentration camps.**

In Japan, military leaders seized power. In the early 1930s, hungry for natural resources such as coal and iron, Japan went to war against China.

During the 1930s, Italy, Germany, and Japan committed acts of **aggression** that threatened world peace. (See chart.) Events were driving the world to another war.

In the United States, people continued to struggle through the Great Depression. Few wanted to get involved in another war. Throughout most of the 1930s, the country remained officially neutral in the growing conflicts of Europe and Asia.

THREATS TO WORLD PEACE IN THE 1930s		
Leader	**Country**	**Action**
Benito Mussolini	Italy	Promised to return Italy to greatness; invaded Ethiopia in Africa
Adolf Hitler	Germany	Claimed that Germany had the right to expand; rebuilt German armed forces and moved troops near French border in violation of Treaty of Versailles
Military leaders	Japan	Wanted to build an Asian empire; seized territory of Manchuria in northeastern China

REVIEW

Answer the following questions on a separate sheet of paper.

1. How did the United States respond to the acts of aggression by dictators?

2. **Chart Skills** Who was the leader in Germany, and what actions did he take?

CHAPTER 27

Section 1 Guided Reading and Review

The Gathering Storm

A. As You Read

Directions: As you read Section 1 in your textbook, fill in the graphic organizer with details of each country's government on the eve of World War II.

Soviet Union	1.
Italy	2.
Germany	3.
Japan	4.

B. Reviewing Key Terms

Directions: Briefly define each term, and note which country or countries it is associated with: use S for the Soviet Union, I for Italy, G for Germany, or J for Japan.

5. totalitarian state _____

_____

_____

6. fascism _____

_____

_____

7. Nazis _____

_____

_____

8. concentration camp _____

_____

_____

CHAPTER

27 Section 2 Guide to the Essentials
World War II Begins

VOCABULARY

appeasement policy of giving in to aggression to avoid war

SUMMARY

During the late 1930s, Italy, Japan, and Germany continued their aggression. The United States and the European democracies did little in response.

In 1938, Hitler annexed Austria. Then he claimed part of Czechoslovakia. Britain and France were eager to avoid war. They made a deal that Germany could keep this land if no additional attempts to expand were made. However, this policy of **appeasement** failed. Germany seized the rest of Czechoslovakia. When Germany invaded Poland in September 1939, Great Britain and France declared war. World War II had begun. By the summer of 1940, German forces had conquered France and were threatening Britain.

When war broke out in Europe, the United States declared that it would remain neutral. President Roosevelt, like most Americans, sympathized with Britain and France. He created programs by which the United States supplied planes, guns, and other supplies to Britain. He quietly began preparing the nation for war.

Tensions between the United States and Japan grew. The United States refused to sell oil and metal to Japan unless it stopped its attacks on other countries. On December 7, 1941, Japanese planes made a surprise raid on the American naval base at Pearl Harbor in Hawaii. The attack destroyed many ships and planes. More than 2,400 people died. An outraged Congress declared war on Japan. The United States entered the war on the side of the Allies. Germany, Italy, and Japan were the Axis powers. (See chart.)

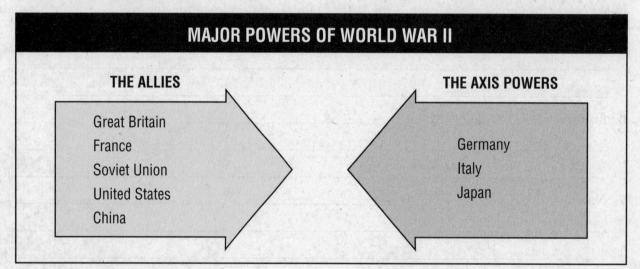

MAJOR POWERS OF WORLD WAR II

THE ALLIES

Great Britain
France
Soviet Union
United States
China

THE AXIS POWERS

Germany
Italy
Japan

REVIEW
Answer the following questions on a separate sheet of paper.

1. How did the United States respond when war broke out in Europe in 1939?

2. **Chart Skills** On which side did China fight in World War II?

CHAPTER

27 Section 2 Guided Reading and Review
World War II Begins

A. As You Read

Directions: As you read Section 2 in your textbook, number the events below in chronological order. List one effect of each event.

_____ 1. Japan bombs Pearl Harbor, Hawaii.

Effect: _____

_____ 2. Hitler and Stalin agree to divide Eastern Europe between their nations.

Effect: _____

_____ 3. The German army invades France.

Effect: _____

_____ 4. Germany invades and annexes Austria.

Effect: _____

_____ 5. Japan declares all-out war on China and begins bombing major cities.

Effect: _____

_____ 6. The United States Congress passes the Lend-Lease Act.

Effect: _____

B. Reviewing Key Terms

Directions: Briefly define or identify each term.

7. Munich Conference _____

8. appeasement _____

9. blitzkrieg _____

10. Axis _____

11. Allies _____

12. Atlantic Charter _____

CHAPTER

27 Section 3 Guide to the Essentials

Americans in Wartime

★

VOCABULARY

rationing limiting the amount of certain goods people can buy

SUMMARY

After the attack on Pearl Harbor, the United States mobilized for war. (See chart.) The military built bases all over the country to train forces for combat. Factories shifted to the production of weapons, ships, and planes. As a result, other goods became scarce. The government **rationed** the amount of certain goods that people could buy. The war quickly ended the Great Depression. Unemployment fell as millions of jobs opened up in factories.

During the war, more than 6 million women entered the work force. They replaced men who joined the armed services. Women also joined the armed forces. While not allowed to fight, women served in other important roles.

African Americans, Native Americans, Latinos, and other minorities contributed to the war effort. Many found jobs in factories. They also served in the military. Although they were placed in segregated units, African Americans served heroically. More than one out of three able-bodied Native American men were in uniform. Thousands of Puerto Ricans and Mexican Americans also served.

Some Americans were treated unjustly during the war. After Pearl Harbor, some people on the West Coast questioned the loyalty of Japanese Americans. No evidence of disloyalty existed. Yet the government forced about 120,000 Japanese Americans to move to "relocation" camps. In 1988, Congress apologized to these Japanese Americans.

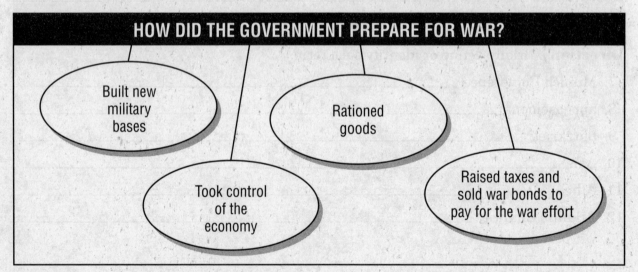

HOW DID THE GOVERNMENT PREPARE FOR WAR?

- Built new military bases
- Took control of the economy
- Rationed goods
- Raised taxes and sold war bonds to pay for the war effort

REVIEW

Answer the following questions on a separate sheet of paper.

1. What happened to Japanese Americans living on the West Coast during the war?

2. **Chart Skills** What actions did the government take to pay for the war effort?

27 Section 3 Guided Reading and Review
Americans in Wartime

A. As You Read

Directions: As you read Section 3 in your textbook, answer the following questions:

1. What did women do in the armed forces during the war? _____

_____

2. Why were American consumer goods rationed during the war? _____

_____

3. Why did America's entrance into the war have the effect that it did on the economy?

_____

_____

4. What kinds of changes did the war bring for women on the home front? _____

_____

_____

5. What caused the race riots in American cities in the 1940s? _____

_____

6. What was the African American experience in the military? _____

_____

7. What happened to Japanese Americans during the war? _____

_____

B. Reviewing Key Terms

Directions: Use each term correctly in a sentence about the homefront during World War II.

8. War Production Board _____

9. victory garden _____

10. Rosie the Riveter _____

11. "Double V" Campaign _____

12. Tuskegee Airmen _____

CHAPTER 27 Section 4 Guide to the Essentials
The Allies Turn the Tide

SUMMARY

In early 1942, it seemed likely that the Allies would lose. Hitler was in control of most of Europe and North Africa. His forces were advancing deep into the Soviet Union. Japan was advancing across Asia and the Pacific. The Japanese had captured Hong Kong and Singapore and had driven the United States out of the Philippines.

However, later that year, the Allies began to have successes. There were several key turning points in the war. (See chart.) The United States Navy won a major victory at the **Battle of Midway** in the Pacific. American planes sank four Japanese aircraft carriers. This prevented Japan from attacking Hawaii again. Allied troops drove the Germans from North Africa and then invaded Italy. Meanwhile, the Soviets slowly pushed the Germans back west. Finally came **D-Day**—June 6, 1944. The Allies landed an invasion force on the beaches of Normandy in northern France. By August, Allied troops entered Paris.

The Allies began moving east toward Germany. By 1945, American troops were closing in on Berlin, the German capital, from the west. Soviet troops advanced from the east. Allied air forces pounded the city. Hitler committed suicide rather than surrender, but Germany had lost the war. On May 8, 1945, the Allies celebrated victory in Europe. Sadly, after leading the country through the Great Depression and World War II, President Roosevelt died one month before the Germans surrendered.

Battle of Stalingrad 1942–1943
Germans try to take Stalingrad, but Russians force their surrender.

Battle of El Alamein October 1942
British drive back German advances, leading to German surrender of African lands.

TURNING POINTS OF THE WAR

Invasion of Italy September 1943
British and American troops invade Italy. Hitler is forced to send troops to help Italy fight the Allies.

Invasion of Normandy (D-Day) 1944
Allied troops land in northern France. They go on to free France.

REVIEW

Answer the following questions on a separate sheet of paper.

1. Why did it seem likely that the Allies would lose in early 1942?

2. **Chart Skills** What happened after the invasion of Normandy?

CHAPTER

27 Section 4 Guided Reading and Review
The Allies Turn the Tide

A. As You Read

Directions: As you read Section 4 in your textbook, list the main events that happened to each country between 1942 and 1945.

1. Soviet Union

_____

_____

_____

2. Japan

_____

_____

_____

_____

3. United States

_____

_____

_____

_____

4. Germany

_____

_____

_____

_____

B. Reviewing Key Terms

Directions: Briefly define or identify each term.

5. Battle of Midway _____

6. Operation Overlord _____

7. D-Day _____

8. Battle of the Bulge _____

CHAPTER

27 Section 5 Guide to the Essentials
The End of the War

★

VOCABULARY

island hopping a military strategy whereby American forces captured a series of Pacific islands that brought them closer to Japan

SUMMARY

After the Battle of Midway, the United States fought to take control of the Pacific from Japan. Through a campaign of **island hopping,** American forces captured islands closer and closer to Japan. American bombers began to shell Japanese factories and cities. Still, the Japanese did not seem ready to surrender. Some American officials warned that an invasion of Japan would be long and bloody.

During the war, American scientists developed the atomic bomb. President Harry S. Truman thought that this weapon could finally end the war. Allied leaders warned Japan to surrender or face terrible destruction. The Japanese ignored this message, not knowing about the atomic bomb. In August 1945, an American bomber dropped a single atomic bomb, destroying the Japanese city of Hiroshima and killing at least 70,000 people. After the United States dropped a second bomb on Nagasaki a few days later, Japan finally surrendered.

World War II was the deadliest war in human history. (See chart.) Bombs had destroyed houses, factories, and farms. Japan had brutally mistreated prisoners of war. Especially horrifying was the

Holocaust, the slaughter of Europe's Jews by the Nazis. The Nazis killed more than 6 million Jews in death camps. Another 6 million Poles, Slavs, and Gypsies were also victims of the death camps.

DEATHS IN WORLD WAR II		
	MILITARY DEAD	**CIVILIAN DEAD**
Britain	389,000	65,000
France	211,000	108,000
Soviet Union	7,500,000	15,000,000
United States	292,000	*
Germany	2,850,000	5,000,000
Italy	77,500	100,000
Japan	1,576,000	300,000

*Very small number

All figures are estimates. Source: Henri Michel, *The Second World War*

REVIEW

Answer the following questions on a separate sheet of paper.

1. What action finally brought an end to the war with Japan?
2. **Chart Skills** What country had the most civilian deaths during the war?

CHAPTER

27 Section 5 Guided Reading and Review

The End of the War

A. As You Read

Directions: As you read Section 5 in your textbook, fill in supporting details under each main idea.

Main Idea A: One goal of the United States was to regain the Philippines.

1. _____

2. _____

Main Idea B: A second goal of the United States was to invade Japan.

3. _____

Main Idea C: Japan surrendered in 1945.

4. _____

Main Idea D: World War II was the deadliest war in history.

5. _____

6. _____

7. _____

8. _____

B. Reviewing Key Terms

Directions: Fill in each blank with the correct term.

9. The Americans captured steppingstones to Japan in a strategy known as

_____.

10. A _____ pilot is one who uses his own plane as a missile, knowing

that he will die when he hits his target.

11. The _____ warned Japan to surrender or face destruction.

12. The deliberate massacre of millions of Jews, Poles, Gypsies, and Slavs is known as the

_____.

13. At the _____, 12 Nazis were sentenced to death for war crimes, and

thousands more were imprisoned.

CHAPTER
27 TEST

Identifying Main Ideas

Write the letter of the correct choice in the answer space.

____ 1. In the 1930s, Germany became a totalitarian state under the control of the dictator
A Harry S. Truman.
B Benito Mussolini.
C Joseph Stalin.
D Adolph Hitler.

____ 2. During the 1930s, Italy, Germany, and Japan committed acts of
A appeasement.
B aggression.
C neutrality.
D justice.

____ 3. In 1939, Great Britain and France declared war after Germany
A invaded Poland.
B invaded Czechoslovakia.
C annexed Austria.
D annexed part of France.

____ 4. Although the United States remained neutral when World War II began, Roosevelt looked for ways to
A persuade Italy to stop cooperating with Germany.
B make peace with Germany.
C convince Americans to support the Axis powers.
D help Great Britain and France.

____ 5. During World War II, African Americans
A fought in segregated units.
B fought in desegregated units.
C were not allowed to fight.
D fought for the Axis powers.

____ 6. During the war, Japanese Americans living on the West Coast were forced to
A leave the country.
B move to "relocation" camps.
C apologize for the actions of Japan.
D live in camps with German Americans and Italian Americans.

____ 7. The American victory at the Battle of Midway
A ended the war.
B was a turning point in the war in the Pacific.
C prevented the Allies from retaking the Philippines.
D caused Germany to surrender.

____ 8. D-Day, the start of the Allied invasion of Normandy, took place on
A August 6, 1945.
B August 14, 1945.
C June 6, 1944.
D December 7, 1941.

____ 9. Japan surrendered after the United States
A dropped atom bombs on two Japanese cities.
B adopted a policy of appeasement.
C released Japanese prisoners of war.
D invaded Japan.

____ 10. The Holocaust, one of the horrors of World War II, was the
A Japanese mistreatment of prisoners of war.
B slaughter of Europe's Jews by the Nazis.
C American bombing of Hiroshima.
D Italian invasion of Ethiopia.

CHAPTER

28 The Cold War Era
(1945–1991)

Vocabulary Development

A word's origin and history is known as its **etymology**. Word etymologies are often very interesting. For instance, the word *salary* comes from the Latin word *salarium*, which was a Roman soldier's allowance to buy salt. Salt, or *sal* in Latin, was a very precious commodity in ancient Rome.

Vocabulary
censure
exile
guerrilla
perjury

Directions: *Look at the table below. In the left-hand column is each of the above vocabulary words along with its definition. In the right-hand column is each etymology for the above vocabulary words. Draw a line from each word to its correct origin and history.*

Word with Definition	Word's Etymology
1. Censure—criticize harshly	A. This word from the early 1800s means a member of an independent group taking part in irregular fighting. It comes from the Spanish word for *war, guerra*.
2. Exile—forced absence from one's native land	
3. Guerrilla—a soldier who uses hit-and-run tactics	B. This word comes from the Latin verb, *perjurare*, which means to "swear to ill effect."
4. Perjury—the act of deliberately telling an untruth when under oath	C. This word comes from the Latin word *censura*, meaning "judgment."
	D. This word comes from an Old French word meaning "banishment."

Directions: *Using the four listed vocabulary words, write a paragraph about the chapter on the lines below. Be sure to use complete sentences and correct spelling in your writing.*

_____

_____

_____

_____

_____

_____

CHAPTER 28 Section 1 Guide to the Essentials

The Cold War Begins

VOCABULARY

satellite nation country dominated by a more powerful country

containment American policy designed to prevent Soviet influence from expanding

SUMMARY

After World War II, the United States and the Soviet Union became rivals. They competed for influence around the world but did not face each other directly in battle. This conflict became known as the Cold War. The United States distrusted the communist government of the Soviet Union, which rejected religion and the idea of private property. The Soviet Union also distrusted the United States, fearing invasion from the West. The distrust between the two sides increased when the Soviet Union did not allow fair elections in the countries it had freed from Germany. By 1948, the countries of Eastern Europe had become **satellite nations** of the Soviet Union.

President Truman decided on a policy of **containment.** Under the *Truman*

Doctrine, the United States helped nations threatened by communist expansion. Under the *Marshall Plan,* the United States helped the countries of Western Europe rebuild from war damage. American aid helped prevent communist revolutions in those countries.

Americans and Soviets clashed over the city of Berlin. (See time line.) The Berlin Wall became a symbol of the Cold War. In 1949, Cold War tensions increased when the Soviet Union tested an atomic bomb and the Communists gained power in China.

The United States joined with Western European nations to form the *North Atlantic Treaty Organization* (NATO). The Soviet Union formed its own alliances, called the *Warsaw Pact.*

COLD WAR TENSIONS IN BERLIN

1945 Allies divide Germany and its capital, Berlin.

1949 Soviets lift blockade.

1949–1961 3 million people flee from East to West Berlin.

1961 Communists build a wall separating East Berlin from West Berlin.

1945   1950   1955   1960   1965

1948 Soviet Union places blockade on West Berlin. United States supplies West Berlin by air.

REVIEW

Answer the following questions on a separate sheet of paper.

1. Why did the United States distrust the Soviet Union?

2. **Time Line Skills** What was the American response to the Soviet blockade of West Berlin?

CHAPTER

28 Section 1 Guided Reading and Review

The Cold War Begins

A. As You Read

Directions: As you read Section 1 in the textbook, list one cause and one effect of each of the following events:

1. After World War II, the Soviet Union's relationship with Britain and the United States was one of distrust.

   Cause: _____

   Effect: _____

2. President Truman decided on a Cold War policy of containment.

   Cause: _____

   Effect: _____

3. Secretary of State George Marshall urged passage of the Marshall Plan.

   Cause: _____

   Effect: _____

4. President Truman approved an airlift to West Berlin.

   Cause: _____

   Effect: _____

5. The East German government built the Berlin Wall.

   Cause: _____

   Effect: _____

B. Reviewing Key Terms

Directions: Complete each sentence by writing the correct term in the blank.

6. The _____ was an intense rivalry and standoff between the forces of communism and democracy.

7. After World War II, many eastern European countries became _____ of the Soviet Union.

8. The _____ was an imaginary barrier between communist nations and democratically governed countries.

9. The _____ set out a program encouraging nations to resist communist expansion.

10. The _____, an international peacekeeping force, was the successor to the failed League of Nations.

CHAPTER 28

Section 2 Guide to the Essentials

The Korean War Period

VOCABULARY

38th Parallel the invisible line of division between North Korea and South Korea

SUMMARY

After World War II, the Korean peninsula in northeast Asia was divided into two zones: communist North Korea and noncommunist South Korea. North Korea invaded South Korea in 1950. The United Nations, an international peacekeeping organization started after World War II, sent armed forces to stop the invasion. Americans led and made up most of these forces.

American forces under General Douglas MacArthur successfully drove North Korean forces back. This action angered China, North Korea's ally. President Truman wanted to avoid another world war. He called for peace agreements. Finally, after a truce was signed in 1953, Korea was divided at the **38th Parallel** into two countries, just as it had been before the war. To help preserve the truce, the United States continues to station thousands of American troops in South Korea.

Although North and South Korea remain divided, this war showed that the United States and its allies would fight to stop communist expansion.

The Cold War led to increased tensions within the United States. (See chart.) From 1950 to 1954, Senator Joseph McCarthy led an effort to search for communist spies within the American government.

THE COLD WAR AT HOME

Between 1946 and 1950, several people are arrested as Soviet spies.

↓

Loyalty of government workers is questioned. Nearly 3,000 are forced to resign.

↓

In 1950, McCarthy announces that he has a list of government officials who are Communists. He receives national attention.

↓

Fear and suspicion spread. Businesses and colleges question employees, and many are fired.

↓

When McCarthy charges that there are communists in the army, his popularity falls.

↓

In 1954, the Senate officially condemns McCarthy.

REVIEW

Answer the following questions on a separate sheet of paper.

1. Why did President Truman call for peace agreements?

2. **Chart Skills** How were government workers affected by the Cold War tensions at home?

CHAPTER 28

Section 2 Guided Reading and Review
The Korean War Period

A. As You Read

Directions: As you read Section 2 in the textbook, answer the following questions:

1. What was the immediate cause of the Korean War? _____

    _____

2. What was the UN response to the outbreak of fighting in Korea? _____

    _____

3. What happened at Inchon? _____

    _____

4. What role did China play in the Korean War? _____

    _____

5. What was the source of the dispute between Truman and MacArthur? _____

    _____

    _____

6. What were the terms of the armistice between the two sides? _____

    _____

7. What effect did the Korean War have on Americans at home? _____

    _____

8. How and why did Joseph McCarthy become notorious? _____

    _____

B. Reviewing Key Terms

Directions: Match each term with its definition.

Column I	Column II
___ 9. 38th parallel	a. officially condemn
___ 10. demilitarized zone	b. lying under oath
___ 11. perjury	c. line of latitude along which Korea was temporarily divided
___ 12. censure	d. an area with no military forces

CHAPTER

28 Section 3 Guide to the Essentials
Regional Conflicts

VOCABULARY

superpower a nation with enough military, political, and economic strength to influence events worldwide

SUMMARY

After World War II, colonies in Asia and Africa demanded independence. New nations, such as India, Pakistan, and the Philippines, emerged in Asia. By 1970, 50 independent states had formed in Africa.

Many regions around the world became battlegrounds in the Cold War struggle between the **superpowers.** The United States developed policies to deal with these countries. (See chart.) Cuba was one of those battlegrounds. In the 1960s, the superpowers clashed over Cuba in the *Cuban Missile Crisis.* In 1962, the Soviet Union began to build a nuclear missile base on Cuba. President Kennedy responded forcefully. The American navy prevented the Soviets from shipping missiles into Cuba. After a tense week, the Soviets agreed to remove the missiles. This was the closest that the United States and the Soviet Union ever came to a nuclear war.

Other parts of Latin America also played a role in the Cold War. The United States intervened throughout the region to stop communism. Between 1950 and 1990, American forces were sent to a number of Latin American countries. In the 1980s, the United States provided military aid to anticommunist groups in El Salvador and Nicaragua. The United States also sought to improve conditions in Latin America. American aid helped in the building of schools, roads, and hospitals.

The Cold War was essentially a rivalry between the two superpowers. By the 1950s, both nations had begun an arms race. Both sides built stockpiles of nuclear bombs and other weapons. By the 1970s, the two superpowers had enough weapons to destroy each other and the world many times over.

United States Cold War Strategies

Encouraging Reform	Stopping Communism
Encourage democratic reforms.	Support governments, even dictators, who oppose communism.
Provide economic aid.	Provide military aid to anticommunist groups.
Send volunteers to help people.	Send troops to put down rebellions.

REVIEW

Answer the following questions on a separate sheet of paper.

1. In which regions of the world did many new nations emerge after World War II?

2. **Chart Skills** How did the United States try to stop communism on Cold War battlegrounds?

CHAPTER

28 Section 3 Guided Reading and Review
Regional Conflicts

A. As You Read

Directions: As you read Section 3 in the textbook, describe the effects of the Cold War in each region or country.

1. Africa

   Effects: _____

   _____

   _____

   _____

2. Asia

   Effects: _____

   _____

   _____

   _____

3. Cuba

   Effects: _____

   _____

   _____

   _____

4. Latin America

   Effects: _____

   _____

   _____

   _____

B. Reviewing Key Terms

Directions: Briefly describe the purpose of each organization.

5. Alliance for Progress _____

6. Peace Corps _____

7. Organization of American States _____

8. National Aeronautics and Space Administration _____

CHAPTER 28
Section 4 Guide to the Essentials
The War in Vietnam

SUMMARY

After World War II, the French colony of Vietnam in Southeast Asia was divided into two nations. North Vietnam received aid from the Soviet Union. South Vietnam was backed by the United States. In the early 1960s, communist rebels in South Vietnam threatened to overthrow the government. President Kennedy believed in the domino theory. He reasoned that if South Vietnam fell to the communists, neighboring countries in Southeast Asia would also fall—like a row of dominoes. Kennedy sent military advisers to South Vietnam. Later, President Lyndon Johnson began to send troops. By 1968, more than 500,000 American troops had been sent to fight in the Vietnam War.

As the war became more intense, Americans divided into hawks and doves. Hawks felt that the United States had to stop the spread of communism. Doves said that the country should not interfere in a civil war among the Vietnamese. Also, they believed that the money spent on the war would be better spent at home. By the late 1960s, many antiwar protests took place, especially on college campuses.

The United States tried to remove itself from the conflict. The turning point was the *Tet Offensive.* Communist rebels, known as the Vietcong, stormed Saigon, the capital of South Vietnam. It was clear that American troops could not win the war. After years of peace talks, American troops finally left Vietnam in 1974. The war had a number of important results in both the United States and Southwest Asia. (See chart.) Many Americans began to wonder how far the country should go in the fight against communism.

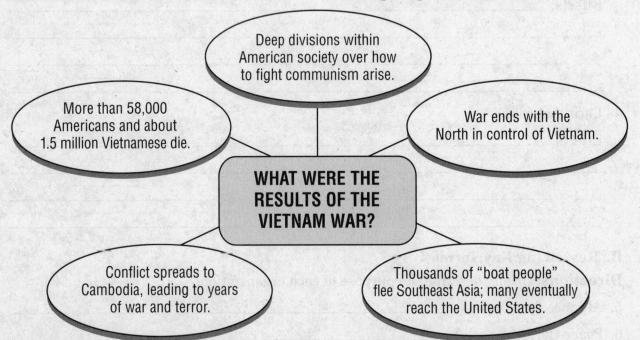

Deep divisions within American society over how to fight communism arise.

More than 58,000 Americans and about 1.5 million Vietnamese die.

War ends with the North in control of Vietnam.

WHAT WERE THE RESULTS OF THE VIETNAM WAR?

Conflict spreads to Cambodia, leading to years of war and terror.

Thousands of "boat people" flee Southeast Asia; many eventually reach the United States.

REVIEW
Answer the following questions on a separate sheet of paper.

1. What was the domino theory?

2. **Chart Skills** How many deaths occurred as a result of the Vietnam War?

A. As You Read

Directions: As you read Section 4 in the textbook, answer the following questions:

1. What were the results of the peace conference after Ho Chi Minh defeated the French in Vietnam? _____

_____

_____

2. Who were the Vietcong? _____

_____

_____

3. Why did the United States become involved in Vietnam? _____

_____

_____

4. What did the Gulf of Tonkin Resolution state? _____

_____

_____

5. How did Americans at home feel about the Vietnam War? _____

_____

_____

6. Why was the Tet Offensive a turning point in the war? _____

_____

_____

7. What effect did the Vietnam War have in Cambodia? _____

_____

_____

B. Reviewing Key Terms

Directions: Briefly describe each person's role in the Vietnam War.

8. Ho Chi Minh _____

9. Lyndon Johnson _____

10. Richard Nixon _____

Section 5 Guide to the Essentials
The Cold War Ends

VOCABULARY

détente effort to reduce tensions between the superpowers

SUMMARY

In the 1970s, President Richard M. Nixon looked for ways to ease world tensions. He improved relations with the People's Republic of China by visiting the country in 1972. Nixon toured the Great Wall of China and attended state dinners with Chinese leaders. This paved the way for formal diplomatic relations between the United States and China in 1979.

President Nixon also sought friendlier ties with the Soviet Union. He visited the country in 1972 in an effort to promote friendlier relations and reduce tensions between the two superpowers. The policy was known as **détente.** It resulted in increased trade and other contacts. More importantly, the two countries signed treaties to limit nuclear weapons. Then, in 1979, the Soviet Union invaded Afghanistan. Tensions increased again.

Cracks began to appear in the Soviet empire in the mid-1980s. A new Soviet leader, Mikhail Gorbachev, started economic and political reforms. Gorbachev called for glasnost, a policy of speaking out openly. Soon, people were demanding change throughout the Soviet Union and the satellite states of Eastern Europe. By 1989, communist governments had fallen in most Eastern European countries.

In 1991, the Soviet Union ceased to exist. It broke up into 15 separate nations. The largest and most powerful of these was Russia. The new countries began the difficult task of introducing democracy

and free market economies. The United States and its western allies attempted to help the transition by providing advice and economic aid. Finally, the long Cold War, which had cost the United States trillions of dollars and often divided the nation, came to an end. (See chart.)

DURING THE COLD WAR

- Arms race between United States and Soviet Union leads to threat of nuclear war.

- Cold War tensions result in armed conflicts.

EFFECTS OF THE COLD WAR

AFTER THE COLD WAR

- United States is world's greatest military power.

- Countries of Eastern Europe are struggling to create democratic governments.

- Other nations have worked to develop their own nuclear weapons.

REVIEW

Answer the following questions on a separate sheet of paper.

1. How did the United States respond to efforts by Russia and other new countries to introduce a free market economy?

2. **Chart Skills** Which nation was the world's greatest military power after the Cold War?

CHAPTER

28 Section 5 Guided Reading and Review
The Cold War Ends

A. As You Read

Directions: As you read Section 5 in the textbook, complete the following sentences:

1. Germans tore down _____ in 1989.

2. The United States had refused to recognize the Chinese communist government led by _____.

3. President Nixon became the first American President since the beginning of the Cold War to visit _____.

4. The Soviets and the Americans worked together on a policy of _____, which eased the tensions of foreign relations for both sides.

5. Soviet troops invaded _____ in 1979 in support of the communist government that had just seized power there.

6. _____ took office in 1981, firmly believing that the Soviet Union was the focus of evil in the modern world.

7. Soviet leader _____ instituted sweeping reforms to help his country solve its vast economic and social problems.

8. In Poland, labor leader _____ led the fight against the communists and later became the freely elected head of the government.

B. Reviewing Key Terms

Directions: Use each term correctly in a statement about the end of the Cold War.

9. SALT agreement _____

_____

10. Star Wars _____

_____

11. Solidarity _____

_____

12. glasnost _____

_____

CHAPTER

28 TEST

Identifying Main Ideas

Write the letter of the correct choice in the answer space.

____ 1. During the Cold War, the United States and the Soviet Union were
A satellite nations.
B allies.
C major trading partners.
D rivals.

____ 2. The Berlin Wall prevented
A people in East Berlin from fleeing to West Berlin.
B Cold War tensions.
C the Soviet Union from influencing East Berlin.
D East Germans from entering Berlin.

____ 3. McCarthy led a search for
A communist spies within the United States government.
B communist spies in Europe.
C anticommunist officials.
D an end to American fear of communism.

____ 4. After World War II, many Asian and African colonies demanded
A an end to the Cold War.
B a role in the Cold War.
C independence.
D a decrease in military aid.

____ 5. During the Cuban missile crisis, the Soviet Union
A successfully placed missiles in Cuba.
B attempted to build a missile base in Cuba.
C forced the United States to remove missiles from Cuba.
D forced Cuba to destroy its missiles.

____ 6. What was one policy that the United States followed in Latin America during the Cold War?
A helping overthrow military dictators
B allowing the Soviet Union a role in the region
C providing military and economic aid
D not intervening in Latin American affairs

____ 7. When communists in South Vietnam threatened to overthrow the government, Kennedy sent
A troops.
B military advisers.
C officials to negotiate peace.
D messages of peace.

____ 8. The Vietnam War resulted in
A the North in control of Vietnam.
B the South in control of Vietnam.
C Vietnam becoming a colony.
D Americans uniting in the fight against communism.

____ 9. Nixon's policy of détente brought
A rejection of arms agreements.
B an end to trade agreements.
C worse relations with communist countries.
D better relations with communist countries.

____ 10. The policies of Mikhail Gorbachev resulted in
A better relations between the United States and China.
B the breakup of the Soviet Union.
C the creation of the Berlin Wall.
D increased Soviet control.

Name_____ Class_____ Date_____

CHAPTER

29 Prosperity, Rebellion, and Reform (1945–1980)

Vocabulary Development

Latin roots are common in the English language. Knowing some common Latin roots makes it easier to guess the meaning of unknown words. For instance, the Latin root meaning "law," *jus*, can be seen in several English words, including *justice* and *judge*. It combines with the prefix *pre-*, meaning "before," to make the word *prejudice*, meaning "an opinion or judgment formed before the facts are known."

Examine the list below to see more examples of Latin roots and prefixes. This list provides the meaning of each Latin root or prefix, plus an English word that comes from it.

bi (two):	*bi*cycle
carn (flesh):	*carn*ivorous
form (shape):	con*form*
grad (to step, to go):	*grad*uation
greg (flock):	cong*reg*ation
her (to stick):	ad*her*ent
inflare (to blow into):	*infla*me
lingua (language):	*lingu*istics
magn (great):	*magn*ificent
mut (to change):	*mut*ilate
port (to carry):	im*port*ant
re (again):	*re*create
spec (to look):	*spec*tator
sub (under):	*sub*conscious
urb (city):	*urb*anization

Directions: *First, write the related Latin root or roots next to each of the vocabulary words. Then, describe how the meaning of the Latin root(s) relates to the meaning of the English word. It may be helpful to review the definitions of the vocabulary words in the textbook.*

Example: segregation   root: <u>greg</u>

Greg means "flock," so *segregate* means "to set apart from the flock."

1. bilingual   roots: _____ _____

    _____

2. inflation   root: _____

    _____

3. reform   roots: _____ _____

    _____

4. suburb   roots: _____ _____

CHAPTER

29 Section 1 Guide to the Essentials

Postwar Policies and Prosperity

VOCABULARY

baby boom increase after World War II in the number of babies being born in the United States

standard of living measurement of the quality of people's lives based on the amount of goods, services, and leisure time they have

suburb community outside a city

SUMMARY

After World War II, the United States faced the challenge of returning to peacetime conditions. Many feared that there would be no jobs for returning soldiers. Congress passed the GI Bill of Rights to help returning soldiers set up businesses, go to college, and build homes. President Truman tried to extend his Fair Deal, but conservatives in Congress blocked his plans. A Republican President, General Dwight Eisenhower, was elected in 1952. Eisenhower tried to follow a moderate course. He believed that the federal government should limit its spending, but he agreed to expand the benefits of Social Security.

The 1950s were a period of prosperity in the United States. One reason for growth

of the economy was the **baby boom** that occurred after World War II. Growing families needed new homes. Factories increased production of building materials, furniture, and other goods. More jobs were created. Government projects, including Cold War military production, also contributed to economic growth. The economic good times led to a higher **standard of living** for Americans.

As the economy grew, American lifestyles changed. More Americans began to live in **suburbs.** As suburbs grew, more people needed cars. Highways were built to link the nation. In cultural life, television brought great change. (See graph.) News and entertainment were brought right into people's homes.

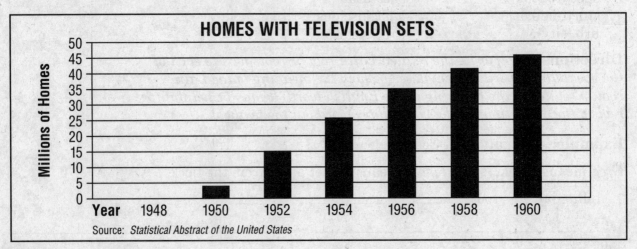

HOMES WITH TELEVISION SETS

Source: *Statistical Abstract of the United States*

REVIEW

Answer the following questions on a separate sheet of paper.

1. How did the American standard of living change during the 1950s?

2. **Graph Skills** About how many more homes had television sets in 1960 than in 1950?

CHAPTER
29 Section 1 Guided Reading and Review
Postwar Policies and Prosperity

A. As You Read

Directions: As you read Section 1 in the textbook, give one cause and one effect for each statement.

1. During World War II, Congress passed the GI Bill of Rights.

   Cause: _____

   Effect: _____

2. President Truman was reelected in 1948.

   Cause: _____

   Effect: _____

3. In the 1940s and 1950s, the American population grew by many millions.

   Cause: _____

   Effect: _____

4. Suburban communities of identical houses and shopping malls became common.

   Cause: _____

   Effect: _____

5. The federal government built thousands of miles of highways.

   Cause: _____

   Effect: _____

6. Television became a major source of news and entertainment.

   Cause: _____

   Effect: _____

B. Reviewing Key Terms

Directions: Use each term correctly in an accurate statement about postwar America.

7. inflation _____

8. baby boom _____

9. standard of living _____

10. beatnik _____

CHAPTER 29

Section 2 Guide to the Essentials

The Civil Rights Movement

VOCABULARY

integration mixing of different ethnic groups

civil disobedience nonviolent protests against unjust laws

SUMMARY

In the 1950s, African Americans and other minorities continued to face discrimination. In the South, laws enforced the segregation of the races. All across the country, African Americans could not get well-paying jobs. Many were kept from living and going to school where they pleased. Latinos faced similar problems.

The movement to win civil rights for all Americans gathered strength. (See chart.) In 1948, President Truman ordered **integration** in the armed forces. When American troops were sent to fight in the Korean War, black and white soldiers fought together in the same units. Meanwhile, civil rights lawyers used the courts to win equal rights. In 1954, the Supreme Court ruled that segregation in schools was unconstitutional in the case ***Brown* v. *Board of Education of Topeka.*** When officials in Little Rock, Arkansas, refused to integrate the schools, President Eisenhower sent troops to enforce the court decision.

Dr. Martin Luther King, Jr., emerged as a leader in the civil rights movement. King believed in nonviolent **civil disobedience.** He led peaceful marches and organized boycotts against companies that practiced discrimination. King led a year-long boycott of a bus company in Montgomery, Alabama, in 1956. The company agreed to integrate the buses and to hire African American drivers. Despite these victories, segregation and discrimination remained widespread in the United States.

Membership in civil rights group NAACP (National Association for the Advancement of Colored People) climbs.

The NAACP challenges segregation in court.

EARLY SUCCESSES OF THE CIVIL RIGHTS MOVEMENT

Jackie Robinson and other players integrate major league baseball.

Segregation in the armed forces ends.

REVIEW

Answer the following questions on a separate sheet of paper.

1. What strategy did Dr. Martin Luther King, Jr., use to protest discrimination?

2. **Chart Skills** What is the NAACP?

CHAPTER

29 Section 2 Guided Reading and Review
The Civil Rights Movement

A. As You Read

Directions: As you read Section 2 in the textbook, explain the importance of each of the following to the civil rights movement:

1. NAACP _____

_____

2. Brooklyn Dodgers _____

_____

3. *Brown* v. *Board of Education of Topeka* _____

_____

4. *Hernández* v. *Texas* _____

_____

5. Montgomery Improvement Association (MIA) _____

_____

6. Southern Christian Leadership Conference _____

_____

B. Reviewing Key Terms

Directions: Briefly define each term.

7. segregation _____

8. integration _____

9. civil rights movement _____

10. boycott _____

11. civil disobedience _____

CHAPTER 29

Section 3 Guide to the Essentials

Protest, Reform, and Doubt

VOCABULARY

counterculture movement a movement of young people who were critical of competition and the drive for success in America

SUMMARY

The 1960s and 1970s were years of crisis and change for Americans and their leaders. (See chart.) In 1961, President John F. Kennedy took office. He hoped to use the government to help the economy and to help poor Americans. His term ended tragically in November 1963, when he was shot and killed. Vice President Lyndon Johnson took office. Johnson proposed the Great Society, his plan to improve the standard of living of every American. Congress created Medicare, which helped people over age 65 pay their medical bills.

Protest movements grew in the 1960s despite social reform. Young people joined the **counterculture movement.** They protested the Vietnam War and called for peace and social equality.

Opposition to the Vietnam War led to the election of a Republican, Richard Nixon, as President in 1968. Nixon faced a number of economic problems, including high unemployment and slow economic growth. During his second term of office, he faced the Watergate Affair. His reelection campaign was accused of sending burglars into Democratic Party headquarters in 1972. Nixon denied knowing about the burglary, but tapes he kept showed that he had tried to cover up the crime. He resigned in August 1974. Vice President Gerald Ford took office.

Jimmy Carter became President in 1977, promising to bring new ideas to government. However, he was unable to bring down the high inflation that made life difficult for many Americans. In foreign policy, Carter took a firm stand on the need to support human rights around the world.

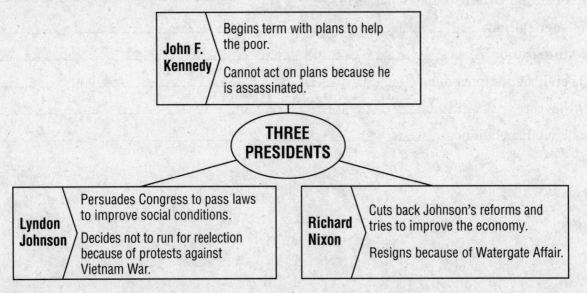

John F. Kennedy
Begins term with plans to help the poor.
Cannot act on plans because he is assassinated.

THREE PRESIDENTS

Lyndon Johnson
Persuades Congress to pass laws to improve social conditions.
Decides not to run for reelection because of protests against Vietnam War.

Richard Nixon
Cuts back Johnson's reforms and tries to improve the economy.
Resigns because of Watergate Affair.

REVIEW

Answer the following questions on a separate sheet of paper.

1. What event led to the resignation of President Nixon?
2. **Chart Skills** What led President Johnson to decide not to run for reelection?

CHAPTER

29 Section 3 Guided Reading and Review
Protest, Reform, and Doubt

A. As You Read

Directions: As you read Section 3 in the textbook, correct each of the following false statements:

1. Americans were concerned that presidential candidate Richard Nixon might be more loyal to the Catholic Church than to the country. _____

   _____

2. Lee Harvey Oswald became President after John F. Kennedy was assassinated.

   _____

3. The Warren Commission ordered that Lee Harvey Oswald be executed for killing the President. _____

4. Lyndon B. Johnson's Great Society programs took money from the poor and gave it to the wealthy. _____

5. The counterculture movement arose as a result of protests against the Vietnam War.

   _____

6. In the 1968 presidential election, Richard Nixon defeated Robert F. Kennedy.

   _____

7. Nixon is best remembered for his economic policies. _____

   _____

B. Reviewing Key Terms

Directions: Match each President with the description of his term of office.

Column I	Column II
_____ 8. John F. Kennedy	a. high inflation; strong support for human rights
_____ 9. Lyndon B. Johnson	b. created Peace Corps; began space program; assassinated in third year of his term
_____10. Richard M. Nixon	c. covered up his connection to burglary of Democratic national headquarters; resigned presidency under threat of impeachment
_____11. Gerald R. Ford	d. pardon of Nixon lost him much public support
_____12. Jimmy Carter	e. goal was for all Americans to achieve decent standard of living; created numerous social programs such as Head Start

CHAPTER
29 Section 4 Guide to the Essentials
The Crusade for Equal Rights

VOCABULARY

affirmative action program meant to provide equal opportunities for minorities and women

bilingual in two languages

SUMMARY

During the 1960s, the fight for equal rights grew stronger. The goals of the civil rights movement included ending segregation and discrimination in jobs, housing, and education. (See diagram.)

Many civil rights groups used nonviolent protest to achieve their goals. Freedom Riders traveled on buses in the South to integrate them. In 1963, Dr. Martin Luther King, Jr., spoke to 200,000 Americans at a march in Washington, D.C. As a result of these efforts, Congress passed civil rights laws. The Civil Rights Act of 1964 outlawed job discrimination. The Voting Rights Act of 1965 guaranteed that all citizens could vote.

During the 1970s, African Americans made some gains. They were elected to government positions. **Affirmative-action** programs helped provide equal opportunities in jobs and education.

Women also struggled to win equal rights. In 1966, the National Organization for Women (NOW) was founded to work for equality in jobs, pay, and education.

Latinos worked for change, too. Mexican Americans formed a union to protect migrant workers. The Voting Rights Act of 1975 provided for **bilingual** elections.

Native Americans fought for their rights, as well. The American Indian Movement (AIM) occupied Wounded Knee, South Dakota, to protest unfair treatment.

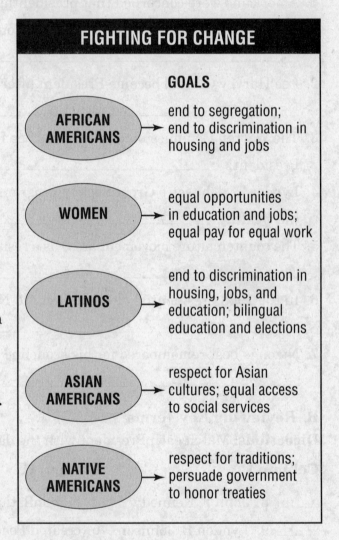

FIGHTING FOR CHANGE

GOALS

AFRICAN AMERICANS → end to segregation; end to discrimination in housing and jobs

WOMEN → equal opportunities in education and jobs; equal pay for equal work

LATINOS → end to discrimination in housing, jobs, and education; bilingual education and elections

ASIAN AMERICANS → respect for Asian cultures; equal access to social services

NATIVE AMERICANS → respect for traditions; persuade government to honor treaties

REVIEW
Answer the following questions on a separate sheet of paper.

1. What were the goals of civil rights laws passed in 1964 and 1965?

2. **Diagram Skills** What were the goals of Native American civil rights groups?

CHAPTER
29
Section 4 Guided Reading and Review
The Crusade for Equal Rights

A. As You Read

Directions: As you read Section 4 in the textbook, identify and briefly describe the various methods people used to protest during the civil rights movement.

1.	
2.	
3.	

B. Reviewing Key Terms

Directions: Briefly identify or describe the importance of each of the following:

4. Greensboro, North Carolina _____

5. Congress of Racial Equality _____

6. Voting Rights Act _____

7. Black Panthers _____

8. Malcolm X _____

9. Watts, Los Angeles, California _____

10. Thurgood Marshall _____

© Pearson Education, Inc. All rights reserved.

CHAPTER
29 TEST
Identifying Main Ideas
Write the letter of the correct choice in the answer space.

____ 1. President Eisenhower believed in
A ending the New Deal.
B strengthening the New Deal.
C increasing federal spending.
D limiting federal spending.

____ 2. One reason for the growth of the economy in the 1950s was the baby boom that occurred
A after World War II.
B during World War II.
C in the 1930s.
D as a result of World War I.

____ 3. The American standard of living is based on the
A growth of American suburbs.
B number of babies being born in the United States.
C American factory output.
D goods, services, and leisure time Americans have.

____ 4. After World War II, President Truman
A continued segregation in the military.
B ended segregation in the military.
C avoided the problem of segregation in the military.
D kept segregation in the military until after the Korean War.

____ 5. In 1954, the Supreme Court ruled that segregation in schools was
A constitutional where it existed.
B a local matter.
C legal.
D unconstitutional.

____ 6. Dr. Martin Luther King, Jr., believed in
A civil disobedience.
B violent protests.
C segregation.
D separate schools for African Americans.

____ 7. Which program did Congress pass to help older people pay medical bills?
A Human Rights laws
B the Great Society
C Voting Rights Act
D Medicare

____ 8. President Carter believed that human rights should
A play no role in American foreign policy.
B be supported by the United States.
C be a minor factor in American foreign policy.
D be supported in some areas but not in others.

____ 9. Affirmative-action programs were designed to provide
A equal opportunities for people who faced discrimination.
B ways for states to continue discrimination.
C jobs for students.
D a way for workers to form a union.

____ 10. Which group was founded to work for equal rights for women?
A AIM
B Freedom Riders
C NAACP
D NOW

Name_____ Class_____ Date_____

30 The Nation in a New World
(1970–Present)

Vocabulary Development

<u>Vocabulary</u>
Earth Summit
Environmental
    Protection Agency
environmentalist
global warming
renewable resource

One of America's first **environmentalists**, or persons concerned with protecting the environment, was President Theodore Roosevelt. In the early years of the twentieth century, Roosevelt encouraged Americans to be mindful of the environment, and he also gave support to the establishment of natural parks. Decades later, the **Environmental Protection Agency (EPA)** was established in 1970. The EPA is an independent agency of the federal government that acts to protect the nation's environment from pollution.

Two major topics of concern to environmentalists are global warming and renewable resources. **Global warming** is a condition that occurs because of the pollutants produced from the burning of fossil fuels. Many scientists believe that as these pollutants build up in the atmosphere, they are causing a slow warming of Earth's temperatures. Another major issue is reducing the rate at which natural resources are used up. Nonrenewable resources, including coal and petroleum, exist in limited amounts and will someday run short. On the other hand, **renewable resources**, such as solar and wind power, are recreated by nature. In 1992, President George H. W. Bush attended a meeting in Brazil called the **Earth Summit**, in which world leaders addressed environmental concerns.

Directions: *Write a letter to a leader in your community, such as your mayor or city councilperson. This letter should use at least four of the vocabulary words from the list. Your letter should suggest a way that your community could help protect the environment.*

_____
_____
_____
_____
_____
_____
_____
_____
_____
_____
_____
_____

CHAPTER
30 Section 1 Guide to the Essentials
The Conservative Revolt

VOCABULARY

deregulation reduction of restrictions on business

SUMMARY

In 1980, Republican Ronald Reagan was elected President. His election began a new conservative era in American politics. Conservatives had a number of goals. (See chart.) Their main goal was to limit the size of the federal government.

President Reagan persuaded Congress to cut taxes. He also cut government spending on social programs. Reagan increased military spending, however. The federal budget deficit soared. Another policy President Reagan pursued was **deregulation.**

George Bush was elected President in 1988. Bush wanted to continue the Reagan policies. He vowed not to raise taxes, but he was not able to keep this promise. A recession took place during his term in office.

Democrat Bill Clinton won election as President in 1992. He succeeded in reducing the federal budget deficit. A Clinton plan to reform the health care system, however, was defeated in Congress. In 1994, Republicans won control of Congress. After many conflicts, Congress and Clinton compromised on a plan to balance the federal budget by the year 2002. Clinton easily won reelection in 1996. The economy boomed.

In 2000, Vice President Al Gore ran against George W. Bush, son of President Bush. Gore won the popular vote by a narrow margin. A number of votes in Florida were questioned, however. Gore called for a selective recount, but Bush opposed it. Both sides went to court. After 46 days, the Supreme Court ruled against Gore. Bush was declared the winner.

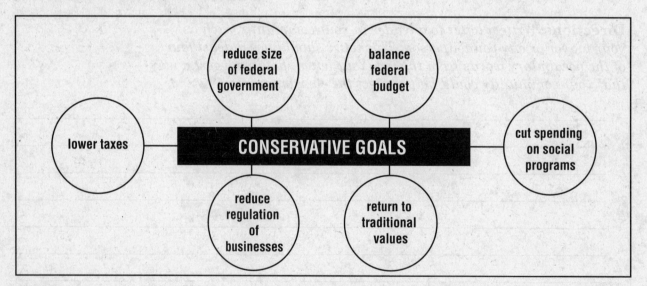

REVIEW

Answer the following questions on a separate sheet of paper.

1. What occurred two years into President Clinton's first term in office?
2. **Chart Skills** Identify three conservative goals.

Name_____ Class_____ Date_____

A. As You Read

Directions: As you read Section 1 in the textbook, answer the following questions:

1. Why did the country become more conservative as the century ended? _____

_____

2. What were the goals of conservative citizens and politicians? _____

_____

3. Why was Ronald Reagan called "the Great Communicator"? _____

_____

4. What were Reagan's economic goals? _____

_____

5. What were the problems in George H.W. Bush's presidency? _____

_____

6. What were the successes in Bill Clinton's presidency? _____

_____

7. What was unusual about the 2000 presidential election? _____

_____

B. Reviewing Key Terms

Directions: Briefly identify or define each term.

8. Moral Majority _____

_____

9. Reaganomics _____

_____

10. deregulation _____

_____

11. Contract with America _____

_____

Section 2 Guide to the Essentials
American Leadership in a New World

SUMMARY

After the Soviet Union collapsed, the United States became the last superpower. In the 1990s, the country assumed new and greater responsibilities. Sometime it acted as a mediator, working to help conflicting parties iron out their differences. American leaders continued to use military and diplomatic power where they thought it necessary. (See chart.)

The United States helped promote democracy by encouraging developing countries to practice economic and political freedoms. Countries such as the Philippines, China, North and South Korea, and South Africa have attempted to open their markets or to employ new political systems.

During the 1990s, conflict erupted in the Eastern European country of Yugoslavia. After the fall of communism, Yugoslavia split into several different countries and many quarreling ethnic groups. In 1995,

American negotiators helped arrange a peace treaty in Bosnia, one of the new countries. American troops went to Bosnia to help maintain the peace.

In 1992, American forces led a United Nations mission to Somalia to help distribute food during a severe famine. The United States also helped arrange a peace agreement in Northern Ireland, a region that had experienced violent conflict between Catholics and Protestants for many years.

Another international challenge has been halting the spread of nuclear arms. In 1996, the United States helped draft a treaty outlawing the testing of nuclear weapons. Some countries, however, refused to sign the treaty. In 1998, India and Pakistan both tested nuclear bombs. People outside those countries feared that the testing might lead to a new nuclear arms race.

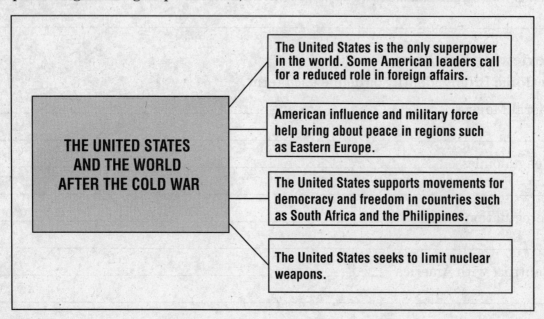

THE UNITED STATES AND THE WORLD AFTER THE COLD WAR

The United States is the only superpower in the world. Some American leaders call for a reduced role in foreign affairs.

American influence and military force help bring about peace in regions such as Eastern Europe.

The United States supports movements for democracy and freedom in countries such as South Africa and the Philippines.

The United States seeks to limit nuclear weapons.

REVIEW
Answer the following questions on a separate sheet of paper.

1. What happened to Yugoslavia after the fall of communism?

2. **Chart Skills** Where in the world has the United States supported democracy since the Cold War ended?

CHAPTER

30 Section 2 Guided Reading and Review
American Leadership in a New World

A. As You Read

Directions: As you read Section 2 in the textbook, complete the following sentences:

1. The United States became the world's only superpower when _____
_____

2. Filipino protest against dictator Marcos resulted in _____
_____

3. China responded to a people's campaign for democratic reforms by _____
_____

4. The United States and Russia continued to work together to _____
_____

5. The Comprehensive Test Ban Treaty failed because _____
_____

B. Reviewing Key Terms

Directions: Match each term with its definition.

Column I	Column II
_____ 6. apartheid	a. competition to have the most weapons
_____ 7. sanctions	b. strict separation of races
_____ 8. global democracy	c. establishment of freely elected governments all over the world
_____ 9. arms race	d. measures designed to make a country change its policies

CHAPTER 30

Section 3 Guide to the Essentials

The Spread of Regional Conflict

SUMMARY

In 1973, the United States experienced an oil shortage. The Arab nations of the Middle East cut back on the amount of oil they exported. They were protesting American support for Israel, a Jewish state founded in 1948 in the land known as Palestine. The oil embargo showed how much the United States depended on foreign oil.

The United States has had a long history of involvement in the Middle East. (See chart.) It strongly supports Israel. It also has ties to the Islamic Arab states in the region. The United States has tried to bring peace between Israel and its Arab neighbors. The United States has also worked for peace between Israel and the Palestinians. Palestinians are Arabs who left Israel when it was founded in 1948.

The United States fought a war in the Middle East. In 1990, Iraq invaded neighboring Kuwait, a country with a large supply of oil. In this Persian Gulf War, the United States led many other nations in a successful effort to drive Iraq's forces from Kuwait.

The United States was shocked by terrorist attacks on September 11, 2001. Thousands of people were killed when airplanes struck the World Trade Center in New York City and the Pentagon near Washington, D.C. The United States reacted by declaring war on terrorism and countries that help terrorists, such as Afghanistan. American and British troops were sent to fight in Afghanistan, in southwest Asia. A majority of Americans supported this effort.

THE UNITED STATES AND THE MIDDLE EAST AND CENTRAL ASIA	
1973	Arab nations cut oil exports. Americans realize how much they depend on foreign sources of oil.
1977	President Carter helps negotiate peace agreement between Israel and Egypt.
1979	Iran takes American hostages and holds them until early 1981.
1991	The United States and UN allies push Iraq out of Kuwait in Persian Gulf War.
1993	President Clinton hosts ceremony at which Israel signs peace agreement with Palestinians.
2001	American and British forces begin war on terrorism by attacking forces in Afghanistan.

REVIEW

Answer the following questions on a separate sheet of paper.

1. Name two ways that oil in the Middle East affected the United States.

2. **Chart Skills** What two peace agreements did the United States help negotiate between Israel and its Arab neighbors?

CHAPTER
30 Section 3 Guided Reading and Review
The Spread of Regional Conflict

A. As You Read

Directions: As you read Section 3 in the textbook, fill in details about each regional conflict. For those conflicts not directly involving the United States, include a brief description of the role the United States has played in each conflict.

Arab-Israeli Conflict
1.

Iran and Iraq
2.

Terrorism and the United States
3.

B. Reviewing Key Terms

Directions: Briefly identify each term. Note to which of the above conflicts it is most relevant.

4. OPEC _____

5. Camp David Accords _____

6. Palestinian Liberation Organization _____

7. Office of Homeland Security _____

CHAPTER

30 Section 4 Guide to the Essentials
A Global Economy

★

VOCABULARY

trade deficit difference that occurs when a nation buys more goods and services from foreign countries than it sells to them

renewable resource resource that can be replaced by nature or people

e-commerce business or trade over the Internet

SUMMARY

Today American companies do business around the world. But American workers are paid more than workers in many other countries. So, many American goods cost more to produce than similar foreign goods. Foreign competition has caused a **trade deficit.** (See graph.)

In 1993, Congress approved the North American Free Trade Agreement (NAFTA). The purpose of this treaty was to end trade restrictions between Canada, Mexico, and the United States. Critics of NAFTA argued that free trade would cause a loss of American jobs. Companies might move factories to Mexico, where workers receive lower pay.

The environment is another issue that affects the world economy. Environmental problems require nations to work together. At the Earth Summit in Brazil in 1992, world leaders focused on rising global temperatures and holes in the ozone layer. At home, environmentalists called on Americans to reduce the energy they use and to develop **renewable resources.**

Technology ties the world together even as it changes the way people do business. In recent years, computers have had the greatest impact on people's lives. Using

pagers, cell phones, personal computers, and the Internet, people around the world can exchange information instantly. **E-commerce** allows businesses to trade online.

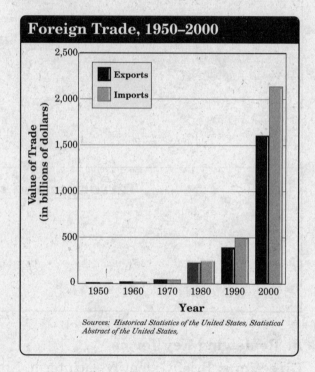

Foreign Trade, 1950–2000

Value of Trade (in billions of dollars)

■ Exports
■ Imports

Year

Sources: *Historical Statistics of the United States, Statistical Abstract of the United States,*

REVIEW
Answer the following questions on a separate sheet of paper.

1. How have computers changed people's live?

2. **Graph Skills** In 1990, did the United States import more or less than it exported?

CHAPTER

30 Section 4 Guided Reading and Review
A Global Economy

A. As You Read

Directions: As you read Section 4 in the textbook, fill in the missing causes and effects.

Causes	Effects
American companies pay workers higher wages than do companies in most other nations.	1.
2.	Trade boomed among Mexico, Canada, and the United States, and new jobs were created.
Environmental reformers called attention to the dangers of industrial waste and chemical pesticides.	3.
A scientist dreamed of a vast inter-connected network of computers.	4.

B. Reviewing Key Terms

Directions: Briefly define each term.

5. trade deficit _____

6. environmentalists _____

7. renewable resource _____

8. global warming _____

9. Internet _____

10. e-commerce _____

CHAPTER

30

Section 5 Guide to the Essentials

New Challenges for the Nation

VOCABULARY

illegal alien person who enters the country without legal permission

SUMMARY

Americans continue to work for equal rights and greater opportunities. In recent years, Native Americans have worked to develop economic independence. African Americans have fought for economic success and political power. Women have continued to press for equal treatment. More women work outside the home than ever before. (See graph.) Americans with disabilities also have struggled for equal rights. The ***Americans with Disabilities Act of 1990*** outlawed discrimination against people with disabilities. Older Americans have, as a political group, developed a powerful voice.

The United States is also being reshaped by new patterns of immigration. In 1965, Congress ended the quota system of the 1920s. Many of the new immigrants came from Asia and Latin America. This was a change from earlier waves of immigrants, who came mostly from Europe. Some immigrants are **illegal aliens.** Congress and the states have passed laws to reduce illegal immigration.

Immigration is just one challenge facing Americans in the twenty-first century. Although greater opportunities exist, racial discrimination and poverty continue. Many lives are being ruined by the abuse of drugs.

Terrorist acts of violence have occurred in the United States. As they face these problems, Americans continue to work together to build a better nation.

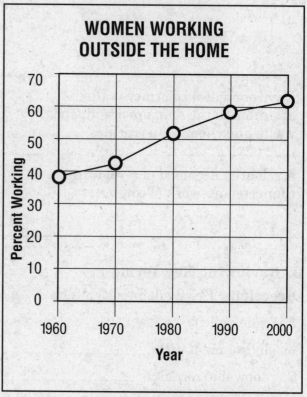

Source: *Statistical Abstract of the United States*

REVIEW

Answer the following questions on a separate sheet of paper.

1. Describe how immigration to the United States has changed since Congress ended the quota system.

2. **Graph Skills** Approximately what percentage of women worked outside the home in 2000?

CHAPTER

30 Section 5 Guided Reading and Review

New Challenges for the Nation

A. As You Read

Directions: As you read Section 5 in the textbook, answer the following questions:

1. Why do so many Asians immigrate to the United States? _____

_____

_____

2. What is the function of the Immigration Reform and Control Act? _____

_____

_____

3. What is the current status of Native Americans? _____

_____

_____

4. What is the Americans with Disabilities Act? _____

_____

_____

5. Why has the population of the United States grown older? _____

_____

_____

6. What are two major challenges the United States faces in the twenty-first century?

_____

_____

B. Reviewing Key Terms

Directions: Briefly define each term.

7. refugee _____

8. illegal alien _____

9. mainstreaming _____

CHAPTER 30 TEST

Identifying Main Ideas

Write the letter of the correct choice in the answer space.

____ 1. What happened to the federal budget deficit during President Reagan's terms in office?

A It fell.

B It stayed the same.

C It rose.

D It was eliminated.

____ 2. Which was a goal of conservatives during the 1980s and 1990s?

A deregulation

B a larger federal government

C increased social spending

D a movement away from traditional values

____ 3. The United States became the only superpower in the world when

A American forces won World War II.

B the Soviet Union ceased to exist.

C the Persian Gulf War ended.

D peace came to the Middle East.

____ 4. During the 1990s, the United States worked to

A help Russia build nuclear weapons.

B spread nuclear weapons.

C help India and Pakistan develop nuclear weapons.

D limit nuclear weapons.

____ 5. In its Middle East policy, the United States attempted to

A ignore events in the Middle East.

B bring peace to the Middle East.

C convince Israel to attack its Arab neighbors.

D help Egypt make peace with its Arab neighbors.

____ 6. The United States led forces to drive the Iraqis out of

A Israel.

B Kuwait.

C Iran.

D Egypt.

____ 7. Some people opposed NAFTA because they feared it would

A raise tariffs.

B reduce automobile production.

C cause a loss of American jobs.

D hurt some industries and the environment.

____ 8. In recent years, which technological device has had the greatest impact on people's lives?

A the computer

B the DVD player

C the cell phone

D the pager

____ 9. During recent decades, the number of women working outside the home has

A increased steadily.

B remained the same.

C decreased slightly.

D gone up and down.

____ 10. In the 1960s, the pattern of immigration changed when

A illegal aliens arrived.

B people from Europe began to arrive.

C Congress ended the quota system.

D the world entered a global depression.

Epilogue The United States Since 1865

Vocabulary Development

Using what you learned from the Epilogue, use the vocabulary words to complete the following sentences correctly.

Vocabulary
civil rights
  movement
Cold War
Homestead Act
isolationism
monopoly
New Deal
terrorism
urbanization

1. After World War I, the United States returned to a policy of _____.

2. _____ has been used by a number groups to promote political goals.

3. When one company creates a _____, the lack of economic competition usually causes prices to rise.

4. The _____ gave free land to settlers in the West.

5. One of the most important trends in the population of the United States in the 20th century was _____.

6. The _____ was designed to lift the economy out of the Great Depression.

7. Soon after the end of World War II, a new international conflict, the _____, began.

8. Some of the most important achievements of the _____, including the Voting Rights Act, came during the presidency of Lyndon Johnson.

Directions: *Using at least four of the listed vocabulary words, write a paragraph about the chapter on the lines below. Be sure to use complete sentences and correct spelling in your writing.*

_____

_____

_____

_____

_____

_____

Epilogue Section 1 Guide to the Essentials

Entering the Modern Times

VOCABULARY

transcontinental railroad railroad that stretches across a continent

corporation a business owned by investors

monopoly a company or group having control of all or nearly all of the business of an industry

urbanization movement of population from farms to cities

SUMMARY

The United States had been expanding westward since the Louisiana Purchase. After the Civil War, this westward expansion sped up. Mining, cattle ranching, and farming attracted people to the West. With the Homestead Act of 1862, the federal government promised free land to anyone who would farm it for five years.

The government also gave land and money to encourage railroad building. In 1869, two railroad companies completed the first **transcontinental railroad**, which linked the Atlantic coast to the Pacific.

Westward expansion was a disaster for Native Americans. Most western Indians were forced onto reservations.

American business and industry boomed after the Civil War. New technology, including electricity, helped this growth. Railroads spurred industrial growth, but some railroad owners abused power by fixing prices and bribing public officials. (See chart.)

Many businesses organized themselves as corporations. A **corporation** sells shares of stock in exchange for capital, or money to help the company grow. Some corporations, such as U.S. Steel and the Standard Oil Company, grew into giant monopolies that controlled entire industries. In response to harsh working conditions, a growing number of factory workers began to organize into unions.

In the late 1800s, millions of people immigrated to the United States. Immigration contributed to the rapid growth of cities. The process of population shifting from farms to cities is called **urbanization**. Living conditions for poor people in the cities were crowded and unhealthy. A variety of reformers worked to improve these conditions.

CAUSES

- Railroad growth helps other businesses grow
- Businesses become corporations
- Nation has rich supply of natural resources

THE RISE OF INDUSTRY IN THE UNITED STATES

EFFECTS

- Steel and oil become giant industries
- Monopolies control important industries
- Factory workers face harsh conditions

REVIEW

Answer the following questions on a separate sheet of paper.

1. How did westward expansion affect Native Americans?
2. **Chart Skills** What were two effects of the rise of industry in the United States?

Epilogue Section 1 Guided Reading and Review

Entering the Modern Times

A. As You Read

Directions: As you read Section 1 in the textbook, answer the following questions:

1. What were some of the reasons people moved west after the Civil War? _____
_____

2. What effect did the westward movement have on Native Americans? _____
_____

3. What effect did technology have on American industry after the Civil War? _____
_____

4. What was the relationship between banks and corporations? _____
_____

5. What are the arguments for and against monopolies? _____
_____

6. What was the importance of the American Federation of Labor? _____
_____

7. What effect did immigrants have on American cities? _____
_____

B. Reviewing Key Terms

Directions: Briefly identify each of the following people.

8. Thomas Edison _____

9. Andrew Carnegie _____

10. J. P. Morgan _____

11. John D. Rockefeller _____

Epilogue Section 2 Guide to the Essentials

A New Role for the Nation

VOCABULARY

Progressives reformers in the late 1800s and early 1900s who wanted to improve American life

Nineteenth Amendment gives women the right to vote

Spanish-American War war between Spain and the United States in 1898

SUMMARY

The period known as the Progressive Era, from 1898 to 1917, was marked by attempts to reduce the power of big business, improve social conditions, and clean up political corruption. The **Progressives** were people who wanted to improve society. The Progressives backed several constitutional amendments, including the **Nineteenth Amendment**, which guaranteed women the right to vote. Presidents Roosevelt, Taft, and Wilson also backed reforms regulating business. (See chart.)

In the late 1800s, the United States purchased Alaska and took over the islands of Midway and Samoa, as well as the Hawaiian Islands. The United States also competed with European nations for trade in China.

In 1898, the United States won a quick victory in the **Spanish-American War** and gained control of Cuba, Puerto Rico, Guam, and the Philippines. Later, the United States began construction of the Panama Canal, connecting the Atlantic and Pacific oceans.

In 1914, World War I broke out in Europe. The war pitted the Central Powers—Germany, Austria-Hungary, and the Ottoman Empire—against the Allied Powers of France, Britain, and Russia. The United States joined the Allies in 1917. American troops landed in France in time to help defeat the Central Powers. The war ended in November. Millions of people had died, and millions more were wounded. President Wilson tried to shape peace settlement with his "Fourteen Points," but many of his ideas were left out of the final treaty.

NEW LAWS BRING REFORM	
LAW	**REFORM**
Pendleton Act (1883)	created Civil Service Commission to make sure that only qualified people got federal jobs
Interstate Commerce Act (1887)	created Interstate Commerce Commission to oversee the railroad companies
Sherman Antitrust Act (1890)	made it illegal for companies to restrict competition

REVIEW

Answer the following questions on a separate sheet of paper.

1. What event set off World War I?

2. **Chart Skills** In which five-year period did American foreign trade grow the most?

Epilogue Section 2 Guided Reading and Review

A New Role for the Nation

A. As You Read

Directions: As you read Section 2 in the textbook, complete the following sentences:

1. The Progressive Era gets its name from _____

_____

2. The Sixteenth Amendment was important because _____

_____

3. Theodore Roosevelt's reforms included _____

_____

4. United States foreign policy began changing because _____

_____

5. Roosevelt's statement that the United States had a right to intervene in Latin American

affairs became known as the _____

_____

6. America declared war on Germany because _____

_____

B. Reviewing Key Terms

Directions: Match each term with its definition.

Column I	Column II
_____ 7. muckraker	a. crusading journalist
_____ 8. isolationism	b. control of several countries by one country
_____ 9. imperialism	c. limited involvement in world affairs

Epilogue Section 3 Guide to the Essentials
The Great Depression and World War II

VOCABULARY

Great Depression worst period of economic decline in United States history, beginning in 1929

New Deal program of President Franklin D. Roosevelt to end the Great Depression

D-Day (June 6, 1944) day of the invasion of Western Europe by Allied Forces

SUMMARY

During the 1920s the U.S. economy grew quickly. Then, in 1929, the stock market crashed, triggering the **Great Depression**. Banks closed, wiping out people's savings, and unemployment soared.

In 1932, Americans elected President Franklin Roosevelt. He instituted a series of new programs called the New Deal, which had three main goals: relief for the unemployed, plans for recovery, and reforms to prevent another depression.

In the 1920s and 1930s, totalitarian governments came to power in several countries. Adolf Hitler and his Nazi party took control in Germany. Hitler's armies began to invade neighboring countries one by one. When Hitler invaded Poland, Britain and France declared war. World War II pitted the Axis Powers—Germany, Italy, and Japan—against the Allies, including Britain, France, China, the Soviet Union, and many other countries. In the early years of the war, Germany took over most of Europe. Japan invaded large parts of Asia. During the war years, Hitler's government systematically killed more than 6 million Jews, as well as millions of others. (See chart.)

The United States remained neutral, but sent economic aid to the Allies. Then, in 1941, Japan attacked the American fleet at Pearl Harbor, Hawaii, bringing the United

DEATHS IN WORLD WAR II		
	MILITARY DEAD	**CIVILIAN DEAD**
Britain	389,000	65,000
France	211,000	108,000
Soviet Union	7,500,000	15,000,000
United States	292,000	*
Germany	2,850,000	5,000,000
Italy	77,500	100,000
Japan	1,576,000	300,000

*Very small number

All figures are estimates. Source: Henri Michel, *The Second World War*

States into the war on the Allied side.

In several key battles the Allies gradually gained the upper hand, and on **D-Day**, June 6, 1944, Allied troops landed on the coast of France and pushed eastward toward Germany. In May 1945 Hitler committed suicide and Germany surrendered. The war against Japan continued until August 1945, when the United States dropped two atomic bombs on Japanese cities, bringing Japan's surrender.

REVIEW

Answer the following questions on a separate sheet of paper.

1. What were the three main goals of the New Deal?
2. **Chart Skills** What country had the most civilian deaths during the war?

Epilogue Section 3 Guided Reading and Review

The Great Depression and World War II

A. As You Read

Directions: As you read Section 3 in the textbook, fill in details about each decade in American life.

1920s: The Jazz Age
1.
1930s: The Great Depression
2.
1940s: World War II
3.

B. Reviewing Key Terms

Directions: Briefly define each term. Note whether it applies to the 1920s, 1930s, or 1940s.

4. flapper _____

5. jazz _____

6. margin buying _____

7. Social Security _____

8. Holocaust _____

9. deficit spending _____

Epilogue Section 4 Guide to the Essentials

The Cold War and the Civil Rights Era

VOCABULARY

Cold War after World War II, long period of rivalry between the Soviet Union and the United States

civil rights movement the efforts of African Americans to win equal rights

SUMMARY

At the end of World War II, tensions increased between the Soviet Union and the United States. The Soviets set up communist governments in Eastern European countries and seemed to intend to spread communism throughout the world. In response, the United States began to send aid to anticommunist governments and groups. This was the start of a conflict known as the **Cold War**. Crises of the Cold War included the blockade of West Berlin and the Berlin Airlift; the Korean War; and the Cuban Missile Crisis. (See chart.)

After World War II, African Americans increased their efforts to gain equal rights. Their struggle became known as the **civil rights movement**. In Brown v. Board of Education (1954), the Supreme Court declared that schools had to integrate. This started the process of ending segregation of other facilities as well. Martin Luther King, Jr., emerged as the most visible leader of the civil rights movement. He urged the use of nonviolent protest against unjust laws.

The civil rights movement grew in the 1960s. Key new civil rights laws included the Civil Rights Act, the Voting Rights Act, and a constitutional amendment that outlawed poll taxes. Other groups, including Mexican Americans and women, also increased their fight for equal rights.

In the 1960s, the United States became involved in the Vietnam War. Between 1961 and 1973, more than 58,000 American troops were killed, and American society was bitterly divided. Finally, in 1974, the last American troops were withdrawn from Vietnam. Soon after, North Vietnam defeated South Vietnam.

United States Cold War Strategies

Encouraging Reform	Stopping Communism
Encourage democratic reforms.	Support governments, even dictators, who oppose communism.
Provide economic aid.	Provide military aid to anticommunist groups.
Send volunteers to help people.	Send troops to put down rebellions.

REVIEW

Answer the following questions on a separate sheet of paper.

1. What were two other groups that were inspired by the African American civil rights movement?

2. **Chart Skills** How did the United States try to stop communism on Cold War battlegrounds?

Epilogue Section 4 Guided Reading and Review
The Cold War and the Civil Rights Era

A. As You Read
Directions: As you read Section 4 in the textbook, fill in the missing causes and effects.

Causes	Effects
Soviet leaders indicated their intent to spread communism throughout the world.	1.
2.	The Marshall Plan allotted $12 billion to help Europe recover.
Communist Fidel Castro seized control of Cuba.	3.
4.	People fought for African American rights in the civil rights movement.
5.	The United Farm Workers gained better working conditions.
More and more American troops were sent to Vietnam.	6.

B. Reviewing Key Terms
Directions: Briefly explain each person's role in the Cold War/Civil Rights era.

7. Fidel Castro _____

8. John F. Kennedy _____

9. Rosa Parks _____

10. Martin Luther King, Jr. _____

11. Lyndon Johnson _____

12. César Chavez _____

Epilogue Section 5 Guide to the Essentials

Into the Future

VOCABULARY

Reaganomics President Reagan's economic program that cut taxes, cut federal spending on social programs, and increased military spending

terrorism deliberate use of violence to spread fear and achieve political goals

SUMMARY

Government programs expanded in the 1960s and 1970s. In the 1980s, President Ronald Reagan cut taxes, reduced spending on social programs, and increased military spending—a policy known as **Reaganomics**. Reagan's Vice President, George H.W. Bush, was elected in 1988 and continued many of Reagan's policies.

In 1992, Bill Clinton was elected President. His improper relationship with a White House intern led to his impeachment. In 1999, the Senate acquitted Clinton. George W. Bush, son of the former President, narrowly defeated Vice President, Al Gore to become President in 2001.

The Cold War, which had dominated foreign policy since the late 1940s, had ended by the mid-1990s. Communist governments in Eastern Europe collapsed, and finally the Soviet Union itself broke apart. (See chart.)

Other hot spots, including the Balkans and the Middle East, presented dangers. In 1991, Iraq invaded Kuwait. The United States led a UN coalition and forced Iraqi troops out of Kuwait. **Terrorism**, the deliberate use of random violence for political reasons, also presented a danger. On September 11, 2001, terrorists crashed two passenger planes into the World Trade Center in New York City, killing more than 3,000 people. American forces successfully invaded Afghanistan, where the terrorists were based, and waged a wider war against terrorism.

The nation faced other changes and challenges. The United States now competes for trade with European and Asian nations that have strong economies. Computers have become common in homes and offices, and the Internet has brought people and nations closer together. New advances have continued in the area of space exploration.

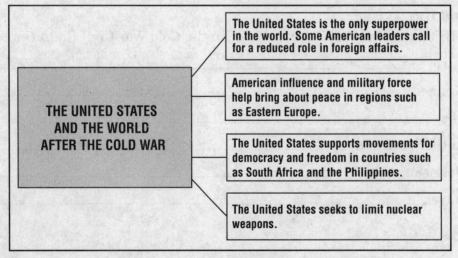

THE UNITED STATES AND THE WORLD AFTER THE COLD WAR

- The United States is the only superpower in the world. Some American leaders call for a reduced role in foreign affairs.
- American influence and military force help bring about peace in regions such as Eastern Europe.
- The United States supports movements for democracy and freedom in countries such as South Africa and the Philippines.
- The United States seeks to limit nuclear weapons.

REVIEW

Answer the following questions on a separate sheet of paper.

1. What happened to Yugoslavia after the fall of communism?

2. **Chart Skills** Where in the world has the United States supported democracy since the Cold War ended?

Epilogue   Section 5 Guided Reading and Review
Into the Future

A. As You Read

Directions: As you read Section 5 in the textbook, answer the following questions:

1. Why was Richard Nixon threatened with impeachment? _____
_____

2. What were the goals of the conservatives who supported Ronald Reagan? _____
_____
_____

3. What actions did Reagan take as president? _____
_____

4. What were some of Bill Clinton's presidential policies? _____
_____

5. How did the Cold War end? _____
_____

6. What are some of the new challenges facing the United States? _____
_____

B. Reviewing Key Terms

Directions: Briefly define each term.

7. Watergate affair _____

8. détente _____

9. North American Free Trade Agreement _____

ogue TEST

Identifying Main Ideas
Write the letter of the correct choice in the answer space.

____ 1. Which of the following was NOT a goal of the New Deal?
A. plans to increase the national debt
B. reforms to prevent depressions
C. plans for recovery
D. relief for the unemployed

____ 2. The Homestead Act
A. set a price for land.
B. promised land only to African Americans.
C. helped farmers settle the East.
D. promised land to people who would farm it for five years.

____ 3. When war broke out in Europe in 1914, the United States
A. remained neutral.
B. favored the Central Powers.
C. entered the war on the side of the Allies.
D. declared war on Russia.

____ 4. In 1954, the Supreme Court ruled that segregation in schools was
A. constitutional where it existed.
B. a local matter.
C. legal.
D. unconstitutional.

____ 5. The United States led forces to drive the Iraqis out of
A. Israel.
B. Kuwait.
C. Iran.
D. Egypt.

____ 6. During the Cold War, the United States and the Soviet Union were
A. satellite nations.
B. allies.
C. major trading partners.
D. rivals.

____ 7. The Nineteenth Amendment
A. allowed women to become doctors.
B. allowed women to go to college.
C. forbade suffragists to protest.
D. gave women the right to vote.

____ 8. In the late 1800s, reformers attempted to
A. force immigrants out of the city.
B. build more tenements.
C. hide conditions in poor neighborhoods.
D. improve conditions for the poor in the cities.

____ 9. The transcontinental railroad
A. led north.
B. led south.
C. crossed the United States.
D. was completed in the 1900s.

____ 10. At the end of the Spanish-American War, the United States
A. acquired overseas territories.
B. helped Filipino rebels gain independence.
C. refused to take over Spanish colonies.
D. gave full independence to Cuba.